Lecture notes

Cavendish Publishing Limited

CHILD LAW

TITLES IN THE SERIES

Administrative Law
Business Law
Child Law
Civil Liberties
Commercial Law
Company Law
Conflict of Laws
Constitutional & Administrative Law
Contract Law
Criminal Law
Criminal Litigation and Sentencing
Criminology
Employment Law
English Legal System
Environmental Law
Equity & Trusts
European Community Law
Evidence
Family Law
Intellectual Property Law
International Trade Law
Jurisprudence
Land Law
Public International Law
Law of Tort
Revenue Law
Succession, Wills & Probate
'A' Level Law - Paper I
'A' Level Law - Paper II

Lecture notes...

Cavendish Publishing Limited

CHILD LAW

Professor Duncan John Bloy, BA, LLM
Head of the School of Law, Glamorgan

First published in Great Britain 1996 by Cavendish Publishing Limited, The Glass House, Wharton Street, London WC1X 9PX
Telephone: 0171-278 8000 Facsimile: 0171-278 8080

British Library Cataloguing in Publication Data.

Bloy, Duncan
Child Law – (Lecture Notes Series)
I Title II Series
344.20615

ISBN 1 874241 59 7

Cover photograph by Jerome Yeats

Printed and bound in Great Britain

Preface

This book is intended to be read by undergraduates studying family law and child law modules as part of their degree studies. It may prove to be useful to those studying for social work qualifications. The modular system of degree study places students under intense pressure to the extent that they are often unable to read as extensively as they would like. Wherever possible, therefore, I have tried to offer guidance on what are the crucial issues and cited relevant snippets of text from various law reports in order to illustrate the point or provide the necessary authority. I have attempted to present the text in such a way as not to encourage students simply to remember and regurgitate information and I hope that lecturers and tutors will find that the book underpins the content of their courses rather than prescribing what ought to be taught.

I offer my sincere thanks to Mrs Glenys Williams for helping to provide some coherence to the draft manuscript and to Mrs Carol Coote of Mid Glamorgan Adoption Agency for her invaluable assistance in the preparation of the chapter on Adoption.

I would like to dedicate this book to my parents Jack and Gladys Bloy for whom this year has extra special significance.

I have endeavoured to state the law as at November 1995.

Duncan Bloy
Llanblethian
Vale of Glamorgan

Contents

Table of Cases

Chapter 1

An Introduction to Child Law

1.1 Introduction

This book is designed to be read by undergraduates who are studying either family law or child law as part of their degree studies, whether on a full-time or part-time basis. It is becoming increasingly common for universities to adopt a semester structure as the model for study, and in consequence, courses which were once studied for an academic session are now designed to comply with a modular ethos lasting at most some 15 weeks. Family law courses once offered on a linear basis have been restructured, giving the student the opportunity to focus attention on difficulties facing the family, and then, in the following semester, delve into the finer points of the law relating to children. Modular courses are often designed to be free-standing in the sense that there is no other module which needs to be studied in order to underpin the study of the current module. It is suggested that the study of the law relating the family will prove of help in assisting an undergraduate quickly to come to terms with some of the problems to be encountered while studying child law. Nevertheless, the subject may be approached in isolation from other aspects of family law, and for that matter, welfare law.

The law relating to children has become increasingly important as a result of statutory developments and case law evolution, both of which have, at times, attracted significant media coverage. The public law dimension has also been prominent, and there is often much press coverage as a result of the actions of social workers and local authorities who have the unenviable task of protecting vulnerable children against inappropriate adult attention, and in some cases against themselves.

The study of child law will require an undergraduate to spend some time examining recent statutory provisions, assessing the finer points of an increasingly voluminous amount of case law and, where relevant, official reports such as the Report of the Inquiry into Child Abuse in Cleveland 1987 (Cm 412 HMSO 1988). Students are invited to become familiar with the Family Law Reports where they will find a range of reported cases with a child law theme. By way of example, the [1995] 1 FLR (No 2) issue contains reports dealing with adoption, child support, contact with children after adoption, care proceedings, and an application for a residence order under the Children Act 1989.

1.2 The hearing of child law cases

If you have previously studied family law, you will probably be aware that the majority of family cases are heard in the family proceedings courts, with some being heard in the county court or Family Division of the High Court. There are two sets of rules, one set relating to the family proceedings court, the other to the county court and High Court; but it must be pointed out that there are not huge differences between them. The Children Act 1989 provides for Children Act cases to be heard in any of the three courts, although only the more important cases are likely to be commenced in the High Court. The recent case of *R v R (Residence order: Child abduction)* (1995) illustrates the point. Stuart-White J was of the opinion that where a case is before the family proceedings court and is found to have an international dimension, then it would be sensible to transfer the case to the county court. The reason for this being that the court is unlikely to have much familiarity with the Hague Convention or with the principles relating to child abduction. (For further information on the working of the Hague Convention on the Civil Aspects of International Child Abduction 1980, as set out in Schedule 1 to the Child Abduction and Custody Act 1985, see Chapter 9). It was further suggested that in cases of 'real difficulty' it would be wise to transfer the matter to the High Court.

The Act differentiates between private and public law cases, with the latter usually being commenced in the family proceedings court, with the potential for transfer to a higher court, dependent upon the complexity of the case. The major difficulty is identifying at an early stage those particularly troublesome cases which should be moved to a more appropriate level at the outset. Ironically, if a case is started at one level and it later becomes apparent that it should be transferred to another, the parties may seek to continue the case without transfer in the hope of achieving a speedier resolution of the case.

The case of *Barking and Dagenham Borough Council v O and Another* (1993) outlined the approach to be adopted in Children Act cases. Douglas Brown J stated:

> 'They are not paternal, they are not administrative and they are not in reality non-adversarial, although they should be conducted in a non-adversarial spirit ... Children Act proceedings are adversarial in the sense that each party is entitled to be heard and to challenge opposing evidence by cross-examination and entitled to representation by an advocate.' (p 655 D-F)

However, within six months of the *Barking* decision, the Court of Appeal had ruled that this was the wrong approach. In *Oxfordshire County Council v M* (1994), Sir Stephen Brown reiterated comments he had made in the case of *B v Derbyshire County Council* (1992) at p 546 A:

> '... I very much hope that the adversarial approach to care proceedings will disappear to a large extent ... the court is concerned with ... the whole welfare of the child and that its task is to investigate, in an inquisitorial manner if necessary, the interests of the child.'

He then went on to say:

> 'The proceedings under the Children Act are not adversarial, although an adversarial approach is frequently adopted by various of the parties. However, so far as the court is concerned, its duty is to investigate and to seek to achieve a result which is in the interests of the welfare of the child. Children's cases ... fall into a special category where the court is bound to undertake all necessary steps to arrive at an appropriate result in the paramount interests of the welfare of the child.' (p 184)

It is as well to be aware of these general comments about the procedural approach to the Act even though it is most unlikely that, as an undergraduate, you will be required to give any detailed consideration to evidential or procedural matters. The above quotations indicate a willingness on the part of the judiciary not to allow proceedings designed to be of benefit to children to become hidebound by long and complex arguments over procedural niceties. Thus wide powers are given to courts with the expectation being that an inquisitorial rather than an adversarial approach will be developed, as this is more consistent with the general philosophy of the Act, which makes the welfare of the child the paramount consideration.

1.3 The role of parents

The Children Act urges parents to adopt a more positive role in making decisions about the future of their children, manifest in the so called 'no order principle and the concept of parental responsibility' defined at s 3 of the Children Act 1989. However, it has been asserted that '... there is a wide divergence of approach between courts in various parts of the UK in the manner in which the Act is being approached and interpreted. Some judges are extremely reluctant to make any orders at all, even in cases in which, under the old law, some form of regulating order would have been highly desirable and generally implemented'. (See *The No Order Principle, Parental Responsibility and the Child's Wishes*, Simon Bennett and Susan Armstrong Walsh (1994) Fam Law 91.)

The concept of parental responsibility is an integral part of the Children Act and seeks to emphasise that parents have duties and responsibilities towards their children rather than possess rights over them. The desire automatically to extend parental responsibility to all parents, married or not, was evident at the initial stage of the Law Commission's deliberations into child law. An overwhelmingly negative response resulted in a policy which allows unmarried fathers to apply for parental responsibility, either with the support of the mother or unilaterally. Bennett and Walsh are critical of what they regard as an 'uneven' approach across courts with respect to awarding parental responsibility orders to unmarried fathers. It is desirable, they argue, for courts to award parental responsibility when making contact orders in respect of fathers, as this will enable fathers

> '... to develop and fulfil a role in the life and upbringing of the child which he can combine with practical contact arrangements as the child grows up. Some courts, however, are unwilling to make parental responsibility orders even where, in some cases, they grant the application for contact'.

1.4 The child's views

Modern child law now stresses the importance of listening to the child's views. The Children Act identifies the wishes of the child as one of the 'checklist' factors in s 1(3) which a court is obliged to take into account when considering whether to make, vary or discharge a s 8 order or any order under Part IV of the Act. With the dramatic increase in the number of divorces immediately after the coming into effect of the Divorce Reform Act 1971, it became apparent that children were being cast as the innocent victims of their parents' divorce. It has been estimated that, at any one time, up to 200,000 children may be affected by the divorce process. The adversarial approach implicit in the Act did nothing to help reduce the trauma of divorce for children, and this led to changes both to the legal principles and the practice of divorce. The so called 'special procedure' was introduced in 1977, and in 1984 the principle of the child's welfare being the 'first consideration' was incorporated into the Matrimonial Causes Act 1973 as it applies to ancillary proceedings relative to the redistribution of the family assets after divorce.

The problem has not been satisfactorily resolved. In 1990, the Law Commission in its Report No 192, entitled The Ground For Divorce, wrote:

> 'There is widespread concern about the current prevalence of divorce in the country and the consequences which this can have both for the couple concerned and for their children. There is also concern that the present divorce process may be making these worse. There have been many calls for the reform of the law, and from many quarters.'

At the time of writing, the government has introduced new divorce legislation which will result in a 'no fault' divorce system in England and Wales, a system which ought not encourage mutual recrimination and will hopefully reduce the trauma currently experienced by those undergoing divorce and that of their children.

The United Nations Convention on the Rights of the Child in 1989 declared that the interests of the child should be placed 'more to the forefront in decision-making'. The Children Act recognises this, not only through s 1(3), but also in other sections, of which s 43(8) is a good example. Section 43 is the first provision in Part V of the Act dealing with the protection of children. Section 43 deals with child assessment orders. These orders can be made in favour of a 'local authority or authorised person' if there is reasonable suspicion, *inter alia*, that the child is suffering, or is likely in the near future to suffer, significant harm. However, s 43(8) establishes that the child may refuse to undergo an assessment provided he is 'of sufficient understanding to make an informed decision'. This subsection alludes to the findings of the House of Lords in the case of *Gillick v West Norfolk and Wisbech Area Health Authority* (1985). A majority of the House of Lords held that children become increasingly independent as they grow older, and in consequence, parental authority dwindles. Parental 'rights' therefore yielded to the child's right of self-determination when there was sufficient understanding and intelligence to be capable of making an informed decision. Thus the common law and the Children Act have recognised that children should be allowed a voice in decision-making although, as is pointed out in Chapter 8, the High Court, in wardship proceedings, may still adopt a paternalistic approach to the welfare of the child which, in consequence, may override the wishes of the child.

The Children Act permits a child to apply for leave to make an application for a s 8 order, and in certain circumstances the child may take part in litigation, either in person or by instructing a solicitor.

1.4.1 Child's self-determination

Child law transcends many of the demarcation lines so beloved of academic lawyers who like to see their subjects compartmentalised for ease of dissemination to their students. The burning issue of consent to medical treatment is a logical corollary to the further recognition to the right of the child to self determination. There has been an enormous amount of judicial energy expended on this issue over the last six years, mainly in the context of wardship proceedings (See Chapter 8). As Michael Nicholls comments in *Keyholders and Flak Jackets:*

Consent to Medical Treatment For Children (1994) Fam Law 81:

> 'Some of the cases have been decided on well settled principles, but in others, particularly those about the power of children to refuse treatment, decisions have been made which have been the subject of considerable criticism and concern to the legal and medical professions.'

Therefore medical law and child law principles are at the heart of this particular issue.

1.5 Child abduction

The ease of international travel has led to an increase in the number of children being abducted from or brought to the jurisdiction. Whilst this country has been at the forefront of good practice in seeking to discourage this behaviour, with the important principles being incorporated into legislation over a decade ago, a cursory glance at the Family Law Reports indicates that the problem is far from being resolved. Child law thus impinges on areas of law traditionally found under the international law banner. Nor can one divorce this issue from international politics, with the law being impotent to ensure basic justice to parents and children where tension exists at a political level between states. And even if states enjoy good relations, it is left to each state to decide whether it wishes to join other nations in recognising the obligations of the Hague and European Conventions on Child Abduction (see Chapter 9).

1.6 The Children Act 1989

In the sphere of child protection the law has been radically overhauled. The oft-criticised Children and Young Persons Act 1969 has been almost totally dismantled, and valuable new provisions designed to ensure a swift and effective response to child abuse and neglect have been introduced through the medium of the Children Act. The Act now provides for action to be taken where there is not only significant harm being suffered by the child but also where there is a reasonable expectation that the child will be on the receiving end of such conduct, thus remedying a significant weakness of the old Act which invariably led to wardship proceedings being commenced. The Act makes it clear that local authorities will have to seek leave of the court if there is a desire to commence wardship proceedings. In other words, parliament has endeavoured to create an all-embracing code to provide maximum protection for a child without the necessity to have recourse to the inherent jurisdiction. The public law sections of the Children Act introduce a radical new approach to resolving questions of long term support and protection of children. Gone is the automatic assumption that a child should be taken into the care of the local authority if the statutory criteria are fulfilled. Now the court will have to make a positive finding that the 'care option' is indeed in the best interests of the child. All possible avenues will be explored, the assumption being that only if it is absolutely necessary, looked at from the child's point of view, will the child be transferred into the care of the local authority. Valuable new rights are also given to parents should their children be removed from their care. There is a presumption in favour of ongoing contact with the child providing it is demonstrably in the child's best interests (see s 34 of the Act).

One of the major problems now facing those charged with the task of implementing the Children Act is that of ensuring that there is as little delay as possible in resolving the particular issue affecting a child's future. The Children Act includes a provision, s 1(2), to the effect that '... any delay in determining the question is likely to prejudice the welfare of the child'. The problem was highlighted by Butler *et al* in *The Children Act and the Issue of Delay* (1993) Fam Law 412. Since then, there has been trenchant comment that the situation is deteriorating rather than improving, particularly in the public law area. Delay of up to 10 months is not unknown, but whether the situation will improve may well depend on the available resources being increased.

1.7 Adoption

In recent years, an international dimension has been introduced into the law on adoption as childless couples have responded to the lack of babies available to adopt by seeking to 'rescue' orphans and destitute children from overseas, particularly war-torn Eastern Europe and certain South American countries. This is one of many aspects of adoption law currently under review by the government prior to an Adoption Bill being laid before parliament. The welfare of the child is not the paramount consideration in adoption proceedings, but it is to be hoped that any new legislation will seek to reinforce the provisions of the Children Act and ensure that decisions are taken which give primacy to the long-term welfare of the child.

1.8 Conclusion

The law as it applies to children and their parents will continue to evolve. The whole question of ongoing maintenance for the child is now the subject public discussion since the implementation of the Child Support Act 1993. As Dr Richard Collier said in his article *The Campaign Against the Child Support Act* (1994) Fam Law 384:

> '[The Child Support Act] ... which had initially been met with guarded praise from across the political divide, has in a matter of months from its enactment become one of the most reviled and potentially damaging of the Conservative government's forays into family politics ... only radical changes ... can now rescue a system that is failing children, rather than helping them.'

Child law will, of necessity, always demand attention, and will consequently be likely to excite the public's interest. The desire to reform the laws relating to children has resulted in a piecemeal approach to legislative change, but nevertheless the Children Act in particular represents a major success in laying down not only a clear philosophy for both private and public law matters but also instituting a comprehensive legal code which addresses in a purposeful and constructive way the difficulties facing parents and children and offers an enlightened approach to their resolution.

Summary of Chapter 1

An Introduction to Child Law

This chapter seeks to give guidance on the approach to be adopted to the study of child law and to draw to your attention some of the major assumptions pervading this area of the law.

The major focus of attention is the Children Act 1989 which should be read together with relevant case law and official reports. It is imperative that constant use is made of the Family Law Reports.

All students should become familiar with the various courts in which child law cases may be commenced ie, the family proceedings court, the county court and the Family Division of the High Court.

The 'golden thread' running through child law cases is that the welfare of the child is the paramount consideration. It should also be noted that children's wishes are increasingly being taken into account by the court, a direct consequence of the House of Lords decision in *Gillick v West Norfolk Area Health Authority* (1985).

It is also stressed by the courts that proceedings should be less adversarial, particularly in child care cases.

There is an increasing body of case law being reported in the context of the Children Act 1989 and it must be appreciated that the Act is radical in both philosophy and approach. This chapter also draws attention to the fact that, increasingly, child law is taking on an international dimension and there is sadly evidence to show that child abduction is on the increase. Not only in this context but throughout child law, it is apparent that delay is inimical to the best interests of the child, and courts are increasingly urging that speedy resolution of disputes concerning children should be a clearly stated objective.

Child law should not be divorced from other areas of family law or from the political ramifications of what, at times, may be highly sensitive legislation affecting large numbers of people, as was seen with the introduction of the Child Support Act 1991.

Chapter 2

The Children Act 1989

2.1 Introduction

The Children Act 1989 represents the culmination of a process of review and reflection undertaken over a four year period from 1985. The Law Commission produced working papers on Guardianship, Custody, Care, Supervision and Interim Orders in Custody Proceedings and Wards of Court, in addition to the Report No 172 entitled Review of Child Law: Guardianship and Custody, in 1988. Lord Mackay of Clashfern LC used the following words when opening the debate in the House of Lords on the second reading of the Children Bill, which subsequently became the Children Act 1989:

> 'The Bill in my view represents the most comprehensive and far-reaching reform of child law which has come before parliament in living memory. It brings together the public and private law concerning the care, protection and upbringing of children and the provision of services to them and their families.'

The learned authors of *Blackstone's Guide to the Children Act 1989* speculated that:

> '... in years to come there can be no doubt that the Children Act 1989 will be viewed as a landmark in the history of child care legislation in this country.'

It may well be premature to conclude that the above remarks were accurate. However, one thing is clear: that for the first time, this jurisdiction possesses a comprehensive code of child law that at first sight appears to promote consistency in approach to both private and public law matters relating to children. The Law Commission concluded that the existing law was 'confusing and unintelligible' and had no doubt that reform was long overdue. 'Public law' is used in this context to denote the child care responsibilities of local authorities, ie care and related procedures, and 'private law' focuses on disputes between individuals which have an impact on children, eg in divorce proceedings or wardship, or, as Hoggett and Pearl put it in Chapter 12 of *Family, Law and Society* , 'when parents part ...' (3rd edn p 500).

The 1989 Act is divided into 12 parts, and it is beyond the scope of this book to consider all of these sections. This book is aimed at those who undertake undergraduate study in child law and who therefore have a limited amount of time available in which to read around the topic. It has therefore been decided to focus on those aspects of the Act which are likely to warrant consideration in the context of an undergraduate degree course which may, of course, be either linear or modular in structure. Attention will therefore be drawn to Parts I, II, IV, V, IX and XII.

The Children Act 1989 repealed eight statutes and significantly limited the ambit of a ninth, the Children and Young Persons Act 1969.

The Act has introduced flexibility as to which court hears 'family proceedings' and the High Court, county court and magistrates' court are given a concurrent jurisdiction. Transfer of cases between courts is possible and, often, will be highly desirable in order to ensure that a case is resolved as quickly as possible at a level consistent with its complexity. Steyn LJ described the importance of the Act in this way:

> '... under the Children Act 1989 the child's welfare is the paramount consideration. This objective is spelled out explicitly in s 1(1). The welfare checklist in s 1(3) underpins it. And the Act contains a framework designed to achieve that purpose. The 1989 Act was a watershed' (*Oxfordshire County Council v M* (1994)).

2.2 The paramountcy principle

One piece of legislation repealed by the Children Act 1989 was the Guardianship of Minors Act 1971, which contained the key principle that determined the majority of cases involving children, ie that the child's welfare is regarded as the 'first and paramount consideration'. Section 1 of the 1971 Act stated:

> 'Where in any proceedings before any court ...
>
> (a) the legal custody or upbringing of a child; or
>
> (b) the administration of any property belonging to or held on trust for a child, or the application of the income thereof,
>
> is in question, the court, in deciding that question, shall regard the welfare of the child as the first and paramount consideration and shall not take into consideration whether from any other point of view the claim of the father in respect of such legal custody, upbringing, administration or application is superior to that of the mother, or the claim of the mother is superior to that of the father.'

That provision has been replaced in s 1 of the 1989 Act by the following words:

> '1(1) When a court determines any question with respect to –
>
> (a) the upbringing of a child; or

(b) the administration of a child's property or the application of any income arising from it.

the child's welfare shall be the court's paramount consideration.'

It will be immediately apparent that the word 'first' has been removed from the previous formula. The Law Commission was of the opinion that its removal was justified because in the past it had caused 'confusion' in that it led some courts 'to balance other considerations against the child's welfare rather than to consider what light they shed upon it'.

However, this view had not held sway since the definitive statement of Lord MacDermott in the case of *J v C* (1970) when he stated that the words in s 1 did not mean that the child's welfare should be treated as the 'top item in a list of items relevant to the matters in question'. The words:

> '... connote a process whereby, when all the relevant facts, relationships, claims and wishes of parents, risks, choices and other circumstances are taken into account and weighted, the course to be followed will be that which is most in the interests of the child's welfare as that term has now to be understood. That is the first consideration because it is of first importance and the paramount consideration because it rules upon or determines the course to be followed.'

The wording in s 1(1) of the 1989 Act is meant to convey the impression that the court's only concern should be the welfare of the child. It is important to recognise that the so-called welfare principle will only apply in the circumstances referred to in s 1(1). Thus it has no application to ancillary relief applications where the child's welfare is the first but not paramount consideration, nor will it apply in adoption proceedings. Nor will the principle be applicable to ouster applications under s 1 of the Matrimonial Homes Act 1983. These are governed by the authority of *Richards v Richards* (1984) and s 1(3) of the 1983 Act. The subsection identifies four matters which should be considered when a court is seeking to decide whether an ouster order should be granted. These are:

- the conduct of the parties in relation to each other;
- their respective needs and financial resources;
- the needs of the children; and
- all the circumstances of the case.

None of these factors was paramount over any other, and the weight given to each depended on the facts of each particular case. An attempt was made in *Gibson v Austin* (1992) to persuade the Court of Appeal that the Children Act 1989 had in effect overruled *Richards v Richards*. Nourse LJ described the argument as 'a hopeless one'. The argument is as follows:

- 'Family proceedings' as defined in s 8(3) of the 1989 includes proceedings under the Domestic Violence and Matrimonial Proceedings Act 1976.
- Then in s 10(1) the court is given power to make a s 8 order in any family proceedings in which a question arises with respect to the welfare of the child.
- The s 8 orders include a prohibited steps order, a residence order and a specific issue order.

The court had no difficulty following the logic of that argument and therefore, if on an application under s 1(1)(b) of the Domestic Violence and Matrimonial Proceedings Act 1976, there was a need to restrain by injunction one party from molesting a child living with the applicant, then there would be no problem in making the child's welfare the paramount consideration. But in circumstances where the application was for a 'straightforward' ouster order, the welfare principle would not apply because the proceedings are not concerned with the upbringing of the child. As Balcombe LJ put it:

> 'If it had been the intention of parliament to reverse the decision of *Richards v Richards* in relation to ordinary ouster applications, I am quite certain they would have said so expressly, and I agree ... that the argument under the Children Act 1989 does not succeed.' (p 443(F))

It has also been held that the welfare principle should not apply to applications under ss 8 and 10(9) of the 1989 Act for leave to apply for a s 8 order. In deciding whether or not to grant leave the court must have regard to the following:

1 The nature of the proposed application for a s 8 order.

2 The applicant's connection with the child.

3 Any risk there might be of that proposed application disrupting the child's life to such an extent that he would be harmed by it.

4 Where the child is being looked after by the local authority

(i) the authority's plans for the child's future; and

(ii) the wishes and feelings of the child's parents.

It is hardly surprising that in *Re A and W (Minors) (Residence Order: Leave to Apply)* (1992) the Court of Appeal should hold that the welfare principle did not apply. Parliament has made it clear that a whole host of factors should be taken into account, and it was quite clear that the child's welfare could not have been intended to be the paramount consideration.

It is possible that a court could be faced with an application where the mother and child are both minors in the care of a local authority. In these circumstances, a court is faced with deciding whose interests are paramount. In *Birmingham City Council v H (a minor)* (1994), the local authority had applied under s 34(4) of the Children Act 1989 for termination of contact between the mother and child on the grounds that the mother was unable to look after her child and that the prospect of rehabilitation between them was not feasible. The House of Lords held that the paramountcy principle should apply only to the mother's child, who was the subject of the application. Their Lordships were not disposed to the view that a court should balance the welfare of one minor against that of the other for the reason that 'the question to be determined does not relate to the applicant's own upbringing'. This decision was applied by the Court of Appeal in *F v Leeds City Council* (1994). The correct approach, said the court, was to identify which child it was 'whose welfare was directly involved'. The welfare of the infant took precedence over that of the child-parent on an application for a care order under s 31 of the Children Act 1989. Lord Slynn of Hadley doubted in the *Birmingham* case whether it was ever intended that a parent be included within the category of 'child' in s 34(2) of the 1989 Act.

A later example is *Re SC (a minor)* (1994) where a 14 year old girl who had been in local authority care for some eight years indicated that she wished to live with a friend's family, on the basis that she would be provided with a settled family home. She applied for leave to apply for a residence order. The local authority, the girl's mother and representatives of the proposed new family all had an interest in the outcome of the application for leave. Booth J rejected counsel's submission that s 1 of the 1989 Act should apply on the basis that an *application* for leave did not raise any question regarding the upbringing of the child. It therefore followed that the child's welfare should not be the paramount consideration. The court was clearly relying upon the authority of *Re A and W* (1992) and in particular Balcombe LJ's comment at p 160 D:

> 'In granting or refusing an application for leave to apply for a s 8 order the court is not determining a question with respect to the upbringing of the child concerned. That question only arises when the court hears the substantive application. The reasoning of this court in *F v S (Adoption: Ward)* (1973) ... supports this conclusion.'

It is also worth noting that the paramountcy principle does not apply to local authorities in the exercise of statutory obligations in respect of children. Section 17 imposes a general duty upon local authorities to:

> '(a) safeguard and promote the welfare of children within their area who are in need; and
>
> (b) so far as is consistent with that duty, to promote the upbringing of such children by their families ...'

The use of the words 'safeguard and promote the welfare of children' quite clearly indicates that the paramountcy principle is meant not to apply.

In conclusion, reference should be made to Lord Wilberforce's speech in the case of *A v Liverpool City Council* (1981), in which he indicates that the word 'paramount' has a long and well established history in the context of legislation relating to children. The word first appeared in the Guardianship of Infants Act 1925 and according to Lord Wilberforce is:

> '... clearly taken from the opinion of Viscount Cave LC in *Ward v Laverty* (1925) ... where he related this test to 'rules which are now well accepted', so clearly not intended as a new or even talismanic word. The speeches in *J v C* provide authoritative guidance which I should not wish to repeat or to gloss.'

The Law Commission's view was that the '... overall needs of the child ... must always prevail' (Report No 172 para 3.16).

2.3 Delay

Section 1(2) states:

> 'In any proceedings in which any question with respect to the upbringing of a child arises, the court shall have regard to the general principle that delay in determining the question is likely to prejudice the welfare of the child.'

At the time of writing, concern is being expressed at a national level that the delay in processing cases involving children can be as long as 10 months. There are obviously resource issues which can contribute to the problem. Sections 11 and 32 impose a requirement upon courts to draw up a timetable with a view to determining questions without delay in both private and public law cases. The Law Commission was of the opinion that there should be a 'clear obligation upon the court to oversee the progress of the case and to ensure that the court regards all delay as prejudicial to the child's interests unless the contrary is shown'. The contents of a welfare report will invariably be of great assistance to a court, but one could question its overall value if the waiting time is unacceptably long. The benefit, though, could outweigh the disadvantage of having to wait, but the implication from the legislation is that normally the opposite will be true. However, note that s 1(2) states that delay is likely to prejudice the welfare of the child, not that it will: ie there is a rebuttable presumption that delay is inconsistent with achieving what is in the child's best interests. Section 1(2) has received recent judicial attention and is undoubtedly a factor to which courts must pay due regard.

In *R v South East Hampshire Family Proceedings Court ex parte D* (1994), Ewbank J was dealing with the Children (Allocation of Proceedings) Order 1991 which provides at Article 8 that a magistrates' court can transfer a case to the county court where:

> '... having regard to the principle set out in s 1(2), it considers that in the interests of the child the proceedings can be dealt with more appropriately in that county court.'

It was held that, while the court had to have regard to the 'delay principle', its main function was always to consider what was in the best interests of the child, and in that context determine whether the transfer should take place. In other words, delay is only one matter to be taken into account, along with which court was the most appropriate and what would be in the best interests of the child. It is worth noting that the father first made an application for contact and parental responsibility in December 1992 and the final determination had not been made by January 1994 when this case was heard and the issue remitted back to the magistrates court for a decision to be made on the correct principle. As the judge commented:

> 'If it was urgent, as the President decided in July 1993, it is more urgent now and ought to be dealt with great expedition.'

Ewbank J was also the judge in *Re B (a minor) (Contact: Interim Order)* (1994). In this case the father made an application for contact and parental responsibility orders. It was agreed that there should be an interim contact order and that the welfare officer would monitor the father's visits to the child. The matter was then scheduled to come back to court four months later. The magistrates were not prepared to consider the proposal as recommended by the welfare officer, on the basis that adjourning the case to the later date disregarded the principle of delay. It was held that a monitored programme of contact could not be regarded as being detrimental to the child. There was likely to be positive benefit to the child from having contact with her father over that four month period.

The approach to be adopted in cases where delay may be a factor was outlined by Hale J in *Re C (Section 8 Order: Court Welfare Officer)* (1995). She said:

> 'Procedural straightjackets in cases of this kind would be most undesirable, especially in light of the balancing act which is required by the paramount consideration of the child's welfare and the provisions as to delay in s 1(2). Many factors will have to be taken into account in the exercise of the court's discretion.'

Providing that 'balancing act' has been attempted and a range of relevant factors taken into account, then it will be extremely difficult successfully to challenge the exercise of that discretion.

Regard should be had to *B v B (minors) (Interviews and Listing Arrangements)* (1994), in which the Court of Appeal emphasised that practitioners and courts had a duty to avoid delay in children's cases. The court concluded that the delay which had occurred 'had undoubtedly prejudiced the welfare of the children and should not have been allowed to happen'.

There is a growing body of opinion which suggests that delay is an issue which is likely to have to be tackled head on by the judiciary. This is evident from the comments of Wall J in *Re JC (Care Proceedings: Procedure)* (1995). The judge expressed concern that a case involving a very young child who had been taken into care within days of his birth should have been unresolved over one year later. It is important that decisions about the long term future of very young children should be taken at an early stage before primary attachments are formed. It should be pointed out that the court was not suggesting culpability on the part of the local authority concerned. Over a period of approximately six months it became apparent that the mother would not be capable of looking after her child. This situation was then compounded by the father 'dropping out' of the assessment process and then another member of the mother's family coming forward seeking to take over the care of the child. The consequence, which was described as 'not unusual' by the court, was that the original hearing date had to be postponed from October until a new date was agreed upon in the following February. A difficult situation was further compounded by the fact that the case then overran its allotted court time. An estimate of four working days had been made. In fact the case lasted seven. It is illuminating to reflect upon the words of Wall J:

> 'The consequence was that a four day child case allocated to me and due to commence on 6 March 1995 had to be taken out of the list. Given the severe and unacceptable delays in hearing child cases in the High Court in London, which is itself in large measure due to shortage of judge power, this case vividly demonstrates the knock-on effect of an overrunning case and the need for there to be accuracy in giving estimates of time' (p 80 C).

Why should a case overrun its allotted time? There are numerous reasons, many of which can be obviated with a modicum of foresight and planning.

Local authority social workers should present evidence in an objective, fair and balanced way. If the case is not presented in such a way the parents may conclude that there is bias on the part of the local authority, and this could lead to delay while the parents' legal representatives seek discovery of the social worker's notes. Secondly, lawyers in public law cases need to give careful consideration to pre-trial discovery of documents. This is not to discount the importance of pre-trial discovery, but merely to emphasise the need for lawyers to think well in advance of the trial about the documentation required for the proper conduct of the proceedings. Pre-trial discovery is an essential part of this process. The final point is that there is a need for lawyers accurately to estimate the length of hearings in such cases. Reference should be made to two practice directions:

- Practice Direction (case management) (1995) 1 FLR 456;
- Practice Direction: Children Act 1989: Hearings before High Court Judge: Time Estimates (1994) 1 FLR 108;

Consideration should also be given to the case of *Re MD and TD (Minors) (Time Estimates)* (1994).

2.4 Presumption of no order

Section 1(5) of the Children Act 1989 has been described by one commentator as 'one of the most innovative and influential principles in the Act' (Bainham A, *Children, The New Law*: Family Law 1990). He states:

> 'Where a court is considering whether or not to make one or more orders under this Act with respect to a child, it shall not make the order or any of the orders unless it considers that doing so would be better for the child than making no order at all.'

In considering the impact of s 1(5) in the recent case of *Re D H (a minor) (Child Abuse)* (1994), Wall J, after stating the terms of s 1(5), went on to comment:

> 'I therefore bear s 1(5) fully in mind when making my order. I am the first to seek to withdraw the shadow of litigation from parties' lives. Parents should obviously be free, wherever possible, to bring up their children without interference from the courts or any other statutory body. The fact remains, however, that there are cases where, in the interests of a particular child, continuing court involvement is necessary' (p 707F).

The Law Commission acknowledged that studies of both divorce and magistrates' courts showed that the proportion of contested cases is very small and concludes that 'orders are not usually necessary in order to settle disputes' (Report No 178, para 3.2). Hence the conclusion that orders should only be made if it was patently necessary in order to serve or secure the best interests of the child. With regard to local authority obligations, it was thought to be appropriate to seek to ensure that 'compulsory intervention [was] confined to cases where compulsion itself is necessary'.

In practice, this means that a court hearing family proceedings must direct itself to consider the likely outcome of making no order by comparison with the predicted effects of making an order. Nor is the court confined to making the order asked for. It could refuse such a request yet still possesses the power to make another order which it deems would best promote the welfare of the child. A court must have regard to 'the range of powers available ... under this Act in the proceedings in question'. This approach is consistent with the philosophy of devolving as much decision-making as possible to parents and acknowledging the significance of the concept of parental responsibility.

Section 1(5) was put under close judicial scrutiny by the President of the Family Division, Sir Stephen Brown, in the case of *K v H (child maintenance)* (1993). In this case, the mother of a two year old child applied to the court for periodical payments from the father for the benefit of the child. The parents, who were not married, agreed £20 per week to be an appropriate amount. The father had been paying this amount for one year prior to the agreement, but on a voluntary basis. The parents sought an order. The question for the court was whether or not s 1(5) was applicable to an application under s 15 and Schedule 1 of the Children Act 1989. Section 15 deals with financial relief and directs attention to Schedule 1, which makes provision for financial relief for children. The justices had considered s 1(5) and concluded that an order was unnecessary because there was in existence a voluntary agreement which was working 'adequately'. The mother's appeal to the Family Division was allowed. The court considered s 1(1) and s 1(5) and concluded that s 1(1) was principally concerned with orders relating to the upbringing of the child, the administration of a child's property or the application of any income arising from it. As such a 'straightforward application for financial provision' did not need to be considered in the context of s 1(5). The magistrates were said to have 'loyally [sought] to apply the general philosophy of the Children Act, that families should wherever possible deal with matters relating to children without recourse to the courts ...'. The judge took the view that even if he was wrong in refusing to acknowledge that s 1(5) should apply to s 15, he would still have made the order sought as it was 'clearly in the interests of the child that proper provision should be made for his financial needs'. Present harmonious relations between the parents could not be guaranteed in the future, and without an order, any problems in enforcing the agreement or pursuing arrears could have presented problems.

Another example of where it was found appropriate to make an order is *B v B (a minor) (Residence Order)* (1992). In this case the maternal grandmother of an 11 year old girl supported by the girl's mother applied for a residence order. The girl had lived for all but six weeks of her life with her maternal grandmother. The mother had left home in 1991 and had endorsed the arrangement. The justices found that there was no risk of the child being taken away from home and refused to make the order relying on s 1(5). The grandmother's appeal to the Family Division was allowed. The court recognised that it was appropriate to apply s 1(5) to this application, but recognised that the grandmother did not have parental responsibility and, given that the grandmother needed the authority of parental responsibility in order to help the child, made a residence order in favour of the grandmother.

The non-intervention principle was also meant to address a difficulty which had arisen in the working of s 41 of the Matrimonial Causes Act 1973, whereby a divorce court had a duty under s 41 to satisfy itself as to the proposed arrangements for any children of the family before making the decree absolute. A similar duty was to be found in s 8(1) of the Domestic Proceedings and Magistrates' Courts Act 1978.

There were two major aims underpinning the s 41 procedure. The first was to ensure an objective assessment of the arrangements proposed for the children, and secondly to 'identify cases of particular concern where protective measures might be needed' (Law Commission Report 172, para 3.6). The Law Commission concluded that neither of these two aims had been satisfactorily achieved, primarily because of the relative paucity of information available to the court upon which to make informed decision. Nor can a court ensure that whatever is approved is, in practice, carried out. The outcome, as reflected in s 1(5), was the recommendation that the court's duty should be to consider the arrangements with a view to deciding whether it should exercise any of its powers under the legislation. The advantages of this proposal are listed at para 3.10 in Law Commission Report 178. The amended s 41 is to be found at Schedule 12, para 31 of the Children Act 1989.

2.5 The checklist

Section 1(3) of the Children Act 1989 introduced a statutory checklist of factors which the court should consider when deciding under s 1(4) whether to make, vary or discharge a s 8 order and where there is opposition to such by 'any party to the proceedings'. The checklist also applies when the court is considering whether to make, vary or discharge an order under Part IV of the Children Act 1989. The factors are not in themselves surprising, and indeed many had been accepted and applied by the judiciary prior to the Act reaching the statute book. The checklist is not meant to be prescriptive, and any other factors which a court deems important may be taken into account. Nor is it generally applicable across the Act. It is not, for example, a mandatory requirement for the checklist to be used when dealing with an application for an emergency protection order.

The checklist details seven points for consideration. No one factor is given greater weight than any other. The checklist comprises the following factors:

- the ascertainable wishes and feelings of the child concerned (in the light of the child's age and understanding);
- the child's physical, emotional and educational needs;
- the likely effect on the child of any change in circumstances;
- the child's age, sex, background and any of the child's characteristics which the court considers relevant;
- any harm which the child has suffered or is at risk of suffering;
- how capable is each of the child's parents, and any other person in relation to whom the court considers the question to be relevant, of meeting the child's needs; and

- the range of powers available to the court under the Children Act 1989 in the proceedings in question.

The benefits of having such a checklist can be stated to be:

- There is a distinct likelihood of greater consistency when judges are obliged to consider the same factors.
- Parties will be aware of which factors are important in the decision-making process.
- Legal advisors will be better equipped to give informed guidance and advice to parents.

One should not immediately discount cases decided prior to the 1989 Act coming into force but they are relevant only insofar as they are not inconsistent with the factors in the checklist. Courts were always careful to emphasise that there was only one principle of law applicable to the resolution of custody and access disputes, ie the welfare principle. The other factors taken into account were not to be elevated to the status of principle and could therefore be relied upon or ignored at the discretion of the judge. However, a substantial body of case law has accumulated over the period since the Act came into force in October 1991, and in the vast majority of cases, precedence ought to be given to post Act as opposed to pre-Act case law (with the notable exception of *J v C*).

2.5.1 The ascertainable wishes and feelings of the child concerned – considered in the light of his age and understanding (s 1(3)(a))

This factor would appear to give credence to the decision of the House of Lords in *Gillick v West Norfolk Area Health Authority* (1985), and the Act recognises, as for example in s 43(8), that the child's wishes should prevail. Section 43(8) provides:

> '... if the child is of sufficient understanding to make an informed decision he may refuse to submit to medical or psychiatric examination or other assessment.'

It is likely that the child's views, for example on which parent should have the residence order, will be put forward in a welfare report. In some circumstances, usually reflecting age and maturity of the child, the judge will actually meet with the child and form an impression based upon personal contact. Butler-Sloss LJ stated in *Re P (Minors) (Wardship: Care and Control)* (1992):

> 'In all family cases it is the duty of the court to listen to the children, ascertain their wishes and feelings, and then make decisions about their future having regard to but not constricted by those wishes' (p 689 H).

See also the comments of Cazalet J in *Re H (A Minor) (Shared Residence)* (1994) where the above passage was cited and the court endorsed the view that it was for the judge to determine what weight to give to the child's wishes. In *Re M (Contact) (Welfare Test)* (1995) the children were aged nine and eight. Their parents had separated in 1989 and the children had remained with their father. Two years later, when the father began to cohabit, the children refused to visit their mother and had on occasions been quite distressed. By 1992 all contact had ceased. The court welfare officer had interviewed the children and indicated that she found the elder child 'mature for his years'. He had made it abundantly clear that he did not wish to continue contact with his mother and gave reasons for his decision. He claimed that his 'security was threatened by contact with the mother and reiterated the allegation that she told him lies ...'. Although the views of the younger child were discounted at the time of the original hearing when she was seven, by 1993, when she was eight, the Court of Appeal was prepared to accept that she was 'no longer a very small child' and was expressing the same sentiments as her older sibling. In upholding the original order refusing contact to the mother, the court had to balance the second element of the checklist against the first, it being quite apparent that significant weight was attached to their view.

Age, though important, will not always be the determining factor as to whether or not the child's views are influential to the eventual outcome of the case. The Court of Appeal made a clear statement of principle in *Re P (A Minor) (Education)* (1992) to the effect that, in family proceedings concerning children:

> '... it was the duty of the court, when making decisions about their future welfare, to listen and to pay respect to the wishes and views of older children' (see p 321 E).

The court was invited to settle a dispute as to whether the teenage son should continue to attend a fee-paying boarding school or, as he wished, attend a local day school, after the parents' divorce. Butler-Sloss LJ expressed her opinion in the following way:

> '... I think that the boy's wishes in this case have to carry, for me, such weight as to tilt the balance and make it necessary that what he has asked for in a sensible way should, in fact, be the decision of this court.'

This case was decided before the Children Act 1989 came into force, but in the judge's opinion, once the Act came into force, courts would have to pay close attention in ascertaining the wishes and the views of children 'of an age and maturity which may give valuable help to the courts'.

The views of boys aged 12 and nine were taken into account in the case of *Re F (Minors) (Denial of Contact)* (1993), a somewhat unusual case resulting from the father having decided that he was 'in effect a woman in a man's body'. Balcombe LJ acknowledged that of the factors in s 1(3) one did not have 'any natural precedence over the others'. The boys were in the circumstances entitled to have 'respect paid to their views'.

Whether or not the judge actually sees the child will be a matter to be determined in light of all the circumstances. It would be extremely unusual for a judge to see a very young child but there is no embargo on that happening if, in exercising discretion, the judge believes it to be necessary in helping to determine the outcome of the case. *Re R (A Minor) (Residence: Religion)* (1993) is a case in point, where the judge decided not to interview a child aged 10 because he was already aware from reading the welfare report of the strong opinions held by the boy concerning the Exclusive Brethren sect of which the father had been a member. Balcombe LJ reiterated the familiar principle to the effect that the exercise of judicial discretion could be successfully challenged only by reference to the principles established by the House of Lords in *G v G* (1985). These are that the judge at first instance had acted on the wrong principles, or that in exercising discretion the conclusion reached was 'plainly wrong'.

There is nothing to prevent magistrates, as opposed to judges in the High Court and county court, from interviewing a child in private. The Children Act 1989 does not give a right to court personnel at any level to interview children in private, but precedent and practice have established the principle that a discretion exists for judges to see children. Guidance on the position in the Family Proceedings Court is to be found in the decision of Booth J in *Re M (A Minor) (Justices' Discretion)* (1993). Justices could not ignore their duty under s 1(3) of the 1989 Act said the judge, but in a case where a guardian *ad litem* was acting for the child, or where a welfare report had been requested which detailed the child's wishes and feeling, then:

> '... it should not be necessary or desirable for the justices to see the child.'

In seeking to determine the true position, looked at from the child's point of view, the court and parties have the opportunity to question the guardian *ad litem* or the welfare officer. In this case the justices were deemed to have erred in seeing the child in private when evidence relating to his wishes had been fully dealt with by the welfare officer. Wall J put it this way in *Re W (A Minor) (Contact)* (1994):

> 'In *Re M (A Minor) (Justices' Discretion)* (1993), Booth J stated that where a guardian *ad litem* or welfare officer is involved it should only be in rare and exceptional cases where justices should themselves see a child in private ... In my judgment, there have to be unusual circumstances before any tribunal interviews any child, and I have to say I find it difficult to conceive of circumstances in which any bench of justices should see a child of W's age [seven] in relation to an issue of contact.'

Strong guidance was given by the Court of Appeal in *B v B (Minors) (Interviews and Listing Arrangements* (1994) on when and how judges should exercise their discretion to interview children. A judge cannot give any assurances to children that what they reveal will remain confidential, despite the assumption that children will only express their true feelings if promised absolute confidentiality. For this reason, ie the inherent contradiction of seeing children but reporting to parents, discretion to see children should be exercised cautiously. It should never be 'automatic or routine', and therefore there should be good reasons for seeing the child after hearing submissions from the parents. The ascertainment of a child's wish was deemed to be within the province of the court welfare officer or guardian *ad litem*, who could be cross-examined as to the contents of their reports. The final point is that in no circumstances should a child be made to feel that the final decision was due to his evidence. The responsibility for the decision rests with the court and a child should at all times be aware of this fact.

2.5.2 The child's physical, emotional and educational needs

A whole range of issues can arise for consideration under this heading, from the material wealth and prosperity of parents to the psychological effect on the child of living and associating with one parent rather than the other. The relative wealth of one particular parent will rarely, if ever, be the determining factor regarding the child's residence after the divorce of his parents. Focus may centre on the sexual orientation of those seeking a residence or contact order and also whether, as a general principle, a mother is better able than a father to look after a young child and respond positively to the child's emotional as well as physical needs. As to this latter point, the balance is in favour of the mother, but courts have fought shy of elevating what is seen as practical consideration to something akin to a rule of law. Heilbron J stated in *C v C (Minors: Custody)* (1988) that 'all things being equal it is a good thing for a young child to be brought up by his mother'. French J in *Plant v Plant* (1983), at p 311, was equally in favour of the mother taking on the responsibility:

> '... in the course of nature, as a matter of good sense, not of law, children who must be deprived ... of one parent or the other, usually suffer the least if left in the care of the mother ... The advantages of the mother's care, in the ordinary case, are obvious.'

Lord Donaldson MR stated in *Re W (A Minor) (Residence Order)* (1992) that there was a rebuttable presumption of fact that the best interests of a baby are served by being with its mother. He went on to stress, however, that the position might well be different with older children. In this case the baby was only one month old and lived with the father and a nanny. The mother, who was not married to the father, had signed a parental responsibility agreement in his favour but later claimed that she had been pressurised into signing. She sought an *ex parte* residence order which was refused by the judge who held that the status quo should be maintained. The mother's appeal was allowed on the basis that three to four weeks was not a long enough period in which to establish a status quo and that, looked at from the child's point of view, her best interests would be served by being with the mother, who, it should be said, already had one child, aged three.

This view will, in all probability, continue to prevail despite the advent of the so-called 'new man' apparently more ready, willing and able to adopt a positive child-rearing role. In *Re S (A Minor) (Custody)* (1991), 388 at p 390, Butler-Sloss LJ said:

> '... it is natural for young children to be with mothers but, where it is in dispute, it is a consideration but not a presumption.'

In *Re A (A Minor) (Custody)* (1991), the judge emphasised that where a child remained throughout with the mother and was very young, '...the unbroken relationship of the mother and child is one which it would be very difficult to displace, unless the mother was unsuitable to care for the child'. If the mother and child have been apart for any length of time and the mother seeks the return of the child, other considerations will apply. The conclusion is that:

> '... there is no starting point that the mother should be preferred to the father and only displaced by a preponderance of evidence to the contrary.' (p 400 A-B).

Courts have been reluctant to encourage fathers of very young children to give up work in order to take on child care responsibilities if the mother is already at home and able to care for the child. It should be emphasised that if this is the preferred solution in order to accord with the principle that the child's welfare is the paramount consideration, then courts will make that decision.

A number of recent cases have focused on the question of whether it is in the best interests of the child to reside with a homosexual or lesbian parent. In *C v C (A Minor) (Custody: Appeal)* (1991), the Court of Appeal held that being in a lesbian relationship did not of itself render the mother unfit to look after her child. The court was of the view that:

> 'Despite the vast change over the past 30 years or so in the attitudes of our society generally to the institution of marriage, to sexual morality, and to homosexual relationships, I regard it as axiomatic that the ideal environment for the upbringing of a child is the home of loving, caring and sensible parents, her father and her mother' (p 228 G).

In circumstances where the 'ideal environment' cannot be perpetuated, the court is faced with a choice of households. The mother was living with another woman, the father had remarried and the child, who lived initially with her mother, became increasingly integrated into the father's household. She was deemed 'happy at both homes'. The decision of the court was strongly influenced by the perceived effect upon the child of learning about her mother's relationship. The judge, said Glidewell LJ, seemed to have disregarded the effect on the child of her school friends making the discovery which would lead to questions being asked of her which 'may well cause her distress or embarrassment'. The impact upon her if she lived with her mother and partner was likely to be greater than if she lived with her father and his wife. The father's home equated to the 'norm' and therefore would be the most appropriate 'setting' in which to raise the child.

This case should be contrasted with *Re H (A Minor)* (1993), where an interim residence order was awarded to one partner of a lesbian relationship. They had brought up the child from birth, having made an agreement with the natural mother very early into her pregnancy that they would bring her up as their own child. At the date of the hearing the child was eight months old and had been in the sole care of the couple from birth. There were no criticisms of the applicants care for the child over the whole of that period. Scott Baker J was of the opinion that:

> 'The fact ... they are lesbians does not, according to the evidence ... make it any less likely that the placement will succeed than if they were an ordinary heterosexual couple ... The fact that they are lesbians adds one more dimension to the considerable difficulties with which this little girl will have to come to terms if she grows up in their household' (p 545 C).

The interim residence order was granted in order to formalise the situation and to allow the local authority to carry out an investigation under s 37(1) of the Children Act 1989 and, in light of the findings, make a decision as to whether a care or supervision order might be necessary. Significantly, the judge also made a prohibited steps order forbidding the natural parents from contacting the child without the court's permission.

Other factors which may be included under this heading include the desirability of keeping siblings together and the educational needs of the child, which, as was seen in *Re P (A Minor) (Education)* (1992), can lead to bitter and acrimonious arguments between parents. The Court of Appeal was prepared to uphold a split custody order in *Re P (Custody of Children: Split Custody Order)* (1991) (decided before the Children Act came into force), despite being referred to a passage from the judgment of Purchas LJ in *C v C (Minors: Custody)* (1988) at p 302 B-C to the effect that:

> 'It is really beyond argument that unless there are strong features indicating a contrary arrangement that brother and sisters should, wherever possible, be brought up together, so that they are an emotional support to each other in the stormy weather of the destruction of their family.'

The headnote to the case states that unless there are 'strong factors' an order giving custody of one child to one parent and custody of another to the other parent should not be made. The 'strong factors' alluded to could include the siblings themselves expressing the view that they should be parted, assuming of course, that they are of sufficient age, maturity and understanding to make an informed choice. See, in addition, *B v K* (1993), where the judge refused to invoke the European Convention on Child Abduction and order the return of a young child to Germany which would have had the effect of parting him from his siblings, aged nine and seven.

2.5.3 The likely effect of any change in circumstances

Prior to the Children Act coming into force, the courts recognised the importance of preserving an element of continuity in the care and control arrangements for children upon their parents' divorce. There is no reason to assume that the pre-Act position has been changed since October 1991. It is relatively easy to imagine that a significant change in the child's circumstances will rarely be to that child's advantage.

The most dramatic example of the caution exercised by judges is to be found in *J v C* (1970). The child's parents were Spanish but the child had been born in London and had, from an early age, been brought up by foster parents. The natural parents had returned to Spain, their financial position had improved and the mother's health, which had been poor for so long, had benefitted from her living in a warmer climate. The boy had lived with the foster parents for some nine years and had not seen his natural parents for many years. The parents sought care and control. The judge took the unusual step of giving care and control to 'strangers' because it was thought that, in the circumstances, to make the necessary adjustments might injure the child's health at what was deemed to be an impressionable age. The boy, who was aged 10, had not seen his family since he was three; he spoke only pidgin Spanish; and would have had to live in a 'foreign' country.

The courts will be reluctant to change the status quo except in a situation where clear benefit will accrue to the child. This was tacitly acknowledged by Ormrod LJ in *Dicocco v Milne* (1983) at p 259 when he commented:

> '... continuity of care is a most important part of a child's sense of security and disruption of established bonds are to be avoided whenever it is possible to do so.'

2.5.4 Age, sex, background and any other characteristics of the child which the court considers relevant

We have already seen that the age of the child can be an important factor in resolving disputes between parents over who has the day-to-day care of the child. The younger the child the more likely it is that a residence order will be given to the mother. There is also a link between s 1(3)(a) and (d), as age is a consideration when deciding if the child's wishes should be taken into account. Courts have in the past paid lip service to the presumption that boys are better brought up by their fathers and girls by their mothers, but there is generally little evidence to support this view, and judges will never fetter their discretion by recognising such a presumption as a principle to be applied in all cases. If a case is finely balanced, in the sense that there is little if nothing to choose between the father and mother's proposals for the child, it is more likely that the maternal claim would carry the day. This proposition is supportable only until such time as the child is able to express a preference, and it may well be that this factor is crucial in tipping the scales one way or the other.

The words 'background and characteristics' may cover a whole range of matters including the religious beliefs of the child and the parents. In *Re K* (1977), the Court of Appeal accepted that the two young children of the marriage should live with the mother who was cohabiting with her lover. The father, a parish curate, strongly objected to this arrangement, fearing that spiritual harm would befall the children where, contrary to the father's religious convictions, the mother was engaged in an adulterous relationship. The judge found the mother to be an excellent mother and the Court of Appeal had no doubt that his decision to award care and control to the mother was correct in the circumstances. The wishes of the unimpeachable parent would not be allowed to prevail if they would work against the best interests of the child.

Re R (A Minor) (Residence: Religion) (1993), discussed above, has illustrated some of the difficulties facing all parties and the judiciary when one or both parents belong to, or share the views of, a minority religious sect. Courts are concerned that a child's development should not be unduly hindered by the adherence to the tenets of a particular group which leads to isolation from a 'normal' existence. It will be of importance to recognise the difficulties which can occur if the child has a parent who is a member of the Jehovah's Witness faith. If a residence order is granted to the parent who adheres to the faith, then that parent is most unlikely to consent to the giving of a blood transfusion to the child should one prove necessary. The other parent may have parental responsibility and could give consent, but this may well depend in an emergency on that parent being aware of the problem. There is no positive obligation imposed by law upon those who have parental responsibility to communicate with each other, and in many cases, time will be of the essence. Resort may be had to another s 8 order, ie Specific Issue, but once again, its effectiveness is likely to depend upon adequate notice of the problem having occurred. In *Re R* (above) the Court of Appeal cited with approval the following extract from the decision of the court in *Re T (Minors) (Custody: Religious Upbringing)* (1981):

> '... it was not for the court to pass any judgment on the beliefs of parents where they are socially acceptable and consistent with a decent and respectable life; there was no reason why the mother should not espouse beliefs and practices of Jehovah's Witnesses for there was nothing immoral or socially obnoxious about them'

> and later

> 'It was not necessarily wrong or contrary to the welfare of children, that they should be brought up in a narrower sphere of life and subject to a stricter religious discipline than that enjoyed by most other people ...'.

Purchas LJ in *Re R* took these statements as authority for the proposition that the provisions of the Children Act 1989 must be applied by reference to the 'normal standards of society'.

2.5.5 **Any harm which the child has suffered or is at risk of suffering**

'Harm' is defined in s 31(a) in the context of care and supervision proceedings to mean 'ill-treatment or the impairment of health or development' and this definition is equally applicable to s 1(3)(e) (see s 105(1)). Undoubtedly, physical and psychological trauma are covered by the definition which specifies that 'development' includes physical, intellectual, emotional, social or behavioural development; 'health' covers physical and mental forms; and 'ill-treatment' includes sexual abuse and non-physical forms of ill treatment. In *C v C* (1991), cited above, the court was concerned not only with the mother's relationship with another woman but also that her partner had convictions for violence and had served a prison sentence in consequence of her activities. In *L v L* (1981), the father had been accused of being over-severe in the chastisement of his daughter although he was commended by Lord Denning for his sterling efforts in bringing up his young daughter whilst still maintaining his employment. Although this was only one of many factors in the case, it is used here to illustrate the point that it is something which could not be ignored in reaching a decision as to with whom the child should live.

2.5.6 **How capable are the parents and any other relevant person of meeting the child's needs?**

It should be emphasised that this subsection poses the question of how capable are the relevant adults in meeting the child's needs. One is not assessing their ability to care for the child in the conventional sense, although that could be relevant to the conclusion. Are the adults capable of identifying and responding to the needs of the child? Within one family the needs of different siblings may, and indeed probably will be, different. Grandparents, therefore, because of the likely age differential, are less likely to be capable of meeting a teenager's needs than the parents, simply because of age and perhaps cultural differences. In *Re DW* (1984), custody of a boy aged 10 was transferred from his stepmother to his natural mother and stepfather, on the basis that the boy's needs could better be met in a family unit which contained his sister rather than with a 'single non-parent'. If one parent is cohabiting, or about to cohabit, then it is legitimate for a court to consider whether or not the new parent is capable of responding positively to the child's needs. So in *Scott v Scott* (1986), the mother's partner was held to have committed indecent acts against the child.

2.5.7 **The range of powers available to the court in the proceedings in question**

This subsection gives the court the power to make any appropriate order, even if the order made was not the subject of the initial application. The court has far more discretion than it did prior to the Children Act 1989, and therefore the whole range of s 8 orders is available, and any can be made in anyone's favour (see s 10(1)). There is also the ability to make a public law order, eg for care or supervision, even though the proceedings were commenced for a s 8 order. Note should also be made of the power to prevent further applications being made. Section 91(14) provides:

> 'On disposing of any application for an order under this Act, the court may ... order that no application for an order under this Act of any specified kind may be made with respect to the child concerned by any person named in the order without leave of the court.'

F v Kent County Council (1993) is authority for the proposition that the discretion should be exercised sparingly, and in *Re T (A Minor) (Parental Responsibility: Contact)* (1993), the court directed that no further application should be made by the father for three years because his efforts to have contact with his daughter were 'likely to place her emotional welfare and stability in real danger ...'.

The Children Act 1989

This chapter seeks to outline the general principles which are to be applied throughout the Children Act in circumstances where: 'the upbringing of a child; or the administration of a child's property or the application of any income arising from it' is being determined.

In such circumstances the Act decrees that the welfare of the child is the paramount consideration.

Reference should be made to the Law Commission Report No 172 entitled Review of Child Law: Guardianship and Custody (1988). This document outlines the Commission's thinking on why the welfare of the child should be 'the paramount consideration' and not 'the first and paramount consideration', which was the general principle under the Guardianship of Minors Act 1971 and which had been applied since the Guardianship of Infants Act 1925 first used those words.

The Children Act 1989 is the '... most comprehensive and far-reaching reform of child law which has come before Parliament in living memory' (*per* Lord Mackay of Clashfern LC).

The paramountcy principle

The wording of s 1(1) of the Children Act is meant to convey the impression that the court's only concern should be the welfare of the child. But note that the principle is not of general application and does not apply, for instance, to adoption proceedings, despite their being designated as family proceedings under s 8(4) of the Act. Another example where the principle does not apply is under the Matrimonial Homes Act 1983 and applications for ouster orders. *Richards v Richards* (1984) is an important case and you ought to be aware of its significance in this respect.

For judicial thinking on the meaning of the word 'paramount' consider the speeches of Lord Wilberforce in *A v Liverpool City Council* (1981) and Lord MacDermott in *J v C* (1970).

The Law Commission's view was that the '... overall needs of the child ... must always prevail'.

Delay

The Act obliges a court to have regard to the general principle that any delay in determining the question in relation to the child's upbringing is likely to prejudice the welfare of the child. Note that the Act does not state that it *will* prejudice the child's welfare. In practice, delay can result for a number of reasons, but the legislation urges the court to set a timetable against which all those involved in the case will be judged. In broad terms, if the upbringing of the child is at issue then everything possible should be done to reduce uncertainty over the future custodial arrangements for the child. See, for example, the Court of Appeal decision in *B v B (Minors) (Interviews and Listing Arrangements)* (1994).

Presumption of no order

Section 1(5) has been described as 'one of the most innovative and influential principles of the Act'. The Act acknowledges, as far as is consistent with the child's welfare, that parents are the best people to look after their children. Therefore, only as a 'last resort' should a court consider making an order that might, for example, remove the children from the care of their parents. Sometimes, though, an order may be welcomed by parents after divorce, so that each knows the precise ambit of their ongoing responsibilities towards the child, eg, *B v B (A Minor) (Residence Order)* (1992).

The checklist

The Children Act sought to promote consistency in respect of decision-making by introducing a list of factors to which all courts must have regard when considering making, varying or discharging s 8 orders, or when any of these matters is being considered in respect of orders under Part IV of the Act. The benefits of having such a checklist are:

- greater consistency possible;
- all parties will be aware of the important factors in the decision- making process; and
- legal advisors will be better equipped to give advice.

Note the significance of *Gillick v West Norfolk Area Health Authority* (1985) in respect of the child's voice being heard in the proceedings and the possibility of it being influential to the outcome. The weight to be placed upon the child's views will be determined on a case-by-case basis reflecting the maturity and understanding of the child. It is, though, a controversial area, and one which deserves an investment of time in order to become familiar with the recent case law, eg *Re M (Contact) (Welfare Test)* (1995) and *B v B (Minors) (Interviews and Listing Arrangements)* (1994). The other factors referred to in s 1(3) are also generating an increasing number of reported cases and attention should be paid to all of them. It may be worth bearing in mind that if the child has suffered, or is suffering, harm, then local authority intervention may be required and a care or supervision order may be made. Do remember, however, that for a public law order to be made, the threshold criterion of 'significant harm' needs to be proved, whereas the requirement under s 1(3)(e) is 'harm'.

Chapter 3

Parental Responsibility

3.1 Rights and responsibilities

It is becoming increasingly apparent that lawyers need to focus both on the rights and responsibilities of *parents* and *children.* The Children Act 1989 has recognised that children do have rights, particularly of self-determination as to their future, but in this chapter we shall focus on the concept of parental responsibility. Parental responsibility is the modern terminology superseding the concept of parental rights. It is worth making the point at the outset that parental rights to control a child do not exist for the benefit of the parent. As Lord Fraser put it in the influential decision of *Gillick v West Norfolk Area Health Authority* (1985):

> 'They exist for the benefit of the child and they are justified only in so far as they enable the parent to perform his duties towards the child, and towards other children in the family.'

In support of the premise, Lord Fraser refers to *Blackstone's Commentaries* (17th ed) (1830) to the effect that 'The power of parents over their children is derived from ... their duty'.

The Law Commission in its Report No 172, entitled Family Law: Review of Child Law: Guardianship and Custody [1988] accepts as a fundamental principle that the primary responsibility for the upbringing of children rests with their parents. The role of the state is to help them to discharge the responsibility and the state should not intervene unless there is an unacceptable risk to the child. The Report goes on to suggest that '... present law (pre Children Act) does not adequately recognise that parenthood is a matter of responsibility rather than rights ...' (para 2:1 p 5).

Historically, the legal right to control a legitimate child lies with the father. The father was viewed as the 'natural' guardian of his child. In *Re Agar Ellis* (1883), Cotton LJ stated:

> '... by birth, a child is subject to a father; it is for the general interests of families, and for the general interests of children ... that the court should not ... interfere with the discretion of the father, but leave to him the responsibility of exercising that power which nature has given him by the birth of the child.'

Nearly a century later, Stamp LJ was able to state the opposite view. In *Re K* (1977), at p 651, he is of the opinion that:

> '... effect should be given to the dictates of nature which

> makes the mother the natural guardian, protector and comforter of the very young.'

A mother's legal standing in respect of her children improved as a result of various enactments, particularly the Guardianship of Infants Acts 1886 and 1925 and the Guardianship Act 1973. However, it is significant that parliament never bestowed upon the mother the power to be equated with the father as to the natural guardianship of her child.

What the Children Act 1989 does is to abolish the rule of law that the father is the natural guardian of his legitimate children (s 2(4)). The reason fathers acquired this right is to be found in the concept of guardianship, which developed as a means of safeguarding a family's property. As the Law Commission states:

> '... [it] later became an instrument for maintaining the authority of the father over his legitimate minor children.'

The Children Act 1989 defines a parent so as to include 'any party to a marriage (whether or not subsisting) in relation to whom the child concerned is a child of the family' (Schedule 1, para 16(2)). To fall within this definition, a non-natural parent, eg a stepfather, must be a party to a marriage and must have treated the child as a child of the family. Therefore, as illustrated in *J v J (A Minor) (Property Transfer)* (1993), a man who had treated the mother's daughter as a child of the family, but who had simply lived with the mother without marrying her, was held not to be a parent within the definition.

This begs the question: what is the extent of a parent's rights and responsibilities and how may they be exercised? It would appear that the degree of control parents may exercise over their children is reduced as the children get older, a situation recognised by Lord Denning MR in the case of *Hewer v Bryant* (1969) at p 585, approved by the House of Lords in the *Gillick* case. After referring to the strict attitudes of Victorian parents and a father's power to control his children, which ceased only when the child reached majority, he went on to state:

> 'The common law can, and should, keep pace with the times. It should declare, in conformity with the recent report on the Age of Majority ... (Cmnd 342) ... that the legal right of a parent to the custody of a child ends at the eighteenth birthday, and even up till then, it is a dwindling right which the courts will hesitate to enforce against the wishes of the child, the older he is. It starts with a right of control and ends with little more than advice.'

Lord Scarman in *Gillick* provided the context. He considered that the law relating to parent and child:

> '... is concerned with the problems of the growth and maturity of the human personality ... If the law should impose on the process of "growing up" fixed limits where nature knows only a continuous process, the price would be artificiality and a lack of realism in an area where the law must be sensitive to human development and social change ... The underlying principle ... is that parental rights yield to the child's right to make his own decisions when he reaches a sufficient understanding and intelligence to be capable of making up his own mind on the matter requiring decision' (pp 421-422).

Prior to the Children Act 1989, the relevant definition of parental rights was contained in s 85(1) of the Children Act 1975. There it was stated that 'parental rights and duties' means 'all the rights and duties which by law the mother and father have in relation to a legitimate child and his property ... and shall include a right of access ...'.

It will be immediately apparent that the definition is conspicuously lacking in detail as to what 'all those rights and duties' actually encompass. Section 3(1) of the Children Act 1989 offers the following definition of parental responsibility:

> 'all the rights, duties, powers, responsibility and authority which by law a parent of a child has in relation to the child and his property.'

As Hale J said in *Re M (Care: Leave to Interview Child)* (1995) at p 826 A:

> 'Until the child is old enough to decide for himself, a parent undoubtedly has some control over whom he may see and who may see him.'

The Law Commission's view was that no useful purpose would be achieved in seeking to establish a definitive list of rights, duties, powers and responsibilities as:

> '... the list must change from time to time to meet differing needs and circumstances. As the *Gillick* case itself demonstrated, it must also vary with the age and maturity of the child and the circumstances of each individual case.'

This may be so, but parents need to have some idea of the limits to their authority, whether they be imposed by statute or recognised by the common law. A trawl through the major textbooks is worthwhile if only for the chance to determine whether a relative consensus exists as to what are or are not recognised as being the major incidents of parental responsibility. In broad terms they can be reduced to the following:

- Acting on behalf of the child by giving or refusing consent to certain courses of action, eg medical treatment, changing the child's surname, marriage, and adoption.
- Creating a 'home environment' within which the child operates. This embraces caring for the child, providing accommodation, providing for the child's education and, at least initially, determining his or her religion. Within this environment, the parent has the ability to exercise common law rights in respect of disciplining the child.
- Parents have a duty to maintain contact with their children providing always that it is consistent with the welfare principle, ie in the child's best interests.

It is not proposed to go into great detail on all of the incidents of parenthood but some have generated much legal controversy and therefore demand further attention.

3.2 Consent to medical treatment

The most controversial is the issue of consent to medical treatment. As a general rule, the consent of a person holding parental responsibility will be required before medical treatment may be given to the child under 16. Consent itself does not mean that treatment *will* be given. It is, to use Lord Donaldson's words in *Re R (A Minor) (Wardship: Medical Treatment)* (1992):

> 'merely a key which unlocks a door ... in general a doctor is not entitled to treat a patient without the consent of someone who is authorised to give that consent.'

That, of course, will usually be a parent; however, it may be a local authority or any other person in whose favour a residence order has been granted. The potential for conflict between those with parental responsibility should not be under-estimated, but from the medical practitioner's viewpoint, he or she may act providing the consent of one person with parental responsibility is granted. Yet this is not the only situation where conflict may occur. To the general principle stated above must be added the caveat that a 'Gillick competent' child under the age of 16 may give or refuse consent to treatment. Where there is a conflict between the parent and child, the court must not give any undue weight to the wishes of the parent and must take the decision which it deems to be in the best interests of the child.

There is a statement by Johnson J in *Re S (A Minor) (Medical Treatment)* (1994) that for a judge at first instance the law is now clear. Johnson J cites three cases upon which the current law is based: *Re R (A Minor) (Medical Treatment)* (1992), *Re W*

(A Minor) (Consent to Medical Treatment) (1993), and *Re T (An adult) (Consent to Medical Treatment)* (1992), and concludes that the court has power to override a decision of a child to refuse medication and treatment, irrespective of whether he or she is competent to give consent. However, the starting point for a court is to give effect to the patient's wishes 'unless the balance was strongly to the contrary effect'. The case concerned a girl aged 15 who had suffered from birth from the disease thalassaemia, a condition which prevents the body from producing red blood cells. The condition, unless treated, is life threatening. She was kept alive with blood transfusions and daily injections. In 1989 the mother and daughter started to attend meetings of Jehovah's Witnesses and in 1994 decided that there were to be no more blood transfusions. The local authority invoked the court's inherent jurisdiction, asking for an order to override the parent's wishes. The mother quite clearly would not give her consent to ongoing transfusions. The question facing the court was whether the girl was 'Gillick competent' and so able to express a considered opinion on the continuance or otherwise of the blood transfusions. After taking detailed evidence, it concluded that her 'capacity was not commensurate with the gravity of the decision'. The court took into account the following points:

- the patient was weak and ill;
- she was subject to considerable pressure from her mother;
- she had lost faith in her long term treatment;
- she did not fully understand the implications of what would happen to her in terms of her inevitable death and the pain and distress leading up to it.

Note, however, that even if she had been found to be 'Gillick competent', the court possessed the power to override her refusal to consent to treatment if it decided that it was in her best interests to go ahead with the treatment.

It is imperative in such cases to appreciate fully the significance of a finding of Gillick competence, and a detailed examination of the *Gillick* decision is called for. It is instructive not only to examine the House of Lords judgment but also that of the Court of Appeal (1985) and the first instance judge, Woolf J (1984) in order to appreciate the diversity of opinion on this issue. The unanimous decision of the Court of Appeal to grant the declarations sought by Mrs Gillick was reversed by the House of Lords.

3.3 The facts of the *Gillick* case

Mrs Gillick had five daughters under the age of 16. She took exception to a Department of Health and Social Security circular issued to health authorities which advised general medical practitioners that they would not be acting unlawfully if they prescribed contraceptives to girls under 16 providing the doctor was acting in good faith and seeking to protect the girl against the harmful effects of sexual intercourse. The DHSS advice urged doctors to seek to persuade the patient to involve her parents, but nevertheless, if she would not, and if, in the doctor's opinion, exercising clinical judgment, the patient required contraceptives, they should be prescribed. The advice was based upon a recognition of the confidentiality principle between doctors and patients.

Mrs Gillick sought an assurance from her health authority that her daughters would not be given advice or treatment without her prior knowledge and consent while they were under the age of 16. The authority refused, and Mrs Gillick approached the court seeking a declaration that the advice contained in the circular was unlawful. She was particularly concerned that it was encouraging doctors to commit a criminal offence contrary to s 28(1) or s 6(1) of the Sexual Offences Act 1956. Section 28(1) makes it an offence for a person to cause or encourage ... the commission of unlawful sexual intercourse with ... a girl under 16 for whom he is responsible. Section 6(1) makes it an offence for a man to have unlawful sexual intercourse with a girl under the age of 16, and Mrs Gillick's contention was that a doctor would place himself in the position of being an accessory to the crime were he to prescribe contraceptives knowing that the girl intended to engage in sexual intercourse.

The House of Lords held by a four to one majority that the law did not recognise any rule of absolute parental authority until a fixed age. It was determined that the law would recognise parental rights only as long as they were needed for the protection of the child. Parental rights 'yielded' to the child's right to make decisions based upon proof that he or she had sufficient understanding and intelligence to be capable of making up his or her own mind. In respect of the facts of *Gillick*, Lord Fraser thought that a doctor would not breach the law by failing to inform parents that their daughter was to be prescribed contraceptives if the following are satisfied:

- that the girl, although under 16, will understand his advice;
- that she cannot be persuaded to inform her parents or give permission for the doctor to inform them;

- that she is likely to begin or continue having sexual intercourse with or without contraceptive treatment;
- that her physical or mental health will suffer if she does not receive contraceptives; and
- that her best interests require her to be given contraceptive advice, treatment, or both, without parental consent.

The intriguing word used by the their Lordships in respect of the exercise of parental rights is 'yielded'. Should this be taken to mean that, once Gillick competence is established, all parental rights cease to exist? Or should it be taken to mean that parental rights co-exist with children's rights?

The medical treatment cases cited above would seem to give primacy to neither, recognising that a court exercising its inherent jurisdiction has the right finally to determine what is in the best interests of the child. Yet *Re S (A Minor) (Consent to medical treatment)* (1994) clearly articulates the view that the patient's wishes should prevail 'unless the balance was strongly to the contrary'. Lord Donaldson MR in *Re R* (1992) also took the view that, in circumstances where the Gillick competent child refuses consent to treatment, both parents (or those with parental responsibility) and the court had the power to provide the necessary consent to treatment. The inherent jurisdiction, and particularly the wardship jurisdiction, bestow on a court wider powers than those apparently possessed by parents and the Gillick competent child.

The word 'yielded' is taken from Lord Scarman's speech in *Gillick*, but there is little in any of the speeches to support the proposition that 'yielded' is synonymous with 'relinquish', although Lord Scarman does use the word 'terminate' in respect of the parental right to determine whether a Gillick competent child will have medical treatment:

> '... I would hold as a matter of law the parental right to determine whether or not their minor child below the age of 16 will have medical treatment terminates if and when the child achieved sufficient understanding and intelligence to enable him or her to understand fully what is proposed' (p 423(j)).

This, of course, should not be taken to mean that all parental rights terminate once competence is established, but there is no reason in principle why that conclusion should not be reached. It may, however, cause a fair measure of friction in a household if children under 18 believe that on all issues their views are sacrosanct and have the support of the law! Despite

Johnson J's view in *Re S* (1994) that the law is 'now clear', it would be helpful if the Court of Appeal were to give a clear statement as to whether parental rights are co-extensive with children's rights once the illusive Gillick competency is established.

Another issue to ponder is whether or not a Gillick competent child may give consent to *any* form of medical treatment, for example sterilisation. In *Re D* (1976), it was established that sterilisation of a child for non-therapeutic reasons could not be sanctioned through parental consent. In *Re B (A Minor) (Wardship: Sterilisation)* (1987) Lord Templeman was of the opinion that 'sterilisation of a girl under 18 should only be carried out with the leave of a High Court judge' and went on to state:

> 'A doctor performing a sterilisation operation with the consent of the parents might still be liable in criminal, civil or professional proceedings' (p 214 h and j).

However a distinction needs to be drawn between a girl requiring a hysterectomy for therapeutic reasons rather than in order to achieve sterilisation. In such circumstances, parents of a minor were in a position to supply the necessary consent. See, for example, Sir Stephen Brown in *Re E (A Minor) (Medical Treatment)* (1991), in which case the parents of a severely mentally handicapped 17 year old girl were advised that she required a hysterectomy as the only effective means of remedying a menstrual condition. The parents were prepared to give their consent, but the girl was made a ward of court in order that the legal position regarding consent could be clarified. The judge said:

> 'I am satisfied ... that there is a clear distinction to be made between cases where the operation is required for genuine therapeutic reasons and those where the operation is designed to achieve sterilisation. That position was recognised by Lord Bridge in *Re F* (1990) ... I think that J's parents are in a position to give a valid consent to the proposed operation' (p 587 B).

At the time of writing, there is no authority to support the proposition that parental responsibility includes the right to consent to a hysterectomy for a child, for non-therapeutic reasons.

3.4 Child's surname

An all-too-familiar problem facing divorced parents is the demand upon the re-marriage of one parent for the children in her care to adopt the surname of the stepfather. Section 13(1) of the Children Act 1989 states that, where a residence order is in force with respect to a child, no person may:

> (a) cause the child to be known by a new surname; or
>
> (b) remove him from the United Kingdom ... without either the written consent of every person who has parental responsibility for the child or the leave of the court.

Therefore those with parental responsibility cannot act unilaterally in this matter. The basic principles are stated in the case of *W v A* (1981), and recently approved in *Re F (Child: Surname)* (1993). The change of a child's surname is regarded as an important matter which should not be undertaken lightly. The mere fact that a child is known by a surname different from that taken by the new family unit will not, of itself, be sufficient reason to warrant a change of surname. Reference should be made to the judgment of Dunn LJ in *W v A*. After stating that any problems over surnames should be resolved by reference to the welfare principle, he stated:

> 'When considering the question of a change of name, that is to be regarded as an important matter. It is a matter for the discretion of the individual judge hearing the case, seeing the witnesses, seeing the parents, possibly seeing the children, to decide whether or not it is in the interests of the child in the particular circumstances of the case that his surname should or should not be changed; and the judge will take into account all the circumstances of the case, including, no doubt, where appropriate, any embarrassment which may be caused to the child by not changing his name and, on the other hand, the long term interests of the child, the importance of maintaining the child's links with his paternal family, and the stability or otherwise of the mother's remarriage. I only mention those as typical examples of the kinds of considerations which arise in these cases, but the judge will take into account all the relevant circumstances in the particular case before him.'

By Practice Direction dated 20 December 1994, any application for the enrolment of a deed poll to change the surname of a child must be supported by the production of the consent in writing of every other person having parental responsibility for the child. In the absence of such consent, the application will be adjourned unless and until leave is given to change the surname by the court first seized of the matter. *Practice Direction (Minor: Change of Surname)* (1977) is revoked. The current Practice Direction can be located at [1995] 1 FLR 458.

3.5 Discipline

Parental responsibility includes the right to inflict corporal punishment on a child so long as it is reasonable and moderate. This suggests that the 'reasonable relationship rule' employed by the criminal law to determine, for example, the success of self-defence will be relevant here. The chastisement should be in proportion to the activity; the parents should be able to demonstrate that they acted in good faith and with reason. Physical factors and mental age should also be relevant in determining the reasonableness of the punishment. Although school teachers act *in loco parentis*, the Education Reform Act 1988 forbids the exercise by them of corporal punishment, irrespective of whether or not they have parental authority. Teachers who breach the law may find themselves in breach of contract and facing disciplinary action for what may amount to 'gross misconduct'.

3.6 Education

Section 36 of the Education Act 1944 imposes a duty upon parents to 'cause [their child] to receive efficient full-time education suitable to his age, ability and aptitude and to any special educational needs he may have, either by regular attendance at school or otherwise'. In practice, the majority of parents or those with parental responsibility will ensure that their children receive full time education via the state system, although they are under no legal obligation to do so.

A child may be kept at home and taught by a tutor or tutors brought to the house for the purpose. However, this is lawful only if it can be established that the s 36 requirements are met. This may be more difficult to establish now that the National Curriculum is operational than prior to its introduction.

It may be confidently asserted that, in line with the *Gillick* principles, the older the child the greater the say he or she will have in determining which school to attend. In *Re P (A Minor) (Education)* (1992), the children were being educated in a fee-paying school. The parents went through an acrimonious divorce and the father, who had assumed the responsibility to continue paying the school fees, declared that he did not have sufficient financial resources to ensure his eldest son could remain at the school until he attained majority. He therefore proposed that the boy attend a good, local, day school. The mother applied for her son's education to be determined by a judge, who decided that the boy should continue at boarding school. The father appealed, and at this point his son, aged 14, put forward his views that he wished to attend the local day school. The Court of Appeal stated that in family proceedings, the court was under a duty to 'listen and to pay respect' to the wishes and views of older children. This boy was described as 'mature, sensible and intelligent', and, having concluded that his wish to go to the local school was based 'on sound reasons', the court acceded to his wishes.

3.7 Parental responsibility under the Children Act 1989

In this section, the focus will be upon the concept of parental responsibility in the context of the Children Act 1989. It should be noted at the outset that there has been criticism of the 1989 Act in that it does not empower a court to vest parental responsibility in an individual, apart from the father of a child, without a residence order under s 8 being made, or by appointing that person as guardian of the child. In *Re W (A Minor) (Adoption: mother under disability)* (1995), Wall J thought that it was 'highly artificial' for a court to make a residence order in favour of a person with whom there was no intention that the child should reside, simply in order to give him or her parental responsibility. The making of such orders, it was said, '... should not be encouraged'. In this case, the mother was suffering from a mental disability which rendered her incapable of caring for the child. The maternal grandmother had been given parental responsibility via the mechanism of awarding a residence order to her, despite the fact that the child was in the care of the local authority.

The first section which demands attention is s 2(1), which states:

> 'Where a child's father and mother were married to each other at the time of his birth, they shall each have parental responsibility for the child.'

Thus parental responsibility is automatically acquired by parents of legitimate children. Even if the parents are not married at the date of birth, parental responsibility may still be automatically acquired if the child is subsequently legitimised by the marriage of the parents. Reference should be made to s 1 of the Family Law Reform Act 1987, which is deemed by s 2(3) of the Children Act 1989 to apply in such circumstances.

Section 2(2) of the Act emphasises that if the mother and father are not married at the time of the child's birth, then only the mother acquires parental responsibility and the father may only acquire it in accordance with the provisions of the Act (s 4).

It will be apparent, therefore, that more than one person may have parental responsibility for a child at any one time. Parental responsibility may be viewed as a shared, or at least potentially shareable, responsibility (see Hale J in *Re M (Care: Leave to Interview Child)* (1995)). So, a person appointed as a child's guardian under the terms of s 5 of the Children Act 1989 shall have parental responsibility, as will a local authority granted a care order under ss 31 and 33(3) of the 1989 Act.

Other examples are where a child becomes a ward of court, when the court itself acquires parental responsibility, and where a person is granted a residence order under s 12(1) and (2).

So the crucial point is that one person does not lose parental responsibility simply because someone else acquires it. Parents who divorce do not relinquish parental responsibility, which is consistent with the principle that parenthood is a long term commitment and not dependent upon marital status. Section 2(7) emphasises that when more than one person has parental responsibility, each may act alone 'and without the other(s) in meeting that responsibility...'. This may lead to difficulties with certain individuals who need to rely upon those with parental responsibility to authorise their actions. An obvious example is the surgeon, who could operate on a child providing he or she has the unequivocal consent of someone with parental responsibility. In practice, if one parent is vehemently opposed to an operation being performed and the other parent is clearly committed to providing the necessary consent, it is likely that some delay will be occasioned while the surgeon seeks clarification from a court, although the operation would appear to be lawful in the light of the latter's consent. This is further complicated by the fact that a Gillick competent child may oppose the operation in any case. In such circumstances, the safest course of action would be to seek the guidance of the court by way of a specific issue order or, if it is an emergency, by invoking the inherent jurisdiction of the court. It will be recalled that the Court of Appeal determined in *Re R (A Minor) (Wardship: Medical Treatment)* (1991) and *Re W (A Minor) (Medical Treatment)* (1992) that the court, in exercising its inherent jurisdiction, could override the wishes of the Gillick competent child. It was, however, pointed out that this would be a last resort and only after the court had approached the matter 'with a strong predilection to give effect to the child's wishes'.

The Law Commission in its Report No 172, Guardianship and Custody (1988), was of the opinion that the law prior to the implementation of the Children Act was 'not clear about whether [parents] may act independently'. It stated that, under the Guardianship Act 1973, married couples could do so, yet under the Children Act 1975, joint holders of parental rights could only act alone if there was no significant disapproval from the other party. The Commission rejected as 'unworkable' the proposition that a legal duty to consult should be established. 'The person looking after the child has to be able to take decisions in the child's best interests as and when they arise. Some may have to be taken very quickly.' The Report went on to recommend:

> '... that the equal and independent status of parents be preserved and, indeed, applied to others (principally guardians) who may share parental responsibility in the future.'

Despite the potential for conflict between those with parental responsibility, it is heartening to note that, at the time of writing, no significant case law relating to this matter has been generated. In the event that disputes should arise, Wilson J in *Re P (A Minor) (Parental Responsibility Order)* (1994) alluded to how they might be resolved. This was a case where the mother and father had not married and the father had sought a parental responsibility under s 4 of the 1989 Act. The judge stated (at p 585 c):

> 'It is to be noted that on any view an order for parental responsibility gives the father no power to override the decision of the mother, who already has such responsibility: in the event of disagreement between them on a specific issue relating to the child, the court will have to resolve it. If the father were to seek to misuse the rights given to him under s 4 such misuse could, as a second last resort, be controlled by the court under a prohibited steps order against him and/or a specific issue order'.

There are two situations where parental responsibility cannot be exercised unilaterally. These are, first, where it would be incompatible with a court order, and secondly, where the proposed exercise of the responsibility would be contrary to statute. An example of the former can be found in the law relating to adoption, where the consent of both parents is needed before an order freeing the child for adoption can be made (see s 16(1)(b) of the Adoption Act 1976). Falling into the latter category would be an attempt to act contrary to an order made under the provisions of the 1989 Act, eg, a s 8 order (see s 2(8)).

The fact that both married parents have parental responsibility does not mean that they must take equal day-to-day responsibility for their children. In fact it could be agreed between them that the care of the child is delegated to a third party, for example a nanny, with the right to make decisions on the child's behalf also being delegated. Section 3(5) of the Children Act states:

> 'A person who (a) does not have parental responsibility for a particular child but (b) has care of the child may (subject to the provisions of this Act) do what is reasonable in all the circumstances of the case for the

> purpose of safeguarding and promoting the child's welfare.'

Ultimately, parents cannot avoid legal responsibility for their children unless they are adopted, and may well face either or both criminal and civil sanctions if they allow a situation to develop where the child is injured or neglected. Section 1 of the Children and Young Persons Act 1933 makes it a criminal offence for a person who has attained the age of 16 '... and has responsibility for any child' to neglect, abandon, ill treat or cause him unnecessary suffering or injury to health. Section 1(2)(a) states:

> 'A parent or other person legally liable to maintain a child or young person or the legal guardian of a child or young person shall be deemed to have neglected him in a manner likely to cause injury to his health if he has failed to provide adequate food, clothing, medical aid or lodging for him, or if, having been unable otherwise to provide such food, clothing, medical aid or lodging, he has failed to take steps to procure it to be provided under the enactments applicable in that behalf.'

It therefore follows that there is a significant obligation placed upon those with parental responsibility to ensure that in delegating care of their child to another they are satisfied that the child will not come to any harm and that the person with care is suitable to accept the responsibility.

There may be circumstances where there is no one with parental responsibility for a child, as when a child is orphaned and there is no member of the extended family who is prepared to take on the obligation of caring. Or indeed there may be no extended family at all. This situation arose in *Re SH (Care Order: Orphan)* (1995). The parents of a boy aged 11 were both dead and no member of the extended family would assume the care function. In order to obtain parental responsibility, the local authority, which wished to place him for adoption, sought a care order. Sections 20, 22, 23 and 24 of the Children Act provide local authorities with extensive powers in respect of accommodation, maintenance, advice and assistance, but they do not confer parental responsibility upon a local authority. Hence the decision to apply for a care order. The problem facing the local authority was the need to satisfy the threshold criteria in s 31 of the Children Act 1989. The boy had been in local authority accommodation for sometime prior to the application, and was therefore not suffering significant harm at the time of the application. The court, following the precedent of *Re M (A Minor) (Care Order: Threshold Conditions)* (1994) accepted that the wording in s 31 was in fact meant in the sense that the child must be shown to have been suffering significant harm when the rescue operation was instigated by the local authority. It was held that the care order should be granted, and therefore parental responsibility would reside with the local authority.

3.8 Unmarried fathers

An unmarried father may seek to acquire parental responsibility in various ways. The most obvious is by invoking s 4 of the Children Act 1989. The father may apply to the court for a parental responsibility order or, and this surely must be preferable, he and the mother may agree that he should acquire responsibility for the child. The fact that a father has to apply to the court would suggest opposition from the mother, who will invariably have day-to-day control of the child as well as parental responsibility. Having said that, it does not automatically follow that maternal opposition will inevitably be in the child's best interests, and in such circumstances the court will have to give full consideration to all the evidence before determining the outcome. The major principle is, of course, that the welfare of the child is the paramount consideration.

What factors will a court take into account in determining the issue? In the leading case of *Re H and Another (Minors) (No 3)* (1991), Balcombe LJ cited three matters which should be considered. They are:

- the degree of commitment which the father has shown towards the child;
- the degree of attachment which exists between the father and child; and
- the reasons of the father for applying for the order.

It was said by the judge that the list was not meant to be exhaustive. The factors listed above were described as being 'material' to the eventual outcome. They were cited with approval by the Court of Appeal in *Re G (A Minor) (Parental Responsibility Order)* (1994). The reasons for the father's application should not be 'demonstrably improper or wrong'. In other words, it was in the best interests of the child that the order should be made.

In this case, the parents of a six year old girl were unmarried, and the mother cohabited with another man. The judge referred to the mother as having led a 'very disturbed lifestyle', having problems with alcohol and drugs. The father had regular contact with his daughter. The daughter came into the care of the local authority and was placed with foster parents. The local authority was given the discretion to determine contact between the father and his daughter. However, the question for the Court of Appeal was whether or not a parental responsibility order should be made in his favour. If so, it would mean that the mother, the local authority and the father would possess parental responsibility. There was, said the Court of Appeal, clearly friction between the father and social workers representing the local authority, but that in itself was not a good reason for refusing to make the order requested by the father. The father was described as 'loving and caring ... who had a positive role to play in [his daughter's] future...' and the court accepted that he had shown sufficient commitment towards the child to warrant a parental responsibility order in his favour.

It should be noted that the court also accepted that 'the overriding or paramount question of the child's welfare applies to the making of a parental responsibility order'. It is instructive to give consideration to a decision of the Family Division reported in the All England Law Reports immediately preceding *Re H*. In *D v Hereford and Worcester County Council* (1991), Ward J was dealing with the question of whether or not a parental rights order should be granted under s 4(1) of the Family Law Reform Act 1987 (the predecessor of the current s 4). He was of the opinion that all relevant factors ought to be taken into account, including the father's character and antecedents. If the child was in the care of the local authority, then the background to the making of the care order could be considered, as could the local authority's plans for the child. In short, the burden of proof appears to be placed firmly upon the father, although it is doubtful if any one particular factor would ever be conclusive in the court reaching its decision.

In conclusion, it may be helpful to summarise the current position by citing Balcombe LJ in *Re E (Parental Responsibility)* (1995). Having referred to the authorities, he stated:

> 'I would certainly approach any application for a parental responsibility order under the Children Act 1989 by a father who has shown the degree of attachment and commitment to his child as this father has shown to C on the basis that such an order would be *prima facie* for the welfare of the child. I would require to be convinced by cogent evidence that the child's welfare would be adversely affected by the making of such an order' (p 398 G).

As Mustill LJ said in *Re C (Minors)* (1992), the question is whether or not the father has shown sufficient commitment to his child and whether the 'association between the parties [is] sufficiently enduring ... to justify giving the father a legal status equivalent to that which he would have enjoyed [had the parties been married]'.

A prerequisite for obtaining a parental responsibility order is proof of paternity. The use of DNA profiling can now establish paternity, whereas the resort to blood testing was able only to show that a particular man could not be the father. The issues were raised in *Re E (Parental Responsibility: Blood Tests)* (1995), where the Court of Appeal refused to order either blood tests or DNA profiling. The jurisdiction to make such an order is found in s 20 of the Family Law Reform Act 1969, and the requirement is for civil proceedings to be extant and the issue of paternity 'falls to be determined by the court hearing the proceedings ...'.

In *Re E*, there were no proceedings in which the child's paternity fell to be determined – only an application by the father for such tests to be undertaken. Relying on *Re F (A Minor) (Paternity Tests)* (1993), the court held there to be no jurisdiction to make a 'free-standing order'. It was accepted by the Court that an order could only be made in proceedings where paternity was an 'ancillary matter'. Examples cited were a father's application for contact with his child, or where the mother has applied for financial provision from the father in respect of the child. A court should exercise its discretion by reference to principles set out by the House of Lords in *S v McC; W v W* (1972). These are:

- the presumption of legitimacy, ie the child of a married woman has been fathered by her husband, merely determined the onus of proof;
- public policy does not demand that any special protection should be given by law to the status of legitimacy;
- in many cases the interests of the child are best served if the truth be determined;
- the interests of justice may conflict with the interests of the child;
- a blood test should not be banned on some 'vague and shadowy conjecture';
- blood samples may not be taken from a person under the age of 16 without the consent of a person having parental responsibility.

Reference should also be made to ss 27 and 28 of the Human Fertilisation and Embryology Act 1990. Section 27(i) deals with the situation of a child being born as a result of *in vitro* fertilisation. The woman who 'carries or has carried' the child is to be treated as the mother of the child. Section 28 refers to the meaning of 'father' and makes it clear that if a married woman has been artificially inseminated then the husband will be deemed to be the father for legal purposes unless he did not consent to his wife's insemination.

3.8.1 Other ways of acquiring parental responsibility

Unmarried fathers may acquire parental responsibility by seeking to invoke s 12 of the Children Act. The section makes it clear that should a father be successful with an application for a residence order, then the court shall also make an order under s 4 giving him parental responsibility. The parental responsibility order will remain in force for as long as the residence order has effect.

Another way is for the father to make an application under s 5 of the 1989 Act to become the child's guardian. This may happen only if the child has no parent with parental responsibility for him or her, or if a residence order has been made with respect to the child in favour of a parent or guardian who has died while the order was in force.

The fact that parental responsibility relates to a person under the age of 18 raises two particular problems. It is legally possible for a 'child' of 16 to marry, and it is therefore questionable whether or not such a person should be governed in any respect by the rights, duties and responsibilities bestowed by law on someone else, usually, of course, a natural parent. Indeed the 16 year old may be a parent and possess parental responsibility in respect of his or her own child. Prior to the Children Act 1989, the authorities suggested that custody rights over a child ended at the time of marriage. See, for example, Lord Justice Sachs in *Hewer v Bryant* (1969).

It will be recalled that Lord Denning thought that parental rights would rarely be enforced against the wishes of the child as he approached the age of majority. Gillick competency would now need to be taken into account, and therefore, if a 16 year old parent is exercising parental responsibility, then it is difficult to imagine circumstances in which that person would fail the Gillick maturity test. Lord Denning did stress that the legal rights possessed by a parent continue until the age of 18, and until the contrary is decided this view should prevail. However, in circumstances such as those outlined above, it could be argued that, in the overwhelming majority of situations, it would not be consistent with the welfare principle to enforce parental responsibility against the wishes of the minor.

The second matter relates to the point at which parental responsibility commences. The Children Act 1989 refers throughout to 'the child' or 'a child', and if one draws an analogy with the criminal law, then responsibility will commence when the 'child' has taken his first breath independently of his mother. Yet if the child were still-born or died before the umbilical cord is cut, parental responsibility must surely exist. Section 4 focuses attention upon the time of birth as the appropriate moment for parental responsibility to commence. Yet attempts have been made on at least three occasions in the last 20 years to persuade the judiciary to extend legal rights to foetuses. The response has been less than enthusiastic. In *Paton v Trustees of the British Pregnancy Advisory Service* (1978), Sir George Baker P stated:

> 'The foetus cannot, in English law, in my view, have any right of its own at least until it is born and has a separate existence from the mother. That permeates the whole of the civil law of this country and is, indeed, the basis of the decisions in those countries where law is founded on the common law.'

The father was attempting to gain legal support in order to prevent his wife from terminating her pregnancy in accordance with the provisions of s 1 of the Abortion Act 1967. Doctors had signed the appropriate certificates and there were no doubts that the termination would have been lawful. The father claimed he had a right to a say in the destiny of his child, that he had not been consulted and did not wish his wife to have an abortion. The conclusion was that English law does not give a father a right to have a say in the destiny of the child that he has helped to conceive.

In a similar case nearly a decade later, the Court of Appeal followed the reasoning in *Paton* and concluded that the father, who was not married to the mother, would not be entitled to an injunction in order to prevent the foetus from being aborted.

C v S (1987) raises a number of points of contention other than the issue of whether or not a father has any cause of action in respect of his unborn child. In particular, consideration was given to whether the proposed abortion would contravene s 1 of the Infant Life Preservation Act 1929, which makes it a criminal offence to 'destroy the life of a child capable of being born alive ...'. The court ruled that the child (foetus) of between 18 and 21 weeks gestation could not properly be described as capable of being born alive as the foetus was incapable of breathing naturally or with the aid of a ventilator. *Re F (In utero)* (1988) decides that a court does not possess any jurisdiction to make an unborn child a ward of court, mainly because of the difficulty of enforcing any rights possessed by the foetus against the mother. Although the case does not decide that the foetus is without any legal rights, May LJ agreed with the passage quoted above from Sir George Baker's judgment in *Paton* and its endorsement by Heilbron J in *C v S*.

3.9 Terminating parental responsibility

Sections 4(3) and 4(4) of the Children Act 1989 establish that a parental responsibility agreement may only be terminated by court order on the application of 'any person who has parental responsibility for the child or, with the leave of the court, the child himself'. Such order will, though, automatically end upon the child attaining the age of majority. If the child were to apply for the termination of the order or agreement, then s 4 makes it clear that leave will be granted only if the court is satisfied that the child has sufficient understanding to make the proposed application. Students would, however, be well advised to refer to s 12(4) of the Act, which makes it absolutely clear that if there is a residence order in force then parental responsibility cannot be lost by the person in whose favour the residence order has been authorised. This principle also applies to non-parents who possess a residence order (s 12(2)).

It is difficult to identify case law which illustrates the circumstances in which parental responsibility will be removed, but it is logical to assume that they could well be similar to those where a court refuses to *bestow* parental responsibility upon the applicant. An example is *Re T (A Minor)* (1993). In this case the parents lived together for a short period prior to the birth, but in consequence of violence perpetrated by the father on the mother, she returned to her parents. She subsequently refused all contact with the father and was anxious that he should not know when the child was born. Throughout a period of two years following the child's birth, there was further violence by the father and a failure by him to comply with court orders regarding access and maintenance. He then applied in April 1992 for a parental responsibility order. The order was refused by the judge at first instance on the basis that the father had treated the mother with 'hatred and violence', had shown scant regard for the welfare of the child, and had failed to comply with the court orders. The rather obvious conclusion is that to authorise a parental responsibility order would have been contrary to the best interest of the child. The Court of Appeal, in dismissing the father's appeal, affirmed the factors determined by Balcombe LJ in *Re H* (1991), which, it will be recalled, places emphasis on the degree of commitment shown by the father towards the child and the degree of attachment between them. One might therefore conclude that the reasons a court might adopt for relieving a person of parental responsibility would be the very antithesis of the Balcombe factors.

A recent example is *Re P (Terminating Parental Responsibility)* (1995). The court stressed that the ability to make an application to terminate parental responsibility should not be used as a weapon by the dissatisfied mother of a non-marital child. The welfare of the child was the paramount consideration in such applications. On the facts of this case, the court found it difficult to imagine that a parental responsibility order would have been made if none already existed. To continue parental responsibility carried with it a real threat to the child. On all the evidence, the father had forfeited his right to continue to have parental responsibility, the child had suffered such violence at the hands of the father that at one point she was admitted to hospital in a 'lamentable and life-threatening condition'.

The judge alluded to the general principle in such cases that once parental responsibility had been obtained, it should not be terminated in the case of the non-marital father 'on less than solid grounds, with a presumption for continuance rather than for termination' (p 1052 C).

It should not be assumed, simply because the parental relationship breaks down, that parental responsibility will be lost, but this could well be the precursor of such an event. If it is indeed a parental responsibility agreement, then the breakdown of the relationship and any ensuing trauma could have potentially devastating effects on the ability of one parent, ie the non-residential or 'caretaker' parent, to carry out his or her responsibilities. As the parties are unmarried, the termination of the relationship and the consequences which flow from that may never attract any judicial investigation, unlike divorcing parents, and the onus will be on one of the parties to bring the issue to court so that a determination as to what is in the best interests of the child can be undertaken.

3.10 Conclusion

In conclusion, it is perhaps worth echoing the words contained in the Department of Health's *Introduction to the Children Act 1989* to the effect that:

> '... the duty to care for the child and to raise him to moral, physical and emotional health is the fundamental task of parenthood and the only justification for the authority it confers. Courts can only do so much to promote the welfare of any child, the real responsibility, legal and moral, is cast upon the parents and others who have parental responsibility.'

Summary of Chapter 3

Parental Responsibility

Parental Responsibility is the term which is referred to in the Children Act but for which there exists no precise definition. Section 3 of the Act purports to provide a definition, but in reality, what we have is a broad 'statement of intent' which refers to 'all the rights, duties, powers, responsibilities and authority which by law a parent of a child has in relation to the child and his property'.

The Act does not inform us as to the scope of these terms, and therefore the common law has to be called upon in order to discover the extent of the duties, rights and responsibilities we, as parents, have towards our children. This chapter outlines some of what the common law decrees, and in practice, the most important issue centres on the ability of parents to give consent in order for their children to receive medical treatment. In the ordinary run of the mill cases, there are no difficulties, but uncertainty has been caused when 'life and death' decisions have to be taken.

The result of the *Gillick* decision has meant that children who have sufficient understanding and maturity may oppose their parents who believe they are acting in their child's best interests by consenting to treatment.

Hewer v Bryant (1969) should be considered, particularly Lord Denning's statement to the effect that the older the child the less inclined the courts will be to seek to enforce the parents' wishes in face of opposition by the child. Parents, he suggested, started out controlling their children, and ended up simply tendering advice.

You should establish the extent of the common law in terms of what has been recognised as falling within the scope of parental responsibility. Bromley and Lowe, *Family Law* (8th edn) 1992, lists 16 aspects of parental responsibility, ranging from the obligation to provide a home for the child to burying or cremating a deceased child.

Parental responsibility is acquired by married couples on the birth of their child. If the parents are unmarried, then only the mother has automatic parental responsibility. The unmarried father can acquire parental responsibility for his child in one of two ways. He may apply to the court, or he may, together with the mother, reach agreement that he should have parental responsibility (a 'Parental Responsibility

Agreement'). Both parents exercise parental responsibility independently and there is no obligation upon parents after divorce to consult with each other before exercising any of the rights or responsibilities bestowed upon them by virtue of their status.

The *Gillick* case must be analysed in some detail. It should be noted that it was a majority decision in the House of Lords, and, as such, the speeches of all the Law Lords ought to be considered. Particular attention must be paid to the speeches of Lords Scarman and Fraser, and in the case of the latter, to the so-called 'Fraser guidelines' in respect of whether or not doctors should inform parents that their daughter is seeking contraceptive advice or treatment.

It is possible for unmarried fathers to have parental responsibility removed from them by the courts. This may happen if it is clearly not in the child's best interests for it to continue and if the father has demonstrated a lack of commitment to his child. In deciding whether parental responsibility should be awarded or removed, pay particular attention to the following cases:

Re H and Another (Minors) (No 3) (1991)

Re E (Parental Responsibility) (1995)

Re T (A Minor) (1993)

Parental responsibility does not extend to a child in the womb (*Paton v British Pregnancy Advisory Service* (1979)). The difficulty envisaged by the courts is one of enforcement against the mother were the foetus to be given rights.

Chapter 4

Court Orders

4.1 Introduction

The Law Commission's Working Paper on Custody (1986) Working Paper No 96 (Part II) identified 12 different provisions under which courts could make final orders for custody and access, and made reference to the 'many gaps, inconsistencies and anomalies amongst them'. The Law Commission Report No 172 outlined three 'main difficulties with the present law'. The first was that orders may differ according to the proceedings. For example, divorce courts could make orders for 'custody', 'care and control' and 'access', with 'joint custody' orders becoming increasingly common in the 1970s and 1980s. Yet domestic courts hearing applications under Domestic Proceedings and Magistrates' Courts Act 1978, and all courts hearing custody or access applications under the Guardianship of Minors Act 1971, could make orders only for 'legal custody' and access. The second difficulty was that the orders were 'no longer clear or well understood'. Judges and solicitors, it was reported, had experienced difficulty in explaining the effects of the orders to clients.

The third difficulty was that 'views and practices of courts differ very considerably, largely because of differences of opinions amongst judges, legal practitioners and clients about the merits of joint custody orders' (1988 Report No 172 paras 4.2–4.4).

The Law Commission, in framing the scheme of the present orders, had in mind the 'clear evidence that the children who fare best after their parents separate or divorce are those who are able to maintain a good relationship with them both ... the law may not be able to achieve this ... but at least it should not stand in their way'.

The objective of the new law in respect of court orders was, as Bainham put it:

> '... to create a consistent and unified scheme in place of the confusing morass of almost incomprehensible orders and procedural niceties which existed before the Act' (*Children: The New Law: Family Law* p 33).

The new orders, which cover both private and public law matters, are meant to reflect the gamut of everyday issues that arise between parents and children. The orders are designed to support the principle of equal parental responsibility (where appropriate) and to give all parties the ongoing opportunity to contribute to the future well-being of their children or those for whom they have responsibility.

The Law Commission's recommendation was for the creation of four new orders, which were named, 'residence', 'contact', 'specific issue' and 'prohibited steps'. A residence order is designed to settle the arrangements as to the person or persons with whom the child should live. The contact order requires the person(s) with whom the child lives, or is to live, to allow the child to visit, or otherwise to have contact with, another person. A specific issue order is available in an attempt to resolve a dispute about a particular aspect of parental responsibility. And a prohibited steps order, requires the consent of the court before a 'specified step' is taken. These were Law Commission recommendations.

The Law Commission was of the view that the court, when making the above orders, should be able to include directions about how the order(s) should be carried into effect. There should be the power to impose conditions, specify the length of the order and to make any other 'incidental, supplemental or consequential provisions the court saw fit'.

The so-called s 8 orders can be made in virtually all types of family law proceedings, either upon application or of the court's own motion. In order to promote flexibility to meet the changing needs of children and families, s 8 orders can be made in other proceedings which may affect the family. An obvious example will be in proceedings where the occupation of the matrimonial home is in dispute. A s 8 order could be made, if appropriate, giving contact to a father who has been excluded as a result of an application under the Matrimonial Homes Act 1983 and the Domestic Violence and Matrimonial Proceedings Act 1976. It has been emphasised elsewhere that in such proceedings questions about the upbringing of the child are not at issue, and therefore the paramountcy test will not apply. The Act identifies those proceedings where s 8 orders may be made and designates them as 'Family Proceedings'. Sections 8(3) and (4) specify the following:

> '8(3)(a) proceedings under the inherent jurisdiction of the High Court in relation to children, and (b) under the enactments mentioned in subsection (4).'
>
> The enactments are:
>
> '8(4)(a) Parts I, II and IV of this Act;
>
> (b) the Matrimonial Causes Act 1973;
>
> (c) the Domestic Violence and Matrimonial Proceedings Act 1976;

(d) the Adoption Act 1976;

(e) the Domestic Proceedings and Magistrates' Courts Act 1978;

(f) Sections 1 and 9 of the Matrimonial Homes Act 1983;

(g) Part III of the Matrimonial and Family Proceedings Act 1984.'

The following points should be noted in respect of the above provisions:

- 8(4)(a): Only three parts of the Children Act 1989 are included. In practice this will embrace the overwhelming majority of child cases, including parental responsibility and guardianship (Part I), s 8 orders (Part II) and care, supervision, contact and education supervision orders including interim orders (Part IV). This means that in emergency protection applications, the court will not be able to make s 8 orders, as emergency protection falls within the scope of Part V of the Children Act 1989.

- The Matrimonial Causes Act 1973 permits parties to petition for divorce, nullity and judicial separation as well as to apply to the court for ancillary matters to be resolved, particularly relating to finance and property; the matrimonial assets of the parties. Section 8 orders may be made in all such proceedings, if appropriate.

- The 1976 Act permits parties to a marriage, or a man and woman living with each other in the same household as man and wife, to apply to the county court for an injunction either restraining the other party from molesting the applicant or excluding the other party from the matrimonial home. In some cases both orders will be sought. It is inevitable that a speedy response will be called for and a court may need to make a s 8 order in order to regulate the contact position between, say, the excluded party and his or her child.

- The court can make a s 8 order as an alternative to an adoption order or on an application to free a child for adoption. A recent example is *Re U (Application to free for Adoption)* (1993). In this case, the judge dismissed an application by Essex County Council for the child, aged 4, to be freed for adoption, and instead made a residence order under s 8 of the Children Act 1989 in favour of the child's grandparents. Section 10(1) clearly states that, in any family proceedings where a question arises in respect of the welfare of the child, a court may make a s 8 order even though no such application has been made. The Council's appeal was dismissed by the Court of Appeal. Balcombe LJ stated that the child's welfare was only the first, not paramount, consideration under s 6 of the Adoption Act. If the court considered that adoption would promote the child's welfare then it should go on to the 'second stage' in the process and consider whether, under s 16 of the Adoption Act 1976, parental agreement had been given or could be dispensed with. This procedure should equally be applied to an application to free the children for adoption under s 18(1). If satisfied at both the s 6 and s 18 stages, then the court should make the order sought. In this case, the judge had come to the conclusion that the child's welfare required that she should be placed with the grandparents, and could find no reason sufficient to warrant interfering with the exercise of the judge's discretion. The effect of the residence order in these circumstances is to discharge the care order held by the Council (see s 91(1) of the Children Act 1989).

- A range of orders is available to applicants to the family proceedings courts, including financial provision and personal protection orders, and in respect of the latter situation, the ability to make a s 8 order is of use.

- The Matrimonial Homes Act 1983 really came to prominence as a result of the House of Lords decision in *Richards v Richards* (1984). The Act applies only to married couples and is designed to provide a framework within which disputes relating to the occupation of the matrimonial home may be resolved. *Richards* decided that s 1(3) of the Act contained the criteria to be applied in seeking to decide the outcome of a dispute. The subsection makes reference to the needs of any children but does not make their welfare the paramount consideration. The availability of s 8 does, in effect, provide the county court with all the powers it requires in order to ensure that the needs of any children are fully addressed.

- If a couple are divorced or their marriage annulled outside the United Kingdom, and the divorce or annulment is entitled to be recognised in England and Wales, either party may apply to the court for an order for financial relief (s 12(1) Matrimonial and Family Proceedings Act 1984). It is unlikely that courts will need to invoke the s 8 orders with any great frequency, but at least the right exists.

4.2 Section 8 orders – who may apply?

Care needs to be taken when seeking to identify those who may apply for a s 8 order. The following persons may apply for any of the four s 8 orders:

- Under s 10(4):

  (i) any parent or guardian of the child;

  (ii) any person in whose favour a residence order is in force with respect to the child, and

- Under Schedule 14 paras 5 and 7(3)(b) – any person who has custody or care and control of a child by virtue of any existing order.

- To this class of persons who are entitled to apply is added by s 10(5) a further group who may apply only for a residence or contact order: that is, by s 10(5)(a), any party to a marriage (whether or not subsisting) in relation to whom the child is a child of the family.

Section 105(1) of the Children Act 1989 defines 'child of the family' as:

(a) a child of both of those parties;

(b) any other child, not being a child who is placed with the parties as foster parents by a local authority or voluntary organisation, who has been treated by both of those parties as a child of their family.

The word 'treat' was judicially defined in the case of *A v A* (1974) to mean 'act or behave towards', and it follows from that ruling that a child unborn cannot be regarded as a child of the family. It also follows that there must have been in existence a 'family unit' to which the child belonged (see *M v M* (1981)). Ormrod LJ stated that the word 'family' was a 'popular, loose and flexible description and not a technical term, and its exact scope must depend on its context'. Whether a child has been treated in a way which brings him within the definition will be a matter of fact to be determined by reference to all the evidence.

- Under s 10(5)(b) – any person with whom the child has lived for a period of at least three years.

- Under s 10(5)(c) – any person who

  (i) in any case where a residence order is in force with respect to the child, has the consent of each of the persons in whose favour the order was made;

  (ii) in any case where the child is in the care of the local authority, has the consent of that authority; or

  (iii) in any other case, has the consent of each of those (if any) who has parental responsibility for the child.

This list may be further extended by rules of court (see s 10(7)).

In keeping with the philosophy that the court should be able to explore all options before deciding which course of action should be approved, the Act allows for persons other than those referred to above to apply for leave from the court to make a s 8 application. This includes the child himself seeking leave to make an application. The child's prospects of success depends upon whether or not the court is prepared to agree that he has 'sufficient understanding to make the proposed application for leave' (s 10(8)).

In *Re C (A Minor) (Leave to seek s 8 orders)* (1994), a girl almost 15 years of age became unhappy at home and, after staying for a fortnight with a friend's family, refused to return home. C made an application for a residence order to enable her to remain with her friend's family, whose father, albeit perhaps reluctantly, agreed to accept her. Johnson J seemed to accept that, as she was almost 15 years old, she had sufficient understanding to make the application. In the circumstances, the judge refused to make a residence order on the basis that 'no identifiable advantage' would accrue to C by making the order she sought. It appeared to the judge that there was every possibility of a reconciliation between the girl and her parents and that a residence order in favour of the friend's father would possibly hinder the process. She had also sought leave to apply for a specific issue order to be allowed to go on holiday with her friend and her family. In refusing to grant leave, the judge was conscious that she might be seen to be gaining an advantage at the expense of her parents, and that the reconciliation process could be hindered. It must be emphasised that, just because the child has sufficient understanding, it does not inevitably follow that leave will actually be granted. As Booth J commented in *Re SC (A Minor) (Leave to seek residence order)* (1994):

> 'It does not, however, follow that the court is bound to grant leave once the test of s 10(8) is satisfied. The court still has a discretion whether or not to do so.' (p 98 H)

If the applicant under s 10(8) is not the child, the court must have regard to the 'mini checklist' of factors found in s 10(9). However, these were held not to be applicable when the child made the application under s 10(8), nor was there any guidance in the Act as to how the judicial discretion conferred by s 10(8) was to be exercised. It will be recalled that the s 1(3) checklist does not fall to be considered on an application for leave because, at that stage, the upbringing of the child is not in issue. Once leave has been obtained and the court moves onto the substantive issues, then at that point s 1(3) is activated.

Section 10(9) was considered by the court in *Re F and R (s 8 Order: Grandparent's Application)* (1995). The maternal grandmother had applied for leave to make a contact application in respect of her four grandchildren. The grandmother's view was that she had regular contact with the children and that there was a close relationship. The parents took the opposite view, saw her as 'interfering' and not at all interested in seeing the children. The magistrates refused the application for leave on the basis that, if it succeeded, family life would be disrupted as the legal process got underway, and this would be to the detriment of the children. The grandmother's appeal was allowed on the basis that the facts in the present case were disputed, and therefore the magistrates, while not carrying out a full investigation, should have heard evidence from the main parties. They had insufficient evidence from which to form a view and the grandmother should be given the opportunity to have her evidence heard by a different panel of justices. Cazalet J was apparently in favour of the approach outlined in the case of *G v Kirklees Metropolitan Borough Council* (1993) where it was held that:

> '... while adopting the criteria in s 10(a) the court was not precluded from considering the overall merits of the case for a s 8 order in order to assess whether or not it had a reasonable prospect of success.'

Grandparents have no automatic right to seek a contact or residence order under s 8 of the Children Act. Attempts had been made during the passage of the Children Bill through parliament to introduce clauses giving grandparents automatic right to seek a contact order. It is clear, however, that unfettered access by grandparents to their grandchildren is not always in the best interests of the children, a fact which was graphically illustrated by the case of *B v W and others (Wardship: appeal)* (1979). The outcome was the one currently contained in the Act, that grandparents must seek leave from the court in order to apply for a s 8 order. Heather Crook, in her article *Grandparents and the Children Act 1989* ([1994] Fam Law 135) is convinced that they should '... have little difficulty in obtaining leave to seek a contact order, and should stand in a favourable position when seeking leave to apply for a residence order'.

The Law Commission held a similar opinion. Obtaining leave would, it felt, 'scarcely be a hurdle at all to close relatives such as grandparents ... who wish to care for or visit the child'. In the vast majority of cases, grandparents will be seeking to apply for leave to seek contact not residence orders. The latter would only seem to be appropriate where the child has been orphaned, the parents are not available to care for the child, or appear to be incapable of providing adequate care for the child. Crook believes that a grandparent seeking a residence order '... will face a heavy burden, both at the leave stage and at the hearing of the substantive application'. Her conclusion is heavily reliant on the decision of the Court of Appeal in *Re W (A Minor) (Residence Order)* (1993). There is, of course, a strong supposition that, other things being equal, it is in the interests of the child to be brought up by his natural parents.

Waite LJ recognised that the judge had faced a difficult choice when reaching his decision in favour of the father rather than the grandparents given '... the high quality of care which [the child] has received from his grandparents' (for a period of three years prior to the application). It should also be pointed out that the social worker involved had recommended that the child should remain with the grandparents. The court was not prepared to conclude that the judge had been 'plainly wrong' in reaching his decision but was prepared to allow fresh evidence to be introduced at the Court of Appeal stage, which cast some doubts on whether the outcome would have been the same had this evidence been available to the judge. The case was therefore remitted back to the county court for a further hearing.

The article also refers to an unreported case, *Re U (A Minor)* (1993), where the welfare of the child demanded that a residence order should be granted in favour of grandparents. It is also true that, should one parent support an application from a grandparent for a residence order, the chances of success are increased (see *B v B (A Minor) (Residence Order)* (1992)).

Although grandparents may be at a significant disadvantage when competing against natural parents, they may enjoy superiority over other non-parental relatives in circumstances, as Crook points out, where '... the need for non-parental residence is likely to be of limited duration'. The article also draws attention to the fact that an order for contact may not be worth the paper it is written on without the cooperation of the those, usually parents, who have day-to-day control of the child. Grandparents are urged not to raise their hopes unduly simply because they have managed to obtain an order.

Grandparents will have a limited interest in the other two s 8 orders. A prohibited steps order might prove to be of value in order to prevent the removal of the child from the jurisdiction, particularly if the parent with day-to-day control is unable or unwilling to act to restrain the removal. It is difficult to give any prediction as to how grandparents may use specific issue orders as these are designed primarily to resolve disputes between parents over major issues connected with the upbringing of the child, eg consent to medical treatment or decisions about which school the child should attend.

4.3 Residence orders

A residence order means an order settling the arrangements to be made as to the person with whom the child is to live (s 8(1)).

The underlying purpose of the residence order is to settle the day-to-day living arrangements for the child or children in question. The residence order does not affect the ability of each parent to exercise parental responsibility and in no way precludes a shared or joint residence arrangement. In fact s 11(4) would appear positively to endorse the practice. It states:

> 'Where a residence order is made in favour of two or more persons who do not themselves live together, the order may specify the periods during which the child is to live in the different households concerned.'

Prior to the Children Act 1989 the Court of Appeal had signalled its disapproval of joint custodial arrangements. *Riley v Riley* (1986) was critical of a sharing arrangement which appeared to have worked with some success for almost five years. *Riley* is clearly inconsistent with the provision in s 11(4), but it serves to illustrate how inflexibility can creep into the law through one decision of the Court of Appeal and why the philosophy underpinning the Children Act 1989 is so important to the long term welfare of children. This is not to say that such orders will become commonplace, only that the courts should have the ability to make such an order if the circumstances warrant it. This point is confirmed by the decision of the Court of Appeal in *A v A (Minors) (Shared Residence Order)* (1994), which considered that *Riley* could no longer be regarded as good law. However, the court was prepared to accept the view expressed in *Riley* that if there were 'competing homes' the child might suffer 'confusion and stress'. Equally the court could find little reason to import an 'exceptional circumstances' test into the law. In addition to the points mentioned above, the principles to come from *A v A* appear to be:

- the usual order to be made will be a sole residence order;
- judges have discretion to make shared residence orders, after careful consideration has been given to the checklist factors;
- if there are issues between the parties which are still to be resolved, then a shared residence order is unlikely to be made. Issues that will be relevant are the amount of contact, whether there should be staying or visiting contact, or broader issues such as how best to respond to the educational needs of the child.

  As Butler-Sloss LJ so succinctly put it:

  '... there has to be positive benefit to the children in making an order which is not the conventional order. Consequently, a shared residence order is an unusual order which should only be made in unusual circumstances. Each case ... must be decided on its own facts.' (p 678 F)

A v A should be compared to *Re H (A Minor) (Shared Residence)* (1994). Purchas LJ, while endorsing the principle that shared orders would rarely be made, thought that it would '... depend upon exceptional circumstances' (p 728 B). This is at odds with the later decision of the Court of Appeal in *A v A*, and it is suggested that the later case is to be preferred as it is consistent with the desire to allow courts maximum flexibility when responding to difficult family circumstances. Ines Weyland, writing in the Journal of Social Welfare and Family Law (1995) (pp 445-459), concludes in respect of current judicial approaches to shared residence orders that '... old assumptions about its unusual nature and undesirability in most cases still prevail ...' though it is not doubted that courts can and do make such orders when clearly for the benefit of the children.

In deciding in whose favour a residence order should be awarded, it is incumbent upon magistrates to state their reasons in such as way as to enable the parties to understand clearly how the task was approached and what their findings were in respect of the major issues. In *Re L (Residence: Justices' Reasons)* (1995), the magistrates had failed to make any findings in respect of the central issue, which was the mother's alcohol addiction and the likely impact upon the children if in fact she was not, as she claimed, cured of the problem. The magistrates had reached a conclusion which differed from that recommended by the court welfare officer and it was held, in allowing the mother's appeal, that the magistrates should have made it absolutely clear why they rejected the solution proposed by the welfare officer. This would have given either party the opportunity to call the welfare officer. The decision was deemed to have been fatally flawed, albeit not plainly wrong (See *G v G* (1985)).

4.3.1 Interim residence orders

As Bracewell J said in *S v S (Custody: Jurisdiction)* (1995) at p 157:

> 'I am satisfied that an interim order of residence is no different in principle from a residence order; indeed the Children Act 1989 does not recognise that there is such an order as an interim order ... I do not find that there is any fundamental different in law between the two types of order. They are both examples of the residence order. It has become common parlance to speak of 'interim residence orders' but in fact there is no such creature within the Children Act 1989.'

It is clear that courts will be slow to accept the desirability of *ex parte* applications for residence orders. For example the *ex parte* interim residence order was set aside by the Court of Appeal in the case of *Re P (A Minor) (ex parte Interim Residence Order)* (1993). The mother's sister had, with leave, obtained an *ex parte* interim residence order based upon an affidavit which it was alleged gave an unbalanced view of the family history. The mother then made an *ex parte* application which the judge adjourned to an inter partes hearing seven days later. The Court of Appeal set aside the interim order in the sister's favour, thus returning control and parental responsibility to the mother. Purchas LJ adopted the approach set out by Butler-Sloss LJ in *Re G (Minors) (ex parte Interim Residence Order)* (1993) at p 912 D, where she said:

> 'In my judgment, it is very rare indeed that it is necessary to have an *ex parte* interim residence order. The only situation that I can think of is where there is a "snatch" situation – child abduction. There obviously will from time to time be other exceptional circumstances in which it is necessary for the protection of the children that there should be an ex parte order.'

Re G proved to be a case in point. After the parents' divorce, the mother lived with the four children of the marriage in London and the father remarried and lived with his new wife and child in Norwich. On an agreed visit, the children, aged between five and 10, informed their father that their mother and her 'associates' were taking drugs and that they had a lot of knowledge about the smoking of cannabis. They also alleged that 'rave' parties were being held at their house, with the full consent and active participation of the mother and her boyfriend. The interim residence order, made on an *ex parte* basis in favour of the father, was continued pending a full investigation by the court welfare officer. The mother's appeal was dismissed. The court was of the opinion that moving the children to school in Norwich without giving the mother the opportunity to be heard was not reasonable, but in this case other considerations were taken into account. The court was concerned about the children's long-term welfare and their short-term protection. For these reasons, this was deemed to be 'one of those comparatively rare cases' where the status quo should not be maintained and an interim residence order was appropriate.

4.3.2 The statutory checklist

Whether or not a residence order will be granted will depend on the application of the welfare principle contained in s 1(1) of the Children Act 1989 and by reference to the statutory checklist at s 1(3).

4.3.3 Contents of a residence order

As has been seen, the effect of a residence order is to settle the arrangements of where the child is to live, and is essentially declaratory in nature. The order may contain directions about how it is to be carried into effect and conditions can be imposed by the court (s 11(7)). Under s 13(1), where a residence order is in force, no person may cause the child to be known by a new surname or remove him from the United Kingdom without either the written consent of every parent who has parental responsibility for the child or the leave of the court.

Reference should be made to the Court of Appeal decision in *W v A* (1981), which has recently been endorsed by the court's decision in *Re F (Child: Surname)* (1993). A judge will need to consider the likely impact upon the child if there is a change of surname and if there is not. Will the child suffer embarrassment if there is a change of surname or is he currently suffering embarrassment? What is the likely long-term impact of a change of name? Will parental attitude change as a result? In deciding whether or not to grant leave, a judge will need to take into account all the circumstances and probably speak with the parties and children.

The person with a residence order is entitled to remove the child from the jurisdiction for up to one month without having to resort to obtaining written consent or the leave of the court. If one parent is living abroad, directions can be given which permit the child to visit a set number of times each year, thus avoiding the necessity to obtain consent if any period is more than one month. There is, however, no limitation on the number of trips which may be undertaken of less than one month duration.

Where there is opposition from the other parent to the proposed removal out of the jurisdiction, the approach of the court is to sanction only realistic proposals unless it appeared that there would not serve the best interests of the child. So, for example, in *Re K (A Minor) (Removal from Jurisdiction)* (1992) the mother's plan to take the child with her to the United States as she pursued her post-graduate education studies was refused on the basis that her proposals 'displayed a quite insufficient attention to practicalities and no sensible plan for achieving any ultimate goal by reasonable stages'. If the mother had been given permission, contact with the father would have become an annual event lasting for 21 days each summer and contact through letters and telephone calls. The Court of Appeal in *M v M (Minors) (Removal from Jurisdiction)* (1992), relying on the case of *Lonslow v Hennig* (1986), confirms that, if the plans to remove the child are reasonable, then they ought to be complied with unless it is clearly shown that the move would be against the interests of the child. It should be noted that in all these cases, the removal of the child to another jurisdiction involves a degree of permanence, and these issues are unlikely to trouble parents seeking to remove a child for holiday or other social or domestic reasons.

M v A (Wardship: Removal from Jurisdiction) (1993) is a clear illustration of where the mother's plans to remove the children permanently to Canada were deemed ill thought-out and little researched. 'They were held not to constitute reasonable plans and certainly did not accommodate the needs and wishes of the children, who had expressed a preference to maintain the status quo and remain in England'. The well established link with their father would have been dramatically weakened and this would be detrimental to their welfare, as the father played an important role in their lives. The wishes of the children obviously will be of importance where they are of sufficient age and understanding to be able to express an informed opinion. The Children Act 1989 has not, in the words of Wall J in *H v H (Residence Order: Leave to Remove)* (1995), 'altered the underlying factors which need to be taken into account in deciding whether or not a parent should be given leave to remove a child from the jurisdiction' (see *Poel v Poel* (1970)).

4.3.4 Duration and discharge

Section 91(10) provides:

> 'A s 8 order shall, if it would otherwise still be in force, cease to have effect when the child reaches the age of 16, unless it is to have effect beyond that age by virtue of s 9(6).'

In practice, this means there will need to be exceptional circumstances if the order is to extend beyond the age of 16.

If parents resume cohabitation for a continuous period in excess of six months, the residence order will cease to have effect.

A residence order will also end if the child is taken into the care of the local authority (s 91(2)).

4.4 Contact orders

This means an order requiring the person with whom the child lives, or is to live, to allow the child to visit or stay with the person named in the order, or for that person and the child otherwise to have contact with each other (s 8(1)). There appears to be a clear judicial trend to allow contact even when a parent may be implacably opposed to it, and Weyland concludes that there has been greater consistency in the judicial decisions on contact following parental separation than before the Act came into force (see Weyland: *Judicial attitudes to contact and shared residence since the Children Act 1989*: Journal of Social Welfare and Family Law (1995) pp 445-459).

4.4.1 Who may apply?

We have already been appraised of the fact that there are two groups of people who may apply for s 8 orders. There are those who have a statutory right to apply and those who must seek leave to apply for an order. Into the first category are placed parents, guardians, any person having a residence order in respect of the child, any party to the marriage in relation to whom the child is a child of the family, and any person who has lived with the child for over three years. The effect of this is that certain blood relatives, such as grandparents, are excluded and must apply for leave, while certain non-blood relatives, such as step-parents, are automatically included. In the case of the latter category, the court, in deciding whether or not to grant leave, must take into account certain factors. These are displayed at s 10(9) of the Children Act 1989, and, in respect of an application for leave to apply for a contact order, would include consideration of the applicant's connection with the child and any potential disruption which might be occasioned to the child's life which might lead to harm – assuming the child not to be in the care of the local authority, in which case there are additional factors to be taken into account.

A good example of the current legal situation as it pertains to grandparents is to be found in *Re A (s 8 Order: Grandparent application)* (1995). A short-lived marriage resulted in the young child being left in his mother's care while the father, who had parental responsibility for the child, gradually lost contact with him and failed to maintain him. The father lived with his mother. Unfortunately there was considerable hostility between the two families, which resulted in the child not having any sort of meaningful relationship with his paternal grandmother, and the mother was indeed fearful of the grandmother. The grandmother applied for leave to make an application for contact, which was refused on the basis that it was premature. Her appeal was dismissed. Counsel for the grandmother sought to convince the court that were leave to apply granted, then, following precedent, there had to be cogent reasons why contact should not be granted – see *Re H* (1992) – in other words, to treat grandparents as though they were in the same position as natural parents. Butler-Sloss LJ was adamant that this was not the approach to be adopted with grandparent applications nor those from any other members of the family such as aunts and uncles. She points out, at p 157, that parliament had ample opportunity to create within the Children Act a special position for grandparents. Parliament chose not to. She goes on to say:

> 'But the idea that once you surmount the hurdle of s 10(9) you are in a position similar to that of the natural parent flies in the face of common sense and also does not represent, in my view, the current state of the law. First of all, an application for leave is almost always an application on the papers. An application for contact, which is hotly contested at the hearing, is almost always heard with oral evidence and, of course, with the court welfare officer's report.'

If the grandparent, having succeeded in obtaining leave, convinces the court that he or she has a good case for contact, then it is up to the natural parent, in this case the mother, to show why there should not be contact.

Reference should be made to the comments of the judge at p 158, as they reflect the fact that the best hope for the child is for the adults to moderate their feelings of antipathy towards each other and recognise that there is little point in having the child '... tossed like a football from one family to another ...'. The judge regarded this as a hopeless appeal and directed some extremely critical comments towards those responsible for granting legal aid.

Three weeks after the decision in *Re A*, the Court of Appeal considered the factors to be considered when a grandparent was applying for leave to seek to apply for a contact order, albeit this time with a local authority dimension to the case. *Re M (Care: Contact: Grandmother's Application for Leave)* (1995) concerned the attempts of the maternal grandmother to have contact with her two grandchildren. The children, who were aged 12 and nine, had been made the subject of care orders in 1987, their mother having a history of psychiatric disturbance. They spent some time in a children's home, where contact with the mother and grandmother took place. The local authority wished to terminate the contact of both women – in the case of the mother, because of her inappropriate behaviour due to her mental problems, and in the case of the grandmother, because she did not share the children's common language, which was English. The judge agreed that contact should be reduced and then terminated altogether once long-term carers were identified. A year later, contact was terminated. Some three years later, the grandmother applied for leave to make an application under s 34 of the Children Act 1989. Her action coincided with the processing of an adoption application in respect of the children, and the judge decided that the two should be heard together. The grandmother appealed. In allowing the appeal, the court pointed out that grandparents were not allowed reasonable contact with children in care as of right. The court went on to rule that, when exercising its discretion under s 34, a court should have in mind the criteria laid out under s 10(9) of the Children Act. Those criteria are clearly articulated in the report of the case (pp 95D to 97D). In outline, they encompass the following points:

- whether the contact sought was frequent, infrequent, direct or indirect;
- the more important and meaningful the connection with the child, the greater the weight to be given to the application;
- a recognition of the need for stability and security in the child's life. The application should not put this at risk;
- the wishes of the local authority and the parents which are likely to be influential but not necessarily determinative of the issue.

The court should also take into account whether or not the application is 'frivolous, vexatious or an abuse of the process'. If it is, it will fail. The application for leave should be dismissed in circumstances where the applicant has failed to disclose 'any real prospect of success'.

In *Re W (A Minor) (Contact)* (1994) Sir Stephen Brown P identified the general principle of contact:

'It is quite clear that contact with a parent is a fundamental right of a child, save in wholly exceptional circumstances.'

This statement is based upon the principle, recognised as well established by the Court of Appeal, in *Re S (Minors) (Access)* (1990). Access was a right of the child, not of the parents. The Children Act 1989 has done nothing to alter the courts' allegiance to that principle. Prior to the Act, the House of Lords had also recognised the pre-eminence of the welfare of the child over a parent's right or claim to access. In *Re K D (A minor) (Ward: Termination of access)* (1988), the House of Lords held that if a child's welfare so dictates, then the parent ought to be granted access, but if the opposite view prevails, access should be terminated irrespective of whether or not that parent believed it should continue.

Access was one of the least satisfactory areas of family law prior to the Children Act 1989. Parents awarded access to their children often felt disenfranchised, as the custodial parent possessed all the legal rights to the child as well as controlling day-to-day affairs. Resistance by the custodial parent to the access parent often resulted in enduring hostility between them, from which little or no benefit accrued to the child. In a majority of cases, contact between the access parent and the child was lost, or, if contact was maintained, it was achieved in a very 'artificial' way. The non-custodial parent would, on divorce, usually acquire reasonable access rights or defined access where the court would dictate when, how and where contact could be maintained.

A contact order under the present legislation places a new emphasis on the parent/child relationship. The order does not seek to provide for the non-custodial parent to have access; rather it will seek to promote contact by the child to the non-custodial parent. This will, in many cases, result in 'staying' contact and, of course, that non-custodial parent will continue to enjoy and exercise parental responsibility over the child whilst they are together.

The Law Commission acknowledged that a court could attach conditions 'if there are particular anxieties or bones of contention, but these should rarely be required'. A normal order is for reasonable contact, which would encompass all types of contact including letters, telephone calls, faxes and presumably, in this 'high tech' age, Internet communications. In the absence of agreement between the parties, the court may 'define' contact. The Court of Appeal has made it absolutely clear that the Children Act has conferred wide and comprehensive powers on a court to ensure contact between the child and the non-custodial parent (s 11(7)).

An intransigent mother has no right of veto over contact, and a court can compel such a parent to send information about the child to the father in an endeavour to promote meaningful contact. So in *Re O (Contact: Imposition of Conditions)* (1995), the Court of Appeal left the mother in no doubt that the judge's order imposing obligations upon her to encourage and maintain contact between the father and child '... means what it says and should be complied with' (p 133D). This is an important case, given that it reviews the precedents under the Children Act dealing with contact and the hostility factor between parents (see below).

Let it not be supposed, however, that simply by redefining the type of order available that the difficulties experienced under the old law will disappear.

4.4.2 Hostility

In *Re B (Minor) (Access)* (1984), Latey J spoke of the mother's 'implacable hostility' to allowing access to the father. The court refused to allow access to the father because '... to seek to impose access would have adverse effects on the child and injure it'. This would appear to cause great injustice to the father, but it must be remembered that contact with the child should only be maintained providing it is consistent with the best interests of the child. In the *Re B* case, the court ordered that the decision should be reviewed within one year.

That decision was taken a decade ago. Let us consider how a court is now likely to respond if it is faced with ongoing hostility between the parents, such that inviting one parent to encourage contact between the child and the other parent is likely to be met with a rebuttal. In *Re D (A Minor) (Contact: Mother's Hostility)* (1993), the Court of Appeal stated that the approach to contact had not changed since the Children Act 1989, and that the authorities which predated the Act coming into force were still relevant. In this case, the parents had never married and had lived together for approximately one year. When the mother was six months pregnant she left the father and returned to live with her parents. She stated that the father was a 'violent and undesirable character'. This had been confirmed by his intimidatory behaviour towards her since she returned to her parents and at subsequent court hearings. The father applied for contact to the child approximately one year after the child's birth. Although there had been an interim supervised contact order, it had proved unsuccessful, and the mother was totally opposed to a full contact order being granted on the basis that it would be unsettling for the child. The father's application was dismissed, as was his appeal. The Court of Appeal followed the decision in *Re H (Minors)*

(Access) (1992) to the effect that a child should not be deprived of access to either parent unless the court was satisfied that it was in the child's best interests. A court should always take into account the amount of time the parents had spent with the child since birth or the date of the parents separation. In this case (*Re D*), the mother's 'implacable hostility' towards contact was a factor the court could not ignore and could increase the risk of major emotional harm to the child if contact were awarded to the natural father against her will.

Given the facts of this case, there could be some justification for the mother's attitude, but it does not follow that the mother's reaction to contact will always be consistent with the child's best interests. In *Re J (A Minor) (Contact)* (1994), the Court of Appeal recognised that there were strong policy reasons for saying that a recalcitrant parent should not be allowed to undermine the course of action deemed by the court to be in the child's best interests. Yet the court was aware that occasionally it might have to 'inflict injustice upon the parent with whom the child was not resident' if that was consistent with achieving what the welfare of the child demanded.

Balcombe LJ in *Re F (Minors) (Contact: Mother's Anxiety)* (1993) spoke of the 'Draconian effort' of denying the children contact with their father, particularly if the children are very young and have never had the opportunity to build a relationship with him through a combination of their age and parental separation.

The older the children, the more influential they will be in helping to determine the outcome of a contact dispute. It will be recalled, for example, that in *Re F (Minors) (Denial of Contact)* (1993), boys aged 12 and nine expressed a clear preference no longer to have contact with their father after the parents' marriage broke down, due to the father's transsexuality.

It remains to be seen how much influence can be brought to bear on custodial parents actively to encourage contact to continue. Should custodial parent be proactive in persuading the child to write or telephone the other parent? Presumably the only way such an order may be implemented is if the custodial parent gives such an undertaking to the court. This issue was thoroughly explored by Wall J in *Re M (A Minor) (Contact: Conditions)* (1994). There was one child, aged three. The parties had never married, but after they had separated there was limited contact between the father and his son. When the child was two, the father was sentenced to three years imprisonment. The justices made a defined contact order, directing contact by post. The form of the order was as follows:

> 'Contact shall be by post. In accordance with s 11(7) of the Children Act 1989 the court imposes the following conditions:
>
> (a) [the mother] shall read to M the contents of any letters addressed to him, received from [the father] and shall given to M any present or card which the father may send;
>
> (b) at least every three months the mother shall write to the father giving an account of M's progress;
>
> (c) the court further orders that the father shall write to M at least every three months;
>
> (d) both parties are to keep each other informed of their respective addresses.'

The mother appealed. It was held that the justices had been correct to order indirect contact by post and had been correct to seek to maintain the link with the father. However, the court was of the view that the order compelling the mother to read the father's letters could not stand. Section 11(7) is the only section of the Act which bestows jurisdiction upon a court to impose directions or conditions on the parties. It is non-specific, leaving a great deal to the discretion of the court. The judge held that the justices did not have the jurisdiction to order the mother to write progress report to the father, simply because a court could not order the parties to maintain contact with each other. There was, though, the power to impose an obligation on the mother to keep the father informed of the child's whereabouts, but this did not need to be done directly. The court welfare service could be requested to act as a 'limited post office and censor for specific communication'. Contact orders which provided for indirect contact were described as 'permissive, not mandatory'. Courts have increasingly adopted the so-called 'not more than' formula when defining such orders, eg 'not more than twice per month' should letters be sent, or telephone calls on 'not more than three occasions per fortnight'.

It was acknowledged that the court did not have a 'coercive power to compel a parent to undertake a facilitative act ...'. Orders should only be made in this respect if the party who is to be the facilitator consents to take on the tasks.

Judith Parker QC and Deborah Eaton have analysed recent authorities in an attempt to identify the reasons for refusing contact between parent and child. (The article – *Opposing Contact* – is to be found at 1994 Fam Law 636.) The major authorities from 1984 onwards are listed in tabular form, detailing the age of the child at separation, age at the hearing, and a multitude of other factors including judicial comments in respect of each case. The authors conclude that there are 13 general principles relating to the issue of contact. These range from the basic premise that it is the right of every child to have contact with both parents to the acceptance of the fact that non-contact between the parent and child '... does not militate against contact; and in a number of such cases the court has introduced, reintroduced or put into action a plan for the assessment of the feasibility of contact'.

In *Contact – Can we do better?* (1993) Fam Law 528, David McHardy, a solicitor, posed the question of how contact arrangements in the UK may be improved in respect of 'post divorce adjustment' of children of the marriage. Reference is made to the study by Martin Richards and Jane Elliott which confirmed the belief that many of the problems which were manifest after divorce had actually occurred '... in the year or several years before the parents' divorce'.

Conflict between parents it is suggested breeds conflict behaviour in children as they model themselves on their parents. It was argued that a 'positive approach' to contact is important, as is the quality of that contact in helping to raise the self-esteem of children. It was reported that in California the use of joint care and control had increased and that many children actually enjoyed shared physical care and control, albeit not necessarily on a 50:50 basis. Interestingly, the Californian experience demonstrates an increasing tendency to agree detailed contact arrangements which, according to the author, '... are of great importance and benefit to the child'. It is suggested that greater use should be made of mediation services, and that changes should be made to the legal aid rules so that mediation is readily available to all sections of the community, something which may, of course, happen once reform of the divorce laws has taken place. The author advocates the creation of 'contact counselling', designed to promote constructive discussion of contact arrangements in a conciliatory environment. This should take place at a very early stage '... before the matter gets out of hand'.

No one would deny that, on occasions, courts are faced with having to make extremely difficult decisions resulting from complex circumstances surrounding the parents. A recent example is the case of *Re L (Contact: Transsexual Applicant)* (1995). The parents had separated and the daughter, aged six, lived with the mother. The relationship had broken down largely through 'gender confusion' on the part of the father. There had been difficulties over contact, but an interim order had been made restoring contact between the father and his daughter. The father dressed as a woman and was undergoing hormone supplement therapy designed to accelerate the transition from male to female. Surgical intervention was planned. However, the father adopted male attire when having contact with his daughter. At the time of the hearing, the father had accepted that there should not be face to face contact with his daughter and that indirect contact by letter and presents was desirable. The judge sought to '... record the reality' of the situation. He went on to state:

> 'The only obstacle to ordinary contact between the applicant and S is transsexuality. That is a huge challenge for any family, particularly when its emergence post dates the breakdown of the relationship and when its progress is so rapid and when its disclosure is through antagonistic and not cooperative channels of communication.'

The court also reached the conclusion that the father's application for parental responsibility (the parties were not married) should be granted, given that there was clear evidence that the father was strongly committed to his daughter.

4.4.3 Enforcement

This, perhaps, is the most difficult of all the issues affecting contact orders. Courts must hope that common sense will prevail, even when the parties are at loggerheads with each other. If the residence parent does everything possible to frustrate the carrying out of a contact order, the court is faced with limited power to enforce its own orders. This is well illustrated in *Re N (A Minor) (Access: Penal Notice)* (1992). It was acknowledged that access to the father was in the child's best interests, but the judge had been obliged to conclude that because of the mother's destructive influence over the child in turning him against his father, access should be terminated because, if the issue were to be forced, the child could suffer emotional damage. The father's appeal was dismissed. The court felt that a defined access order, endorsed with a penal notice putting the mother at risk of imprisonment, was an act of last resort, but whether it would be enforced would always be a question for the judge hearing the case. It is reasonable to assume that mothers of very young children are unlikely to face imprisonment for contempt, and, as such, the court is virtually powerless, in practice, to enforce its own orders.

It is suggested that s 34 of the Family Law Act 1986 could be invoked so that a third party such as a police officer could collect the child and thus allow contact to take place. Yet in circumstances such as those outlined in *Re N*, if the child has been so turned against his father, then to be brought by a third party to meet a person he does not wish to see is unlikely to have the desired effect. Perhaps the only remedy in such circumstances is to allow nature to take its course, and hope that with time and increased maturity the child may understand what has occurred and seek to remedy the situation. Conversely, of course, the parent may have completely disappeared from the child's life before the change of heart occurs.

4.4.4 Restrictions

These are similar to those listed above for residence orders with one exception. Section 34 provides for parents to continue to have reasonable contact with their children in care, providing the authority is satisfied that it is in the child's best interests for contact to be ongoing.

4.5 Prohibited steps orders

A prohibited steps orders means 'an order that no step which could be taken by a parent in meeting his parental responsibility for a child, and which is of a kind specified in the order, shall be taken by any person without the consent of the court'. The Law Commission put forward the opinion that prohibited steps orders were modelled on the wardship jurisdiction, in the sense that no important step in a child's life may be taken without the consent of the court. We have seen that much of the former wardship jurisdiction has now been incorporated into the statutory jurisdiction (see Chapter 8). The Commission expected prohibited steps orders to be issued relatively infrequently, and certainly this order will be much more 'directed' than the wardship order where 'no important step' can be taken without the consent of the court.

The prohibited steps order should not be used if the result can be achieved by making a residence or contact order (s 9(5)). This was illustrated in the case of *Re H (Prohibited Steps Order)* (1995). The case is also authority for the proposition that a prohibited steps order can be made against someone who is not a party to the proceedings nor present at court. This is subject to the proviso that such action was necessary in order to protect the child and there was no other means of achieving the same objectives.

In *Re H*, the mother of six children cohabited between 1990 and 1994 with a Mr J. During this period he was found to have sexually abused one of the children. The local authority sought supervision orders for five of the children and a care order in respect of the abused child. The applications were granted. The judge made a condition under the supervision order of no contact with Mr J. He also made a prohibited steps order against the mother to prevent contact between the children and Mr J, but declined to make one against Mr J on the basis that he was not a party to the proceedings nor present at the family proceedings. The guardian *ad litem* appealed. In allowing the appeal, the Court of Appeal had to decide whether or not the prohibited steps order against Mr J contravened s 9(5) of the Children Act 1989, and secondly whether such an order can be made against someone who is not a party to the proceedings.

The court felt that the order against the mother did in fact contravene s 9(5), since it achieved the same result as could be achieved by a contact order requiring the mother not to allow contact with Mr J, and could be enforced in exactly the same way. But the order against Mr J was held not to contravene s 9(5). The court was concerned that an order of no contact against the mother put the responsibility upon her to prevent contact. Therefore an order against her would not achieve the desired result of preventing contact with Mr J who, it was stated, posed 'a risk to all the children if he has contact with them'. The wording of s 8 was sufficiently broad to include 'a person' who was not a party to the proceedings.

Prior to this decision, the only case to consider the interrelation of ss 8 and 9(5) was *Nottinghamshire County Council v P* (1993). That case decided that a contact order includes an order that there shall be no contact, but it must be pointed out that the circumstances of that case were entirely different from the *Re H* case.

This decision would appear to go some way towards meeting some of the criticisms levelled against the prohibited steps order by Clare Moxon in her article entitled *Prohibited Steps Orders* (1994) Fam Law 271. Case law, she asserts, has produced 'conflicting dicta in the definition and limitations of prohibited steps orders ... which require clarification as quickly as possible ...'. The decision that a prohibited steps order can be made against someone who is not a party to the proceedings meets one of those criticisms.

At the time of writing, the main provisions of the Family Homes and Domestic Violence Bill have been incorporated into the Family Law Bill (1995) which is under consideration in parliament and seeks to provide new remedies to assist in the protection of one family member against molestation or violence perpetrated by another member, as well as regulating the occupation of the matrimonial home. In consequence, should the Bill reach the statute book in its current form, domestic violence should be controllable without the need for recourse to s 8 orders. See below and the discussion of the case of *Pearson v Franklin* (1994) in the context of specific issue orders and ouster orders. Certainly a local authority cannot utilise a prohibited steps order as a means of excluding a parent from the family home on the basis of his being a threat to the children. This was seen as a device to circumvent the restrictions placed on local authorities in applying for residence or contact orders by s 9(2) of the Children Act 1989. In the case of *Nottinghamshire County Council v P* (1993), Sir Stephen Brown P went further and commented '... it is very doubtful indeed whether a prohibited steps order could in any circumstances be used to "oust" a father from a matrimonial home'. The Court of Appeal confirmed that a court is precluded from making a prohibited steps order which was designed to achieve the same result as a residence or contact order.

A prohibited steps order may be made on an *ex parte* basis, and this is consistent with view that this order should possess many of the attributes of a wardship order. An illustration of how prohibited steps and residence orders were granted on an ex parte basis is to be found in *Re M (Jurisdiction: Forum Conveniens)* (1995). The parents had separated in 1994 and the family home was in Malta. Interim shared care orders had been made by the Maltese court. The mother came to England, leaving the children and the father in Malta. A short period later, the father visited England, bringing the children with him. The mother, on discovering that the children were in this country, obtained *ex parte* residence orders in respect of the children and a prohibited steps order preventing the removal of the boys from the jurisdiction. Malta was not a signatory to the Hague Convention, and so no issue arose in respect of the Child Abduction and Custody Act 1985. Not surprisingly, at the *inter partes* hearing the interim orders were discharged given the fact that the children were habitually resident in Malta and were subject to court orders in that jurisdiction. The Court of Appeal stated that, in theory, there was no limit to the jurisdiction of the English court to act in the best interests of children who were within the jurisdiction. Nevertheless, if the child is habitually resident elsewhere the court will, in practice, decline jurisdiction.

4.5.1 Restrictions

In keeping with the other s 8 orders, a prohibited steps order may not be made in respect of children over the age of 16 except in exceptional circumstances. Nor can such an order be made in respect of a child in the care of the local authority pursuant to a care order (s 9(1)). The only order that is available here is the residence order. Under s 9(5)(b), no court shall exercise its power to make a specific issue order or prohibited steps order in any way which is denied to the High Court (by s 100(2)) in the exercise of its inherent jurisdiction with respect to children (see s 100(2)).

The making of a care order will discharge a prohibited steps order (s 91(2)).

4.6 Specific issue orders

A specific issue order means 'an order giving directions for the purpose of determining a specific question which has arisen, or which may arise, in connection with any aspect of parental responsibility for a child'. A specific issue order may be made in conjunction with either a residence or contact order or it may be free-standing.

Disputes between parents over the upbringing of their children, formerly dealt with under the Guardianship Act 1973, would now fall to be determined in the context of a specific issue order. Section 9(5) of the 1989 Act places an embargo on courts preventing a specific issue order being made if it is with a view to achieving a result for which a residence or contact order would be more appropriate. In examining the case law on specific issue orders, one is struck by the range of issues and the fact that, prior to the Children Act 1989, they would have been resolved by recourse to the wardship jurisdiction. Thus in *Re R (A Minor) (Blood Transfusion)* (1993), the parents were Jehovah's Witnesses and their beliefs prevented them from consenting to blood transfusion treatment. The local authority obtained leave to apply for a specific issue order and was ultimately successful in achieving the order sought. Booth J had no doubt that this was an appropriate case for a specific issue order. There was no need for the local authority to seek to invoke the inherent jurisdiction of the High Court because there was only one issue to be determining and the all-embracing nature of the inherent jurisdiction was deemed unnecessary. This case also decides that such an order can be granted *ex parte*, although 'strenuous efforts' should be made to achieve an *inter partes* hearing.

A specific issue order was deemed to be appropriate in the case of a 17 year old, severely epileptic girl who had a chromosomal deficiency – which meant that she was an infant in terms of abilities – whose parents feared she would become pregnant and desired her to be sterilised. As a matter of practice, it was stated that applications for a specific issue order relating to sterilisation should be commenced in the District Registry of the High Court and not in a family proceedings or county court. It has recently been decided that while a specific issue order is suitable for determining where a child should live, it was not appropriate to make such an order where a right of occupation of the family home was at issue. It had not been parliament's intention to allow an ouster order to be made under the guise of a specific issue order.

In *Pearson v Franklin* (1994), the unmarried parties were joint tenants of a housing association property, and they occupied the premises with their two young children. Nine months after the birth of the children the mother left and set up home with her parents, and the father continued to live in the property. In March 1993, six months after leaving, the mother applied for a specific issue order to allow her to reside in the house with the children but in the absence of the father. The parties' relationship had irretrievably broken down, but there had been no violence or any form of molestation. The judge declined jurisdiction. The mother appealed, arguing that if she could not have successful recourse to the statutory provisions to oust her former partner the requirements of the children meant that jurisdiction should be accepted under s 8 of the Children Act 1989. The court was of the view that the only remedy available to the mother in these circumstances was to be found at s 15(1) and para 1(2)(e)(i) of Schedule 1 to the 1989 Act. Under these provisions, an order could be made requiring the father to transfer to her, for the benefit of the children, his interest in the joint tenancy of the house.

4.6.1 Restrictions

Those restrictions referred to above in relation to prohibited steps order are equally applicable to specific issue orders.

4.7 Family assistance orders

Where a court has power to make an order under Part II of the Children Act 1989, then it may, in any family proceedings, make an order requiring a probation officer or a local authority officer to be available to 'advise, assist and (where appropriate) befriend any person named in the order' (s 16(1)).

These orders may only be made in exceptional circumstances and with the tacit agreement of all those involved. The orders are designed to provide practical help to families in the throes of marital breakdown, but only for a relatively short period. There are one or two examples of how such an order may be utilised to be found in the law reports, for example *Leeds City Council v C* (1993) and *Re V* (1994).

Summary of Chapter 4

Court Orders

Section 8 orders

In this chapter, attention has been focused on the different types of orders available under the Children Act 1989, together with an outline of the purpose of each of the major orders. The new orders, covering both private and public law, are an attempt to move away from the position prior to the Children Act where, according to Bainham: *Children: The New Law* (1993), there was a 'confusing mass of almost incomprehensible orders and procedural niceties'. The new private law orders are:

- The residence order
- The contact order
- The specific issue order
- The prohibited steps order

These so-called 's 8 orders' can be made in virtually all types of family law proceedings, either upon application, or of the court's own motion. Section 8 orders may be made in Family Proceedings as defined by s 8(3) and (4) of the Children Act 1989.

The persons able to apply for s 8 orders are listed at s 10(4) and at Schedule 14 paras 5 and 7(3)(b). In addition, any party to a marriage, in relation to whom the child is a child of the family, may apply.

The definition of 'child of the family' is to be found at s 105(1), and the test is based upon whether or not the child has been treated as a child of the family.

'Treated' has been judicially defined to mean 'act or behave towards', and it follows that an unborn child cannot be a 'child of the family'.

In keeping with the philosophy of the Children Act, the child may make an application for a s 8 order, providing that he has 'sufficient understanding to make the proposed application for leave' (see *Re C (A Minor) (Leave to seek s 8 orders)* (1994)).

Residence order

A 'residence order' means an order settling the arrangements to be made as to the person with whom the child is to live, ie the day-to-day living arrangements for the child. The usual order to be made would be a sole residence order, but if the circumstances warrant it, a shared residence order may be made (see *A v A (Minors) (Shared Residence Order)* (1994)).

The power resides in the court to make an 'interim' residence order, and there is no difference in principle between this and a 'full' residence order. What is clear, however, is that the courts will be reluctant to proceed on an *ex parte* basis. There is authority which suggests that the only time an *ex parte* interim residence order ought to be made is in a case of child abduction. Restrictions are placed on those with a residence order against the removal of the child from the jurisdiction for periods in excess of one month.

Contact order

A 'contact order' requires the person with whom the child lives, or is to live, to allow the child to visit or stay with the person named in the order, or for that person and child otherwise to have contact with each other.

Contact arrangements can be defined by the court, and it does not necessarily mean that parent and child must actually meet each other.

One of the biggest problems faced by courts is how to ensure that contact takes place when there is ongoing hostility between the parents. The courts always stress that contact is a right of the child and not the parent, and thus will do everything possible to ensure that contact is maintained providing it serves the best interests of the child (see *Re D (A Minor) (Contact: Mother's Hostility)* (1993)).

The older the child, the more his or her views may be influential in helping to resolve a contact dispute, and not necessarily in favour of the residential parent.

Prohibited steps order

A 'prohibited steps order' means that no step which could be taken by a parent in meeting parental responsibility for the child, and which is of a kind specified in the order, shall be taken by any person without the consent of the court. This type of order is modelled on the wardship jurisdiction, and much of the former wardship jurisdiction has been incorporated into the Children Act.

A prohibited steps order should not be used if the result can be achieved by making a residence or contact order.

Specific issue order

A 'specific issue order' allows the court to give directions for the purpose of determining a specific question which has arisen, or which may arise, in connection with any aspect of parental responsibility for a child. These orders may be made in conjunction with a residence or contact order or may be free-standing, eg *Re R (A Minor) (Blood Transfusion)* (1993).

Family assistance order

A family assistance order may be made under s 16(1) in any family proceedings in order to 'advise, assist and (where appropriate) befriend' any person named in the order.

Chapter 5

Public Law Orders

5.1 Introduction

Increasing concern was voiced throughout the 1980s as to the effectiveness of the public law system in protecting children from abuse and providing the necessary support to families in need. Following a review of child care law in 1985, the government produced a White Paper (1987 Cm 62) entitled *The Law on Child Care and Family Services*. Paragraph 5 of the White Paper outlines the principles which were eventually to underpin the public law provisions of the Children Act 1989. They were stated to be that:

- the prime responsibility for the upbringing of children should rest with parents;
- the state should be ready to help parents to discharge their responsibilities, thus reducing the number of family breakdowns;
- where a child is being cared for by a local authority, the legal responsibilities of the authority for the child should be clear, as should be the powers and responsibilities of parents in these circumstances; and that
- close contact should be maintained whenever possible between parents and children in circumstances where the child is being looked after away from home.

The Children Act 1989 places a general duty upon every local authority to:

- safeguard and promote the welfare of children within their area who are in need; and
- so far as is consistent with that duty, to promote the upbringing of such children by their families ...

by providing a range and level of services appropriate to those children's needs (s 17(1)).

There was a substantial number of criticisms levelled at the law and practice of 'child care' in the period leading up to the Children Act. The law was primarily to be found in two statutes, the Children and Young Persons Act 1969 and the Child Care Act 1980, which replaced the Children Act 1948. Statutory duties imposed upon local authorities made these bodies responsible for 'taking' children into care and for providing 'voluntary' care provision when a parent or parents could not give the necessary support to their family, eg because of ill-health or an emergency situation having arisen. There had, over a 20 year period, been a number of enquiries which highlighted deficiencies in the working practices of care organisations and associated agencies, often resulting in tragedy. The case of Maria Colwell in 1973 is, in all probability, still etched in many people's minds as the most notorious failure of the 'system' to protect a young child (from the excesses of her stepfather). She was eventually to die at his hands. (See the *Report of the Committee of Inquiry into the Care and Supervision provided in relation to Maria Colwell*, 1974, HMSO.) The Jasmine Beckford enquiry in 1985 also attracted much media attention, as did that set up to enquire into the death of Kimberly Carlisle in 1987. (See *A Child in Trust: The Report of the Panel of Enquiry into the circumstances surrounding the death of Jasmine Beckford 1985* and *A Child in Mind: Protection of Children in a Responsible Society. The Report of the Commission of Enquiry into the circumstances surrounding the death of Kimberley Carlile*, London Borough of Greenwich, December 1987.)

The problems experienced were highlighted in the *Report of the Inquiry into Child Abuse in Cleveland* (1987) HMSO Cm 412. In a period of five months, two consultant paediatricians at a northern hospital had diagnosed sexual abuse in 121 children from 57 families, relying mainly on premise that physical signs could help to identify sexual abuse and assist those seeking to protect abused children. In the conclusion to her report, Lord Justice Butler-Sloss described the reasons for the crisis as being complex and that the doctors, by 'separating children from their parents and by admitting most of the children to hospital, ... compromised the work of the social workers and the police ... The medical diagnosis assumed a central and determining role in the management of the child and the family.'

She identified certain key reasons including:

> '... the lack of a proper understanding by the main agencies of each others' functions in relation to child sexual abuse; the lack of communication between the agencies; and differences of view at middle management level which were not recognised by senior staff. These eventually affected those working on the ground.'

The recommendations were extensive and influential, and many were adopted by parliament and included in the Children Act 1989, for example, in relation to emergency protection orders. It is incorrect to state that the Children Act

1989 is based upon the recommendations of the Cleveland Inquiry Report, but parliament was certainly influenced by the report. The Act was actually based, in this respect, on the recommendations contained in the 1987 White Paper. The White Paper had concluded that the law was 'confusing and inconsistent in an area where the opposite is required', and thus a major objective of the Act was to ensure greater clarity and consistency in the law.

Against the background of uncertainty in respect of role and function there were difficulties encountered by the courts in construing parts of the key legislative provisions. Reference has already been made to the use by local authorities of the wardship jurisdiction in order to supplement, where appropriate, statutory powers. This, in part, could be explained away by reference to the decision of Dunn J in *Re D (A Minor) (Justices' decision: Review)* (1977) where it was held that the welfare of the child was not the first and paramount consideration in care proceedings under the Children and Young Persons Act 1969, although it was in wardship proceedings. It followed that different considerations could be taken into account in wardship proceedings from those which were taken into account by a juvenile court when making or discharging a care order. The House of Lords held in the case of *A v Liverpool City Council* (1981) that the wardship jurisdiction could not be invoked in order to review the exercise by a local authority of its discretionary powers. This decision was made against a background of dissatisfaction in that parents appeared to be marginalised once a local authority had obtained a care order. If a parent wished to challenge a local authority's exercise of its discretionary powers over a child in its care, then the parent would have to invoke the supervisory jurisdiction of the High Court. There were only very limited rights of appeal under the statutory code.

Another difficulty encountered by local authorities in seeking to protect children at risk was the present tense wording of the main statutory provision relating to care orders, ie s 1(2) of the Children and Young Persons Act 1969. It had to be established by the authority that the child's proper development 'is' being avoidably prevented or neglected or his or her health 'is' being avoidably impaired or neglected or he or she 'is' being ill-treated. While this would not cause too many problems where there was clear evidence of abuse, it did create many difficulties in cases where social workers suspected that at some point in the future the child was likely to suffer harm. Local authorities were obviously susceptible to criticism if there was a failure to prevent harm from occurring, and once again the response was to seek to invoke the wardship jurisdiction. This was graphically illustrated by the case of *D v Berkshire County Council* (1987) where the House of Lords adopted a benevolent approach to the construction of s 1(2), holding that although the apprehension of harm was not enough by which to satisfy the statutory provision, the court could look to the past, even while the child is developing in the womb, in order to determine whether he or she 'is' being ill-treated. The court could also look to the future in order to determine whether the problem identified was likely to continue. The House had accepted that the three concepts referred to above were 'continuing concepts' and therefore it would be wrong to focus upon any one in particular. The wording of the Children Act 1989 (s 31(2)) relieves a court from having to adopt a strained construction in order to provide the necessary legal protection for the child. In this case the child's parents were both drug addicts, and at the time of birth, the child was already suffering from drug withdrawal symptoms.

Such, then, were some of the difficulties with the pre Children Act legislation. It is by no means, nor is it meant to be, a comprehensive catalogue of the problems encountered over a period of two decades and more. Readers wishing to gain a fuller picture are referred to the 1985 Review, the 1987 White Paper, the Cleveland Report 1988, and the Law Commission Report No 172.

One effect of the Children Act 1989 is the repeal of the whole of the Child Care Act 1980 and the repeal of a substantial number of sections of the Children and Young Persons Act 1969 including s 1.

5.2 The Children Act 1989 – key principles – public law

The following is an attempt to outline the key principles of the Act as they apply in a public law context before moving on to a more detailed assessment of the current provisions.

5.2.1 Intervention

The obligation placed upon local authorities is to provide support to the family and do everything possible to ensure its survival as the primary unit within which children may flourish.

As responsibility for the care of children is cast upon their parents, it follows that intervention into family life should result from the making of a court order under the relevant provisions of the Act. All those who have any connection with the child should be offered the opportunity to participate in such proceedings. As will be seen, the child's views may also be taken into account on the basis that this is child centred legislation and in recognition of the impact of the *Gillick* decision. A clear example is in s 20(6). Section 20 deals with the provision of accommodation for children in need and, subsection 20(6) states that, before providing accommodation, the local authority must:

> '... so far as is reasonably practicable and consistent with the child's welfare
>
> (a) ascertain the child's wishes regarding the provision of accommodation; and
>
> (b) give due consideration (having regard to [the child's] age and understanding) to such wishes of the child as they have been able to ascertain.'

A second principle is that compulsory care or supervision should be considered as a last resort action. In other words, only when there is no other way that the child's welfare can be better served than by a care or supervision order. There is now only one way of receiving children into care, and that is by meeting the statutory 'threshold' criteria specified by s 31(2). This approach, of seeing removal from the family as a last resort, is consistent with the s 1(5) principle of non-intervention.

A third principle is that parental responsibility is an important concept in public law as well as private law. If a care order is made in favour of a local authority, then parental responsibility will be shared with the parents. However, in the event of a dispute, the local authority will have the final say. The Department of Health's guidance document (Vol 3, 1989) stated:

> 'Partnership will only be achieved if parents are advised about and given explanations of the local authority's powers and duties and the actions the local authority may need to take ... this new approach reflects the fact that parents always retain their parental responsibility. A local authority may limit parents' exercise of that responsibility when a child is looked after by a local authority as a result of a court order, but only if it is necessary to do so to safeguard and promote the child's welfare' (paras 2.10 and 2.11).

A fourth principle which follows logically from the third is the inclusion in the Act of a presumption of reasonable parental contact (see s 34). A parent, for example an unmarried father, who does not have parental responsibility, is still entitled to presume that reasonable contact will continue unless there are good reasons, consistent with promoting the child's best interests, why such contact should not be maintained.

Finally it is worth mentioning that the so-called threshold criteria which have to be satisfied before a care order can be made includes reference to the likelihood of future significant harm as well as to present significant harm, thereby allowing local authorities to act at an early stage if they believe the child will be at risk.

5.3 Care and supervision orders

One of the major recommendations of the Cleveland Report was that inter-agency cooperation needed to be improved so as to ensure a more effective response to the problems of child abuse. The Children Act 1989 works on the basis that full inter-agency cooperation is vital. Section 47(1) places local authorities under a duty to investigate when informed that a child who lives or 'is found' in its area:

- is the subject of an emergency protection order; or
- is in police protection;

or has reasonable cause to suspect that a child who lives, or is found, in its area is suffering, or is likely to suffer, significant harm …

The authority shall make, or cause to be made, such enquiries as it considers necessary to enable it to decide whether it should take any action to safeguard or promote the child's welfare.

Section 47(a) makes it absolutely clear that should the local authority conduct enquiries under the section, it is the duty of 'any person mentioned in the subsection (11) to assist … if called upon to do so'. Those 'persons' are

- any local authority;
- any local education authority;
- any local housing authority;
- any health authority;
- any person authorised by the Secretary of State for the purposes of the section.

The Act has limited applications for care orders to local authorities or an 'authorised person' (s 31(1)). At present, this means the National Society for the Prevention of Cruelty to Children (NSPCC). A care order or supervision order can only be made in respect of someone who is under 17 years of age. A care or supervision order cannot be made if the child has reached the age of 16 and is married. The court cannot, on its own motion, make a care or supervision order. Prior to the Act it was able to do so under several enactments when the exceptional circumstances of the case justified that course of action. See for example s 7(2) and 7(4) of the Family Law Reform Act 1969 or the Matrimonial Causes Act 1973, s 43(1). It was said by Glenn Brasse in his article entitled *The Section 31 Monopoly* (1993) Fam Law 691:

> 'These powers provided a safety net for children whose needs may not have yet come to the notice of the social services, or else may have been overlooked. They were abolished, at a stroke, by Sch 15 to the Children Act 1989.'

It is also worth pointing out that since the Children Act came into force, a local authority is not under a positive duty to bring care proceedings. The situation prior to the Act was that a local authority must bring proceedings 'unless it was not in the child's or the public's interest so to do' (p 691).

The local authority must first make an application. This has caused some judicial disquiet as evidenced by the comments of the Court of Appeal in *Nottinghamshire County Council v P* (1993). The local authority had continually declined the judge's invitation to invoke the care and supervision jurisdiction under Part IV of the Act because it did not wish to remove the children from the home, despite the real risk that they would be sexually abused by their father. The reason given was that it would not be able to control the children if they were to be taken into care. The judge had no jurisdiction to make a care or supervision order; he had given a s 37 direction ordering the local authority to undertake an investigation into the children's circumstances, and the local authority had declined to use the Part IV powers. Instead it had sought a prohibited steps order, which was subsequently refused by the judge on the basis that he had no power to grant it when it was merely designed to achieve what a contact or residence order could achieve (see s 9(5)). The local authority was precluded from applying for a residence or contact order because of the provisions of s 9(2). Sir Stephen Brown P said that the local authority had 'persistently and obstinately refused to undertake what was the appropriate course of action, and it thereby deprived the judge of the ability to make a constructive order'. He went on to comment:

> 'This court is deeply concerned at the absence of any power to direct this authority to take steps to protect children. In the former wardship jurisdiction it might well have been able to do so. The operation of the 1989 Act is entirely dependent upon the full cooperation of all those involved. This includes the courts, the local authorities and the social workers, and all who have to deal with

children ... [In circumstances such as these] ... the local authority may perhaps lay itself open to an application for judicial review ...' (p 828G).

In *F v Cambridgeshire County Council* (1995), the local authority was directed to conduct a s 37 investigation into the circumstances of a man who had served 18 months imprisonment for indecent assault. The conclusion was that the man, F, presented a serious risk to the children and there should be no unsupervised contact between him and the children. F applied for a contact order. The local authority did not make an application for a care or supervision order. Instead the justices' clerk allowed the local authority to be made a party to the proceedings. It was held that he had been wrong to do so as it was not open to a local authority to seek private law orders under s 8 of the Children Act 1989. However, the matter had been dealt with properly and the decision to deny contact to F was upheld. The Nottinghamshire case may be distinguished from this case on the basis that the court in the former case had invited the authority to apply for a s 31 order, whereas in the latter case this course of action had not been adopted by the judge. Nor is it the case that judges are seeking the power to make care or supervision orders; rather they appear to be seeking the power to have greater influence over a local authority as it exercises its discretion in light of any s 37 findings.

Brasse concludes that the *Nottinghamshire* decision:

'... neatly illustrates the weakness of the new regime; the combined effect of ss 31 and 47 of the CA 1989 appears to be that not only is the local authority not obliged to make care and supervision order applications when the s 31 factual threshold has been crossed, and it would be in the child's and the public's interest to do so, but if it considers that it lacks the resources to act it need do nothing more. The Court of Appeal regretted the absence of power to compel the local authority to take appropriate steps to safeguard the interests of the children. In the event, they were left without the protection of any court orders' (p 692).

The Children Act thus gives any local authority an unfettered discretion as to how to discharge its statutory duty in respect of children who appear to be at risk of significant harm. Brasse outlines certain courses of action which could remedy this apparent deficiency in the law, including restoration of the power of the court to recommend that a care or supervision order should be made. It is suggested that if a court forms this view, then a local authority could be informed and be given the chance to make representations as to its own position in respect of the matter. For further information about the use of the s 37 procedure see *Re CE (Section 37 Direction)* (1995), where it was said that the court should not order the local authority to conduct a s 37 investigation unless it appeared that it might be appropriate to make a public law order.

The respondents in care proceedings under the Family Proceedings Rules 1991 and the Family Proceedings Courts (Children Act 1989) Rules 1991 are:

- every person whom the applicant believes to have parental responsibility for the child;
- if the child is already subject to a care order and the application is for a supervision order, any person having parental responsibility immediately prior to the making of the care order;
- the child;
- the parties to the original proceedings if the application is to extend, vary or discharge the order.

5.3.1 The statutory grounds

The grounds which have to be satisfied before a care or supervision order can be made are to be found at s 31(2) of the 1989 Act:

> 'A court may only make a care or supervision order if it is satisfied
>
> (a) that the child concerned is suffering, or is likely to suffer, significant harm; and
>
> (b) that the harm, or likelihood of harm, is attributable to
>
> (i) the care given to the child, or likely to be given to him if the order were not made, not being what it would be reasonable to expect a parent to give to him; or
>
> (ii) the child's being beyond parental control.'

The court must apply the s 1 principle to an application for either a care or supervision order. If the s 31(2) criteria are proved, it does not follow that a care or supervision order will be made. In the light of the 'no order principle', a court may decide not to make an order because, in its opinion, the welfare of the child does not demand it. The circumstances may have changed, eg the mother's partner may now have left the home and the initial source of the danger to the child no longer presents a threat. In such circumstances, it may be deemed appropriate to make no order.

Although the word 'harm' is defined in the Act to mean 'ill treatment or the impairment of health or development' the word 'significant' is not defined. The dictionary definition of significant is 'noteworthy, important, notable', none of which appears at first sight apposite to qualify the word harm. The Department of Health's guidance document suggests that the harm may be significant in terms of the likelihood of having a 'serious and lasting' effect on the child. Section 31(10) advises that:

> 'Where the question of whether the harm suffered by a child is significant turns on the child's health or development, his health and development shall be compared with that which could reasonably be expected of a similar child.'

Judicial reflections on the meaning of 'significant' are extremely rare. There appears to be little authoritative judicial guidance as to the meaning of 'similar child'. As Victor Smith said in his article *Significant Harm* (1994) Fam Law 197:

> '... in comparing the health or development of one child with that of another those factors which are intrinsic to the child, such as sex and age, are certainly to be considered. It would not be meaningful to compare, for example, the development of a three year old girl with what is expected of a four year old boy.'

However, it would be worth giving a moment's attention to the judgment of Ewbank J in *Re O (A Minor) (Care Order: Education: Procedure)* (1992), where he offered the following opinion as to the meaning of 'similar child':

> 'In my judgment, in the context of this type of case, 'similar child' means a child of equivalent intellectual and social development, who has not gone to school, and not merely an average child who may or may not be at school' (p 12E).

Booth J in *Humberside County Council v B* (1993), at p 263, said:

> 'Significant harm was defined (by counsel) in accordance with dictionary definitions, first as being harm that the court should consider was either considerable or noteworthy or important. Then she expressed it as harm which the court should take into account in considering the child's future. I think that is a very apt and helpful submission' (p 263 A).

In *Newham London Borough Council v AG* (1993), Sir Stephen Brown P warned against a 'strict legalistic analysis of the statutory meaning of s 31'. Whilst not doubting that the words of the statute must be considered, he thought that parliament could not be taken to have intended the words to be unduly restrictive 'when evidence clearly indicates that a certain course should be taken in order to protect the child' (p 289 D).

Judges appear to have taken Sir Stephen Brown's words to heart and studiously avoided making pronouncements as to the meaning, in this context, of the word 'significant'. The crucial point to remember is that intervention into family life should only occur if there is sufficient justification to warrant it. The choice of the word 'significant' is meant to reflect this point, ie that the harm must be, in the words of Professor Hoggett, 'sufficiently significant to justify intervention' (*Parents and Children*, 4th edn, Sweet and Maxwell 1993 p 181).

The largest single issue to be considered by the courts relates to the meaning of the words '... is suffering, or likely to suffer, significant harm'. This raises the question of when must it be proved that the child is suffering significant harm. This is somewhat reminiscent of the issue that faced the House of Lords in *D v Berkshire County Council* (1987) in the context of s 1(2)(a) of the Children and Young Persons Act 1969. Whereas the issue took nearly 20 years to arrive at the House of Lords, their Lordships have already been given the opportunity to consider the wording of s 31(2)(a) and give authoritative guidance on the point in the context of the Children Act 1989. The case in point is *Re M (A Minor) (Care order: Threshold conditions)* (1994). In 1991 the child's mother was murdered by his father when the child (G) was four months old. G was then placed with foster parents but retained contact with his older siblings. They were looked after by the mother's cousin (Mrs W) who initially felt unable to care for G. In May 1992 the local authority applied for a care order in respect of G. Three months later, Mrs W believed that she could, after all, care for G and applied for a residence order in respect of all four children. The local authority did not pursue the care application and instead gave support to the application for a residence order. However, the father and the guardian *ad litem* appointed for G supported the application for a care order, with a view to G being adopted.

The judge decided that the threshold criteria for the making of a care order had been satisfied because the murder of G's mother had 'deprived him of her love and care, thereby causing him harm' and that the care order should be made. Mrs W applied to the Court of Appeal which allowed the appeal and made a residence order in her favour. The Court of Appeal held that as parliament had chosen to use the present tense wording, 'is suffering', the court had to be satisfied at the time of the hearing that the child was then suffering significant harm and that it was not enough to show that some event in the past had caused the child to suffer harm if, before the hearing, the child had ceased to suffer such harm.

The House of Lords allowed the father's appeal. The threshold condition was satisfied if the child is suffering significant harm or likely to do so at the time the local authority decides to take temporary measures to protect the child from immediate harm, which in turn led to the care or supervision proceedings. If, by taking interim measures to protect the child, an authority is no longer able to proceed to a full care order, then the ability to provide effective protection for the child and to plan for the future will be jeopardised. The relevant date, therefore, for establishing the threshold criteria is the date the local authority initiates the procedure for protection under the Act. The care order was restored, thus enabling the local authority to monitor the child's placement with Mrs W. Lord Mackay of Clashfern LC commented:

> 'There is nothing in s 31(2) which in my opinion requires that the conditions to be satisfied are disassociated from the time of the making of the application by the local authority' (p 305E).

Lord Mackay went on to endorse the approach to this matter taken by Ewbank J in the case of *Nottinghamshire County Council v P* (1993) at p 140. He said:

> 'In my judgment, the words "is suffering" in section 31(2)(a) of the Children Act 1989 relate to the period immediately before the process of protecting the child concerned is first put into motion, just as in the Children and Young Persons Act 1969. That means that the court has to consider the position immediately before an emergency protection order, if there was one, or an interim care order, if that was the initiation of protection, or, as in this case, when the child went into voluntary care. In my judgment, the family proceedings court was quite entitled to consider the position when the children were with the mother prior to going into care and was correct in doing so.'

This departure from the reasoning adopted by the Court of Appeal means that the reasons for the decision of the court in *Oldham Metropolitan Borough Council v E* (1994) are unsound, being based, as they were, on the Court of Appeal's decision in *Re M* (1994), which is now reversed.

Lord Templeman in *Re M* was concerned at the 'preoccupation with the present tense' wording of s 31(2). Hollis J in *Re SH (Care Order: Orphan)* (1995) considered that the effect of the decision was that the word 'is' in fact means 'was', in the sense that 'the child was suffering significant harm when the rescue operation was initiated'.

Judicial attention has also been focused on the meaning of the words 'likely to suffer' in s 31(2)(a). The White Paper (1987) suggested that 'likely harm' is aimed at cases where there is an unacceptable risk of harm in the sense of balancing the likelihood of the harm occurring against the magnitude of that harm if it does occur. The Court of Appeal decided in *Newham London Borough Council v AG* (1993) that 'likely to suffer' should not be equated with 'on the balance of probabilities'. A court is always projecting forward in these circumstances rather than seeking to apply the test to events which had happened in the past. In looking ahead, all that can be done is to evaluate the chance of significant harm occurring. In this case the mother was aged 18 at the time of the birth and had already had two earlier pregnancies terminated. After the birth she became seriously mentally ill and neglected herself and the baby. The local authority considered the circumstances and ruled out any possibility of the baby being cared for by the maternal grandmother. The court was also of the opinion that the grandparents did not fully appreciate the extent of their daughter's illness, and, if they had care of the child, would experience a real difficulty protecting the baby from the 'serious danger' presented by the mother. Evidence was placed before the court showing the mother to be unpredictably violent and that the child was the 'central person in her delusional system'. The judge concluded that the child was likely to suffer significant harm if a care order was not made. The grandmother's appeal was dismissed, the Court of Appeal accepting that there was abundant evidence that 'if a care order were not to be made, this child would not be adequately protected and would be likely to suffer significant harm'.

The *Newham* case, and the approach to 'likely harm' advocated in it, was approved by the Court of Appeal in *Re H and R (Child sexual abuse)* (1995). Sir Stephen Brown P considered that 'the future risk of likely harm should be considered on a basis which was not necessarily that of the balance of probabilities'. In his dissenting judgment, Kennedy LJ stated:

> '... you cannot prove that a future event will happen, and the law is not so foolish as to suppose that you can. A child can therefore be said to be likely to suffer significant harm if there is acceptable evidence of a real risk that such harm will be sustained' (p 654 E).

In this case, the mother's cohabitee was alleged to have sexually abused her eldest daughter. He was charged with rape but acquitted. The local authority sought care orders in respect of the three other children in the household, two of whom were the man's own children. The judge formed the view that the mother and her cohabitee were lying in respect of the alleged abuse, but he held, on the balance of probabilities, that the allegations were true. He saw this finding as preventing him from taking further action to consider whether the children were likely to suffer significant harm and dismissed the applications for care orders. The local authority appealed on the basis that the allegation itself and the judge's suspicion ought to have been taken into account in order to fulfil the requirements of s 31. The appeal was dismissed, albeit by a two-to-one majority. The majority held that once the judge had reached his conclusion at the first stage of the procedure, it was not open to him on the evidence to move to the second stage and consider the likelihood of future harm to the children. Lord Justice Kennedy was in favour of allowing the appeal. He was of the opinion that the task of the court was to consider whether or not the threshold criteria had been established, not whether or not the children had been sexually abused. By refusing to go beyond stage one, the judge had failed to comply with his statutory duty and had not given himself the opportunity of considering each of the children separately, the judge suggesting that in the context of the 13 year old, the court might well have come to the conclusion that she was likely to suffer significant harm (see now the House of Lords decision in this case at [1996] 1 All ER 1).

'Harm' means 'ill-treatment or the impairment of health and development', and under s 31 the court has to be satisfied by evidence that the significant harm suffered by the child was attributable to the care or absence of care given to the child by the parent against whom the order is sought. In *Re O (A Minor) (Care Order: Education)* (1992) the subject of the application was a girl aged 15 who had truanted from school for a number of years and had attended for only 28 days in one year. The local authority had given the family support but the girl still failed to attend school. Eventually the local authority brought care proceedings. The magistrates concluded on the evidence that, because of the impairment to her education and 'social and intellectual development', they were justified in making a care order. The High Court held that magistrates were entitled to conclude that in such circumstances the harm was likely to be significant enough to warrant a care order being made. One conclusion was that the teenager was beyond parental control in that they could not exert sufficient influence to persuade the girl to attend school.

Conversely, the view could be taken that the girl was not receiving the care that it was reasonable to expect. Nor does it seem to matter whose fault it actually was that the state of affairs existed. In *Re G (A Minor) (Care Proceedings)* (1994), the question arose as to what weight, if any, should be given to statements made by the father in criminal proceedings in which he was subsequently acquitted. The local authority submitted that it was in the interests of the child that the court should reinvestigate in order to determine whether the threshold criteria had been met. The court held that there was a duty to investigate, and that findings of fact should be made – but that the nature of the investigation depended upon the facts of the particular case. In this case, the parties had actually agreed that a care order was appropriate, and therefore no useful purpose would have been served by carrying out a full investigation.

It is quite clear that fulfilment of the threshold criteria does not automatically lead to the making of a care or supervision order or, for that matter, any order at all. An example of this is to be found in *Re M (A Minor) (Appeal) (No 2)* (1994). In this case, the judge had found that the threshold criteria had been satisfied by the local authority, but found that it was not in the child's best interests to make a care order. Despite the misgivings felt by the judge, he believed it was in the child's best interests to 'give the parents a chance', and granted a residence order in favour of the mother rather than the care order that the local authority had requested. The court also indicated there was no need for judges to carry out a 'separate appraisal' specifically related to the itemised heads of s 1(3).

5.3.2 Interim care orders

In many circumstances, it will be impossible to proceed immediately to a hearing for a full care order, and therefore an interim order may be made. This does not contradict the principle of 'no delay' in s 1(2) because the action taken is deemed to be in the child's best interests at the time, and it ought to give time for documentation to be prepared and evidence collected to ensure the child's welfare is the paramount consideration at the hearing. There is a fair measure of authority to support this proposition, most notably the decision in *Hounslow London Borough Council v A* (1993) and *C v Solihull Metropolitan Borough Council* (1993). In the former case, the delay in moving towards a final hearing was described as 'planned and purposeful' and the most appropriate order was an interim one with directions leading to a resumed hearing on the completion of the local authority's assessment. In the latter case, Ward J commented:

> '... delay is ordinarily inimicable to the welfare of the child, but ... planned and purposeful delay may well be beneficial. A delay of a final decision for the purpose of ascertaining the result of an assessment is proper delay

> and is to be encouraged. Therefore, it is wholly consistent with the welfare of the child to allow a matter of months to elapse for a proper programme of assessment to be undertaken' (p 304 G-H).

An interim order bestows on the local authority the same powers as a full order. This means that the local authority will acquire parental responsibility for the child, and contact between the parents and child should continue unless there are good reasons to terminate it at that stage. In *A v M and Walsall Metropolitan Borough Council* (1993), an interim care order was made and the justices, having concluded there was no prospect of the mother being rehabilitated with the child, made an order terminating contact. Ewbank J held that to be wrong in principle. It was for the court making the final adjudication to decide whether or not contact should continue. It was only in circumstances of 'exceptional and severe risk' that contact should be stopped at the interim stage.

The court can, though, give directions at the interim stage when no such power exists in respect of a full care order. Section 38(b) of the Children Act 1989 states that if an interim care or supervision order is made the court:

> '... may give such directions (if any) as it considers appropriate with regard to the medical or psychiatric examination or other assessment of the child; but if the child is of sufficient understanding to make an informed decision he may refuse to submit to the examination or other assessment.'

An example is *Re O (Minors) (Medical Examination)* (1993), where the magistrates made an interim care order and gave directions under s 38(b) for medical tests to be carried out in order to determine whether or not the children were HIV positive. The local authority challenged the direction on the basis that the power under s 38(b) was permissive, and a local authority could not be directed to carry out a medical examination. It was held that given the 'mandatory language' of the subsection, the court did have the power to make such a direction with which the local authority had to comply.

Re T (A Minor) (Care Order: Conditions) (1994) is authority for the proposition that a court does not have the power to impose conditions on a care order under s 31 of the Children Act. It was 'clear beyond peradventure that the court had no power under s 31 to impose any conditions on a care order'.

Reference should also be made to the decision in *Re G (Minors) (Interim Care Orders)* (1993), and in particular the passage from Waite LJ's judgment at p 845A, where he neatly summarised the purpose behind the making of an interim care order:

'The regime of interim care orders laid down by s 38 of the Act ... is designed to leave the court with the ability to maintain strict control of any steps taken or proposed by the local authority in the exercise of powers that are by their nature temporary and subject to continuous review. The making of an interim care order is an essentially impartial step, favouring neither one side nor the other, and affording to no-one, least of all the local authority in whose favour it is made, an opportunity for tactical or adventitious advantage.'

It follows from this that the interim care order is quite different from the position resulting from the making of a full care order under s 31.

5.3.3 Discharge of care orders

Normally, a care order will remain in force until the child attains the age of 18 'unless it is brought to an end earlier' (s 91(12)).

If either a residence order or an adoption order is made by a court, the care order will be automatically discharged. Section 39 states that a care order may be discharged by the court on the application of:

- any person having parental responsibility;
- the child himself; or
- the local authority designated by the order.

Section 39(1)(b) was the subject of judicial scrutiny in *Re A (Care: Discharge Application by Child)* (1995). The question for determination was whether a child seeking to apply to discharge a care order was required to obtain the leave of the court before making an application. It was held that s 39(1)(b) was unambiguous. There was nothing within that section which stated, or even suggested, that the child's right to apply for discharge was to be subject to some 'preliminary screening'. In practice, this means there is a clear distinction between application for the discharge of public law orders and applications for private law orders. Section 39 confers a right upon the child to apply. Section 10 requires leave to be granted before the child can apply for a private law order.

The ultimate decision as to whether a care order should be discharged will be taken after an assessment of the s 1(3) checklist criteria and applying the welfare principle. The court does possess the power to substitute a supervision order on an application for discharge of a care order. *Re MD and TD (Minors) (No 2)* (1994) decides that the burden of proof of showing that the welfare of the child demands the relocation of the care order is on the person applying for the order. *Re T and E (Proceedings: Conflicting Interests)* (1995) is an example of a situation where it was held to be consistent with the child's welfare to discharge the care order and to make a residence order in favour of her father.

5.4 Care order or supervision order?

Supervision orders will be made only if the threshold criteria in s 31(2) are satisfied and, at the second stage of the process, a determination is made that a supervision order is consistent with the welfare needs of the child. It will be evident from the above discussion of care orders that many of the rules applicable to those orders will be equally applicable to supervision orders. There are differences enough in terms of the effect of supervision orders because the supervising person does not acquire parental responsibility for the child. Reference should be made to Parts I and II of Schedule 3 to the Children Act 1989 which detail the various responsibilities and obligations of the supervisor and the 'responsible person'. A 'responsible person' means 'any person who has parental responsibility for the child; and any other person with whom the child is living'. The supervisor's duties are stated at s 35(1) of the Act:

'(a) to advise, assist and befriend the child;

(b) to take such steps as are reasonably necessary to give effect to the order.'

If the order is not wholly complied with, then the supervisor must consider whether or not to apply to the court for a variation or discharge. A supervisor may also give directions and require the supervised child to comply with those directions which relate to place of abode, participation in specified activities, and to attend at particular locations. The supervisor may not give directions in respect of psychiatric and medical examinations or treatment, but the supervision order may require the child to submit to examination subject only to a child of sufficient understanding to make an informed decision giving consent.

Schedule 3 Part II para 6(1) indicates that the duration of a supervision order will be one year, but this can be extended at the supervisor's request for a period of up to three years from the date the first order was made, ie for two further years.

Obligations may be imposed upon a 'responsible person' and these are to be found at Schedule 3 para 3(1). Do note, however, that the person must consent to accept these obligations. A supervision order therefore may include a requirement:

- that (the responsible person) take all reasonable steps to ensure that the supervised child complies with any direction given by the supervisor;
- that all reasonable steps are taken to ensure the supervised child complies with any requirement included in the supervision order, eg regarding medical treatment.

How should a court respond when faced with the question of whether a care order is more appropriate than a supervision order or vice versa? Judge Coningsby QC in *Re S (J) (A Minor) (Care or Supervision Order)* (1993) very helpfully outlined the major differences between the two orders. In his view, a court needed to be clear as to what the future risks were for the child, bearing in mind that a court will have decided that the threshold criteria in s 31(2) were satisfied. In reflecting on this, the judge thought that 'careful scrutiny of what had happened in the past' should be undertaken in order to reach a view of future risks. It was noted that a great deal of protection could be provided by a supervision order. Access to the child's home could be guaranteed exercising powers under s 102 of the Act (warrant), and there could also be a care plan for the child. Parental responsibility for a child would rest with the parent(s) in most cases, and certainly not the local authority if a supervision order were to be made or continued. In the court's opinion, the concept of parental responsibility was 'at the heart of the difference between a supervision order and a care order', in the sense that the local authority has parental responsibility under a care order. A supervisor had no duty to assist parents or offer them advice. Neither was the supervisor under an obligation to safeguard or keep the child safe under a supervision order, whereas under a care order, as soon as the child was in care it was the duty of the local authority to safeguard the child's welfare.

The conclusion to be drawn from this analysis is that where a grave risk exists, then the court should make a care order. In the case itself, the facts clearly indicated that a care order was more appropriate than a supervision order. Three other cases have considered the issues. In *Re D (A Minor) (Care or Supervision Order)* (1993) the court had no doubt that a care order was the more appropriate order. In this case, there had been a history of non-accidental injury to children, culminating in the death of a child whilst in the care of the father. He was subsequently convicted of cruelty and imprisoned. The child was born to the father's new partner, and although the local authority was of the opinion the child was 'thriving', the court emphasised that the protection of the child was the decisive factor and rejected the local authority's assertion that to make a care order would undermine cooperation between the mother and social services.

The Court of Appeal in *Re T (A Minor) (Care or Supervision Order)* (1994) pointed out that even if a care order is made, the Children Act 1989 envisaged that children could remain at home either when proceedings were pending or after the granting of a care order. Neither did parents lose parental responsibility, although, of course, it was 'limited in scope'. Thus to grant a care order is not necessarily inconsistent with the local authority's desire to build a good partnership arrangement with the family concerned. This view, initially recognised prior to the Children Act 1989 in the case of *M v Westminster City Council* (1985), was deemed correct by the Court of Appeal and was to be applied whenever appropriate under the Children Act 1989. The court stated that the 'nature of a supervision order was to help and assist a child where the parents had full responsibility for its care and upbringing'. A supervision order had obvious deficiencies if parents exercised their parental responsibilities in a way which merited criticism. This was because any conditions attached to a supervision order could not be enforced by the court, but only used as evidence in further proceedings. Therefore more positive obligations were imposed upon a local authority under a care order in order to ensure the continued well being of the child.

Not only may a court be faced with choosing between the full orders, it may have to make a decision at an interim stage. This issue was addressed by Ewbank J in *Re R and G (Minors) (Interim care or supervision orders)* (1994). In this case, the children were aged six, five and four. Following an incident in which the eldest child suffered serious injuries at home, the local authority applied for interim care orders in respect of all the children. The authority's reasoning was that it wished to share parental responsibility with the parents and thereby to control the situation. The magistrates made a supervision order and ordered that the children should comply with directions given by the supervisor as to the place of residence. It was then realised by the local authority that there would be difficulty in enforcing the order. The local authority appeal was dismissed. It was acknowledged that insofar as the magistrates had intended the local authority to have the power to take the children into care, the supervision order was inappropriate. However, in the circumstances, the order was being adhered to and therefore should not be altered.

5.5 Contact with children in care

The issue of parental contact with children in the care of the local authority caused much controversy in the period leading up to the implementation of the Children Act 1989. Parents seemingly had few rights and even fewer opportunities to challenge the exercise of discretion by local authorities over their children in care. Belatedly, changes were introduced by the Health and Social Services and Social Security Adjudications Act 1983, but it was argued this was 'too little, too late'. Under the Children and Young Persons Act 1969, parents had no right to appeal against the making of a care order; that right was reserved for the child.

The Children Act has dramatically improved the legal position of parents, particularly in respect of contact with their children in care. Schedule 2 para 15(1) introduced a 'wide' provision seeking to promote and maintain contact between child and family. It states:

> 'Where a child is being looked after by a local authority, the authority shall, unless it is not reasonably practicable or consistent with his welfare, endeavour to promote contact between the child and
>
> (a) his parents;
>
> (b) any person who is not a parent of his but who has parental responsibility for him; and
>
> (c) any relative, friend or other person connected with him.'

This schedule is underpinned by s 34(1) of the Act which provides:

> 'Where a child is in the care of a local authority, the authority shall (subject to the provisions of this section) allow the child reasonable contact with –
>
> (a) his parents;
>
> (b) any guardian of his;
>
> (c) where there was a residence order in force with respect to the child immediately before the care order was made, the person in whose favour the order was made; and
>
> (d) where, immediately before the care order was made, a person had care of the child by virtue of an order made in the exercise of the High Court's inherent jurisdiction with respect to children, that person.'

The amount of contact can be defined on an application by the authority or the child (s 34(2)). By s 34(3), those listed above at (a) to (d) may also apply, as may anyone with leave of the court, such as grandparents, and the court may make such order as it thinks appropriate.

The first question to be answered is: should a contact order be made at the same time as the care order? Section 34(10) states that if there is to be an order, it can be made then or later. Section 34(11) places the court under a duty before making a care order to 'consider the arrangements which the authority have made or propose to make, for affording any person contact with a child to whom the section applies; and invite the parties to the proceedings to comment on those arrangements'. In *Re J (Minors) (Care: Care Plan)* (1994), it was held that the court is required to scrutinise the local authority's care plan for the child. That plan must accord with the best interests of the child, and if the court is of the view that it does not, then it could refuse to make a care order. The care plan ought to be agreed after consultation with parents and other parties and should be made before the final hearing. The care plan should, if possible, accord with the factors contained in Chapter 2, para 2.62 of volume 3 of the *Children Act 1989 Guidance and Regulations: Family Placements*. These are listed at p 259 B-F in the report, and include reference to 'arrangements for contact and reunification'.

The Court of Appeal in *Re B (Minors) (Care: Contact: Local Authority's Plans)* (1993) endorsed the presumption of continuing reasonable contact between parent and child 'unless or until' a court order under s 34(4) of the 1989 Act was made. Section 34(4) permits an authority or the child to apply to the court for an order refusing to allow contact. In this case, the authority's plans were for the two young girls to be adopted and applied for a s 34(4) order on the basis that the prospective adopters were not willing to accept ongoing contact with the mother. The order was made but overturned on appeal by the guardian *ad litem* representing the mother, who had sought, at the initial hearing, increased contact with her children. The court was adamant that parliament had given the courts, not local authorities, the duty to decide on contact, and, as such, the court could require the local authority to justify its long term plans for the child, but only to the extent that the plans excluded contact with the parents. The courts had no wish to become too involved in scrutinising the care plans of local authorities, but in respect of contact there was a legal duty to do so in order to ensure that the child's welfare was not subordinated to local authority discretion. *Re B* also cast doubt upon the approach to s 34 taken by Rattee J in the case of *West Glamorgan County Council v P (No 2)* (1993) on the basis that the judge had introduced restrictions which parliament had chosen not to include in the Children Act 1989. That view was shared by the Court of Appeal in *Re E (A Minor) (Care Order: Contact)* (1994). It was said that the Glamorgan 'test' had placed too much emphasis on the care plan of the local authority and should no longer be regarded as authoritative. This case dealt with an application under s 34(4) to terminate contact on the basis that rehabilitation with the parents was unlikely to be achieved and the 'level and quality of the contact was low'. The judge granted the application, but this was subsequently reversed on appeal. The court once again emphasised that it was parliament's intention that there should be a presumption in favour of continuing parental contact. It followed that even if the local authority's plans were disrupted by allowing contact to continue, then this should be done providing it was warranted by reference to the best interests of the child. The court must be seen to be discharging the duty placed upon it by parliament. Nor should it be assumed that continuing contact between parent and child would necessarily jeopardise local authority plans for a permanent placement for a child. The court was of the opinion that contact with the natural family could enable the child to 'commit himself to a substitute family with the seal of approval of his natural parents, and give the child the necessary sense of family and personal identity'.

It is vitally important in contact cases that reasons are given for the decisions, particularly if contact is to be denied. Recently the Court of Appeal has been critical of the failure of justices to give full reasoning for their decisions. In *F v R (Contact) (Justices' Reasons)* (1995), the justices had 'failed to comply with the duty upon them to give clear reasons'. There was no analysis of the court welfare officer's report and evidence, nor were there any findings of fact. As Wall J stated:

> 'This court has said on numerous occasions that even when making interim orders it is incumbent on justices to set out their reasons in full ... this process including recording their findings of fact or, if they have deliberately refrained from making findings, the fact that they have so refrained, and the reasons why' (p 231 B).

He repeated the warning in *Re D (Contact: Interim Order)* (1995), stating that the justices' reasons must be 'in clear and unambiguous language so that the parties and the court could understand what they had done and why'. Justices were obliged to apply the s 1(3) welfare criteria in every case and 'were well-advised to go through it in their reasons'.

Great care needs to be taken when deciding whether or not to make an interim contact order. If, for example, there was genuine controversy over whether contact should be continued and there were still substantial factual issues to be resolved, then it would be in the child's best interests not to make an interim order. Such an order could have an influence on the outcome of the case and may indeed be prejudicial to the very issue being decided. The strategy would appear to be to place the interim contact in the context of a coherent plan for the child which would need to be implemented with great care if circumstances of bitterness and acrimony existed between the various parties.

Section 34(7) permits a court to 'impose such conditions as [it] considers appropriate', although it does appear that courts will not seek to be too prescriptive where the 'nature and extent of the contact is an integral part of the local authority's care plan' (see *Re S (A Minor) (Care: Contact Order)* (1994)).

The most sensitive and contentious issue is likely to be the prohibition of contact with children in care, given that the presumption is in favour of contact and is seen as a right of the child. The right to apply is vested in the local authority and the child only. Under s 34(b), an authority may refuse to allow contact if satisfied:

- that it is necessary in order to promote or safeguard the welfare of the child; and
- the refusal is decided upon as a matter of urgency and it does not last for more than seven days.

If it is the authority's wish that contact should be refused for more than seven days, then application must be made to the court for an order permitting the period to be extended and, of course, under s 34(4), the court would appear to have a complete discretion in the matter. Thorpe J in *Re N (Contested Care Application)* (1994) adopted the following passage in *Re B* (1993) (above p 116), from the judgment of Butler-Sloss LJ as reflective of the way to approach s 34(4) applications:

> 'The presumption of contact, which has to be for the benefit of the child, has always to be balanced against the long-term future welfare of the child and particularly where he will live in the future. Contact must not be allowed to destabilise or endanger the arrangements for the child, and in many cases the plans for the child will be decisive of the contact application.'

The judge believed that it was tempting to 'keep doors open against possible developments in an uncertain future, but the future must be surveyed in terms of probabilities and not low possibilities'. He reached the conclusion that contact should be terminated. See also the case of *Birmingham City Council v H (A Minor)* (1994), where the House of Lords, after confirming the applicability of the welfare principle to s 34(4), emphasised that an order prohibiting contact between a mother and young child should rarely be made.

In conclusion, it is perhaps worth echoing the words of Balcombe LJ in *Re J (A Minor) (Contact)* (1994) where he stated, at p 735:

> 'Contact with the parent with whom the child is not resident is a right of the child, and very cogent reasons are required for terminating such contact.'

5.6 Emergency protection

Reform of the child protection laws was long overdue. The Inquiry Reports referred to above allude to the difficulties, both legal and procedural, in maintaining and enhancing a child protection system which is compatible with the needs of the children it is designed to serve. While the Children Act 1989 advocates most strongly the desire for partnership between families and local authorities, this cannot be allowed to hinder an effective response to child abuse and, where necessary, the immediate removal of a child from his or her parents. The Cleveland Report drew attention to the deficiencies in the law and helped to ensure that the Children Act would contain a new legal framework for child protection.

Prior to the Children Act 1989 coming into force, reliance had been placed upon the use of the place of safety order under s 28 of the Children and Young Persons Act 1969. This allowed 'any person' – in practice the local authority – to approach a magistrate and be granted, usually on an *ex parte* basis, a place of safety order which provided the necessary authority to detain a child for up to 28 days in a place of safety. The Cleveland Report states that between 1 January and 31 July 1987, 276 place of safety orders were applied for by social workers. '[T]hese place of safety orders were not identified by the grounds upon which they were applied for ...'. Of these orders 227 were applied for by the Emergency Duty Team. Of the 227, '... 174 were heard by a single magistrate at home, during the hours of court sittings, despite a clear understanding between the clerk to the justices and the Social Services Department that social workers would make these applications in the first instance to the full court'. The Cleveland Inquiry concluded that for 'a number of reasons the place of safety order does not sufficiently meet the needs of a child at risk. We welcome ... the proposals for a new emergency protection order in the government White Paper, The Law on Child Care and Family Services'.

5.6.1 Children Act Part V

Part V of the Children Act contains the new legal framework for the protection of children at risk, ie those who find themselves in an 'emergency' situation.

Section 43 introduced a new Child Assessment Order which allows action to be taken even though there is no immediate risk of significant harm requiring resort to an Emergency Protection Order. A court, on the application of a local authority or authorised person, may make an order, but only if it is satisfied that:

- the applicant has reasonable cause to suspect that the child is suffering, or is likely to suffer, significant harm;
- an assessment of the state of the child's health or development, or of the way in which he has been treated, is required to enable the applicant to determine whether or not the child is suffering, or is likely to suffer, significant harm; and
- it is unlikely that such an assessment will be made, or be satisfactory, in the absence of an order under this section (s 43(1)).

Note s 43(8), which permits a child of sufficient understanding to make an informed decision to refuse to submit to a medical or psychiatric examination of the assessment.

A court may treat an application under the section as an application for an emergency protection order, if required. At the time of writing, no cases on either s 43 or s 44 have been reported in the Family Law Reports or the All England Reports. There is no statutory definition of the word 'assessment', but in light of other sections in the Act, most notably s 38(6), it is reasonable to assume that it will focus on physical and mental well-being. However, an assessment order can only be made once a determination has been made that there is reasonable cause to suspect the child is suffering, or is likely to suffer, significant harm. Reference will still need to be made to s 1 and, of course, to whether it is in the child's best interests for the order to be made at all. Section 1(4) of the Children Act does not refer to Part V of the Act, and as a consequence, the checklist factors will not apply to s 43 or s 44 applications.

The effect of a child assessment order is to require that the child be produced for assessment, and secondly that any person authorised to carry out the assessment should do so in accordance with the terms of the order. The making of an order does not impact upon existing parental responsibility obligations. Thus the local authority does not acquire parental responsibility. Directions may be given by the court, and this may involve ensuring that contact is maintained between the parents and child if the assessment is to take place away from the child's home.

Section 43(12) governs applications for variation or discharge of the order.

5.6.2 Emergency Protection Orders (EPOs)

Section 44 seeks to maintain a fair balance between the protection requirements of a child and the legitimate interests of parents and others. These orders are designed for use in situations of genuine emergency and their duration is strictly short-term. The major features of the Emergency Protection Order are:

- Protection is offered to children on a limited time basis, placing the onus on the local authority to take immediate steps to decide on its next course of action.
- The concept of significant harm is equally applicable to the right to obtain an EPO as it is to care and supervision orders.
- Section 45(1) states that an EPO shall have effect for no more than eight days. It is possible to apply for an extension for seven days, but only if the applicant has parental responsibility as a result of the EPO and is entitled to apply for a care order. This means, in practice, only a local authority and the NSPCC have the right to apply.
- Whilst the EPO is in force, the applicant will be given parental responsibility for the child.
- It is possible to seek to discharge the order after only 72 hours, the time commencing with the making of the order.
- Applications for EPOs can be granted on an *ex parte* basis, and often it will be vital, looked at from the child's point of view, that this should be the case.
- Section 45(10) prohibits any appeal against the making of, or refusal to make, an EPO or against any direction given by the court in connection with such an order. In practice, this means that if magistrates were to act unreasonably, the only remedy would be via judicial review proceedings. In *Essex County Council v F* (1993), the court thought it 'regrettable that [it] could not interfere in a case like the present case, which cried out for the intervention of the

court'. However, because of the unambiguous wording of s 45(10), the court could not assist. Similarly, because of s 45(10), any direction regarding contact with the child who is subject to the emergency protection order cannot be challenged.

Overall, it should be emphasised that the emergency protection order should never be viewed as a routine stepping stone towards the making of a care order.

5.6.3 Police protection

Reference should be made to s 46 of the Act, which gives a constable who has reasonable cause to believe that a child would otherwise be likely to suffer significant harm, to remove the child to suitable accommodation and keep him there; or to take reasonable steps to prevent the removal of the child from any hospital, or other place, in which he is then being accommodated.

5.7 Postscript

The conclusions of eight research publications are gathered together in one document and published by HMSO. Entitled Child Protection: Messages from Research (1995), this document focuses on the need for improved training and the desirability of realigning some resource provision away from investigatory work into family support.

Summary of Chapter 5

Public Law Orders

Increasing concern expressed throughout the 1980s over the inadequacies of the state system of child protection and family support led to a review of child care law in 1985 which culminated in the White Paper, The Law on Child Care and Family Services (Cm 62). Its recommendations were to form the basis of the public law provisions of the Children Act 1989. The overriding principles are:

- parents should assume the primary responsibility for the upbringing of their children;
- the state should provide as much assistance as possible to help parents fulfil their obligations;
- if a child has to be taken into local authority care then the powers and responsibilities of both parents and local authority should be clear;
- where the child is in the care of the local authority or being looked after away from home, contact with the parents should be maintained whenever the circumstances permit.

The duty cast upon local authorities is to 'safeguard and promote the welfare of children within their area and ... to promote the upbringing of such children by their families'.

Some of the difficulties in protecting children at risk of abuse are outlined in official reports such as those into the deaths of Maria Colwell, Jasmine Beckford and Kimberly Carlile. Attention should also be given to the problems identified in the Cleveland Report (1988) and the criticisms levelled at the various agencies responsible for investigating child abuse for their failure to implement an effective coordination strategy, which culminated in the Cleveland crisis.

The Children Act introduced a new Emergency Protection Order as a replacement for the discredited Place of Safety Order under the Children and Young Persons Act 1969. The Act also introduced at s 34 a presumption in favour of reasonable contact between parent and child if the latter was in the care of a local authority. This is designed to help avoid the difficulties encountered by parents who were often denied contact by the local authority if their child was in care. See, for example, the House of Lords decision in *A v Liverpool City Council* (1981). It should be noted that parental responsibility for a child is not lost as a result of the child moving into the care of the local authority. The responsibility is shared, but in practice, this means that the parents' rights and duties are suspended for the period in which the child is in care.

Care orders

A care order may be made in favour of a local authority or 'authorised person' once it is established that the child concerned is suffering, or is likely to suffer, significant harm. It also has to be proved that the significant harm is attributable to the care not being that which would be given by a reasonable parent or that the child is beyond parental control.

Once these threshold criteria have been established, it does not automatically follow that a care order will be made. The court will have to consider the range of options available to it, including making no order at all, and make a care order only if it is in the child's best interests. The following cases should be considered as they highlight some of the difficulties which have confronted the courts since the Act came into force in 1991:

Re M (A Minor)(Care order: Threshold conditions) (1994)

Humberside County Council v B (1993)

Newham London Borough Council v AG (1993)

Nottinghamshire County Council v P (1993)

Re S H (Care Order: Orphan) (1995)

Re H and R (Child sexual abuse) (1996)

Re M (A Minor) (Appeal) (No 2) (1994)

Applications may be made for interim care orders which bestow upon the local authority the same powers as a full care order. Contact between parent and child should continue except in circumstances of 'exceptional and severe risk'.

Re T (A Minor) (Care Order: Conditions) (1994) is authority for the proposition that a court does not have power to impose conditions on a care order.

A care order or a supervision order?

The answer, of course, depends upon the circumstances, as was made clear in *Re S (J) (A Minor) (Care or supervision Order)* (1993), it being suggested that a care order would be appropriate where the local authority required the ability to exercise parental responsibility. Parental responsibility would usually rest with the parents in the case of a supervision order. So if the court believes the child to be at great risk, then a care order would be warranted.

The Children Act has dramatically improved the position of parents in respect of the ability to continue contact with their children once received into care. The relevant provisions are to be found at s 34 of the Act. Contact is seen as a right of the child not the parent. The important cases to consider are:

Re B (Minors) (Care: Contact: Local Authority's Plans) (1993)

Re E (A Minor) (Care Order: Contact) (1994)

Contact

It is vitally important that in 'contact' cases, reasons must be given for the decisions, particularly if contact is to be denied.

See *Re D (Contact: Interim Order)* (1995)

Emergency Protection

The new provisions (ss 43-52) seek to maintain a fair balance between the protection requirements of a child and the legitimate interests of parents and others. The major features of the EPO are:

- the order lasts only for eight days with the possibility of renewal for a further seven, thus forcing local authorities to make early decisions about the need to apply for a full care order;
- the concept of significant harm is applicable to s 44;
- the applicant has parental responsibility whilst an EPO is in force;
- an order can be discharged after only 72 hours; and
- an EPO should never be seen as a routine stepping stone towards the making of a care order.

Chapter 6

Financial Provision for Children

6.1 Introduction

There are numerous statutory provisions which allow courts to make financial provision for children of the family. In this chapter, we shall be concentrating upon the financial provision and property adjustment elements of the Children Act together with an assessment of the Child Support Act 1991 which came into force in 1993 and has rarely been out of the headlines ever since. Historically, the law sought to differentiate between financial provision available to children during the course of matrimonial breakdown, eg divorce, and other proceedings where parents were in dispute over a private law matter connected with the child. With the advent of the Child Support Act 1991, the basis of support has dramatically changed from a 'contest' based approach to one which has a 'formula' as its foundation.

6.2 Matrimonial proceedings

The Matrimonial Causes Act 1973 provides that upon divorce, nullity or judicial separation, the court may make financial and property adjustment orders in respect of a child of the family (see ss 23 and 24). Section 25 details the matters to which a court is to have regard in deciding how to exercise its powers under those sections. It must be determined that a child is a 'child of the family' otherwise the relevant provisions will not apply.

6.2.1 'Child of the family'

The Children Act 1989 defines a 'child of the family' in the following way:

> '(a) a child of both of those parties;
>
> (b) any other child, not being a child who is placed with those parties as foster parents by a local authority or voluntary organisation, who has been treated by those parties as a child of the family' (s 105(1)).

The important words in this definition are 'treated' and 'family'. The test changed in 1973 from having to decide whether the child had been 'accepted' as a child of the family to the current assessment based upon whether he or she has been 'treated' as a child of the family. (See s 52(1) of the Matrimonial Causes Act 1973.)

This was held to mean that a party to a marriage must receive the child into the family, and in order to do this must be in possession of all the material facts. The material fact could be paternity of the child, eg the husband believing that he was the father of the child that he has maintained over a number of years.

The current test is less dependent upon knowledge than upon what has actually occurred. The High Court ruled in *A v A (Family: Unborn child)* (1974) that the word 'treat' means to 'act or behave towards' but does not include knowledge of the material facts. In this case, the husband had married believing that he was the father of his wife's child. It was conclusively proved at the time of birth that he could not have been. The wife moved into her father-in-law's house and her husband saw the child when he visited his father. He neither maintained her nor took any interest in her. The wife claimed that she was entitled to financial provision for the child on the ground that she was a child of the family, and that by marrying her the husband had treated the child as a child of the family. It was held that she was not a child of the family for the reason that a man could not 'act or behave towards' a child unborn.

In *D v D* (1981), the husband was held not to have treated his wife's daughter as a child of the family because she lived for most of the time with her grandparents and was, in essence, a visitor to the matrimonial home. The stepfather had always acted with kindness towards the girl, but this was not enough to warrant a conclusion that he had undertaken responsibility for her. The Court of Appeal has held that the test should be an objective one.

In *Teeling v Teeling* (1984), the fact that the child had 'lived as part of the family' for some six months was sufficient evidence from which to conclude the existence of a legal obligation towards the child. Lord Justice Ormrod commented:

> 'The husband did various things for the child and was obviously willing and prepared, if the wife had been prepared, to accept the child as his own child and live together as a family, and they did so for six months.'

6.2.2 Family

A prerequisite to applying the 'treated' test is a finding that there is indeed a family unit that either is, or has been, in existence. In *M v M* (1981), the husband and wife separated, and one year later the wife gave birth to a child of which the husband was not the father. He did not repudiate the wife's implied suggestion that he was the father. The Court of Appeal held that there was no longer a family once the separation had occurred, and in consequence the child had never been a child of the family. The reasoning in *M v M* was applied in *W v W* (1984). The husband had married his wife knowing that she was pregnant by another man. There was, however, only limited contact with the child, at birth and for two weeks when the the husband was home on leave from his army unit. He then brought the marriage to an end. The wife sought financial assistance for the child. The husband argued that there had never been a family unit within which the child could have been treated as a child of the family. The Court of Appeal had regard to the parties' initial intention to live together, combined with the two weeks they spent together, and concluded that 'a family, even though an exiguous one, came into existence at the date of the marriage'. Ormrod LJ in *M v M* thought that the word 'family' connoted a 'popular, loose and flexible description and not a technical term and ... its exact scope must depend on its context'. It follows that to hold that a family exists simply because a marriage subsists can lead to unjust results.

Section 23 of the Matrimonial Causes Act 1973 permits the court to make the following orders:

- periodical payments;
- secured periodical payments;
- lump sum.

The above orders can be made in favour of a party to the marriage for the benefit of the child of the family, or directly to the child.

Section 24 of the Matrimonial Causes Act 1973 permits the court to make the following orders:

- property transfer;
- property settlement;
- ante or post nuptial settlement variation.

There are, however, restrictions imposed by s 29(1) and (3) on the making of property transfer orders where the child has attained the age of 18.

In deciding which, if any, order should be made under these sections in favour of the child, the court must have regard to the factors in s 25. The court must consider all the circumstances, first consideration being given to the welfare of any child of the family who has not attained the age of 18, and then go on to consider the following:

Under s 25 (3)

(a) the financial needs of the child;

(b) the income, earning capacity, if any, property and other financial resources of the child;

(c) any physical or mental disability of the child;

(d) the manner in which he was being, and in which the parties to the marriage expected him to be, educated or trained;

(e) the considerations mentioned in relation to the parties to the marriage in paragraphs (a) (b), (c) and (e) of subsection (2) of s 25.

Those paragraphs relate to:

- the income, earning capacity, property or other financial resources which each of the parties to the marriage has or is likely to have in the foreseeable future;
- the financial needs, obligations and responsibilities which each of the parties to the marriage has or is likely to have in the foreseeable future;
- the standard of living enjoyed by the family prior to the breakdown of the marriage;
- any physical or mental disability of either of the parties to the marriage.

In circumstances where there is a 'child of the family' who is not a child of the party against whom the order may be made, then the following factors must additionally be taken into account:

(a) whether that party assumed any responsibility for the child's maintenance, the extent and the basis upon which responsibility was assumed and the length of time for which the responsibility has been discharged;

(b) whether, when discharging the responsibility, the party knew the child was not his or her own; and

(c) the liability of any other person to maintain the child.

Section 29(3) of the Matrimonial Causes Act 1973 permits a financial provision order to be made in favour of a child over 18 years of age providing the child is receiving instruction at an educational establishment. The case of *Downing v Downing* (1976) decides that the 'child' may be given leave to intervene in matrimonial proceedings if one parent is not prepared to act against the other in order to seek financial provision for the child who is in full-time education or receiving vocational training.

The approach to financial provision for children has been outlined in numerous cases. In *Harnett v Harnett* (1973), Bagnall J said that in the vast majority of cases the 'financial position of a child of a subsisting marriage is simply to be afforded shelter, food and education according to the means of his parents'. In the later case of *Kiely v Kiely* (1988), Booth J stated that:

> '... the provisions of the 1973 Act make it clear that the statutory scheme is to enable the court to make proper financial provision for children as children or dependants ...'
>
> Additionally, the point was made that there is a ...
>
> 'distinct trend against making lump sum payments or property adjustment orders in favour of adult children who have ceased their full time education'.

The above comments in respect of unsecured and secured periodical payments must be read subject to the provisions of the Child Support Act 1991, which came into force in April 1993. The Child Support Act is concerned only with the obligation between parent and child, a 'parent' for the purposes of the Act, is defined as 'any person who in law is the mother or the father of the child'. The Act does not concern itself with anything other than maintenance, and therefore the court will retain jurisdiction in respect of lump sum orders, settlement of property for the benefit of the child, and transfer of property for the benefit of the child. In the Family Proceedings Court, the maximum amount that may be awarded under a lump sum order is £1,000. However, the court will retain jurisdiction for maintenance orders in the following circumstances:

- where the prospective payer is a step-parent, providing always that the child has been treated as a child of the family. This is in keeping with the principle of the Child Support Act that the provisions apply only to parent/child obligations;
- if one of the child's parents is not habitually resident in the United Kingdom. See, for example, the case of *A v A (A Minor) (Financial Provision)* (1994);
- if the parents of the child still live together as one household;
- if the child is 19 years of age or over;

- if the child is aged between 16 and 19 but is not in receipt of full-time, non-advanced education.

The Child Support Act also allows the court to retain jurisdiction in respect of child maintenance in the following situations:

- the so-called 'topping up' cases, where the carer is seeking maintenance for the child which exceeds the maximum amount payable under the formula introduced by the Act (s 8(6));
- where an order is required in respect of the payment of school fees (s 8(7));
- if the child suffers from a disability and, as a result of extra costs incurred in caring for the child, an additional payment is required (s 8(8)).

It should be noted that jurisdiction is retained in the case of applications for lump sum, property adjustment and property settlement orders under the Matrimonial Causes Act 1973, the Domestic Proceedings and Magistrates' Courts Act 1978 and the Children Act 1989. The final situation where jurisdiction is retained is where a residence order has been made in favour of the carer and the application for an order is against that person (s 8(10)). The welfare of the child is not the paramount consideration, and it was held in *Suter v Suter and Jones* (1987) that to make the child's welfare the overriding consideration was wrong in principle. The Court of Appeal acknowledged the importance of making the child's welfare the first consideration, but the objective it was said was to try 'to obtain a financial result which is just as between husband and wife'. The court ordered a nominal order of £1 per year as a measure of the husband's maintenance contribution to his former wife. She had already received capital transfers and, on the facts, there was 'no reason ... to expect that the children will find themselves without a roof over their heads if periodical payments for the wife came to an end'. The wife's cohabitee was expected to contribute to the household expenses.

The Matrimonial Causes Act imposes an obligation on the court to consider whether a 'clean break' between the parties is attainable. This was described by Lord Scarman in *Minton v Minton* (1979):

> 'There are two principles which inform the modern legislation. One is the public interest that spouses, to the extent that their means permit, should provide for themselves and their children. But the other – of equal importance – is the principle of the "clean break".'

He went on to state:

> 'The law now encourages spouses to avoid bitterness after family breakdown and to settle their money and property problems. An object of the modern law is to encourage each to put the past behind them and to begin a new life which is not overshadowed by the relationship which has broken down.'

There can never be a clean break from the obligation to maintain one's children, but the court has, on many occasions, either reduced the obligation between the parties to a purely nominal amount, as in *Suter* above, or terminated the obligation altogether, usually as a result of a lump sum payment to the other by one of the parties to the marriage.

6.3 Domestic Proceedings and Magistrates' Courts Act 1978

During the course of the marriage, financial provision may be made under the provisions of the 1978 Act. These provisions apply to children of the family, defined in the same way as in the Matrimonial Causes Act 1973 (s 88(1)). In deciding whether or not to make an order for financial provision for a child under s 2 of the 1978 Act, for either periodical payments or a lump sum order, the court must have regard to exactly the same factors as specified in the Matrimonial Causes Act. These, however, are repeated at s 3(3) and (4) of the 1978 Act. Under s 8(4) of the Children Act 1989, proceedings under the 1978 Act are deemed to be 'family proceedings' in which s 8 orders may be made. However, with the advent of the Child Support Act 1991, the jurisdiction has been severely curtailed in respect of unsecured and secured periodical payments. (See above for comment in the context of the Matrimonial Causes Act 1973.)

6.4 Inheritance (Provision for Family and Dependants) Act 1975

Section 1 of the Act permits a 'child of the deceased' to make an application for reasonable financial provision from the deceased's estate, providing the person dies domiciled in England and Wales (s 1(1)(c)). Any person (not being a child of the deceased) who has been treated by the deceased as a child of the family is also permitted to make a claim against the estate (s 1(1)(d)). 'Reasonable financial provision' is defined by s 2 to mean 'such financial provision as it would be reasonable in all the circumstances of the case for the applicant to receive for his maintenance'. Section 2 details the very wide powers possessed by the courts, including the ability to award periodical and lump sum payments and to transfer property to the applicant. Section 3 lists the matters to which the court is to have regard in exercising its powers under s 2 of the 1975 Act.

A parent, through his or her will, may make reasonable financial provision for a child in the event of his or her (ie, the parent's) death during the child's minority or beyond, in which case there ought to be few problems for the child. However, the converse may be true in that the parent may actively seek to avoid making any sort of financial provision for the child. Those who have reached majority are still entitled to apply, but as Henry LJ pointed out in *Re Jennings (Deceased), Harlow v National Westminster Bank Plc and Others* (1994), at p 546, those powers should be exercised '... circumspectly and in relatively rare circumstances' if the applicant is in good health and economically self-sufficient. The Act emphasises that the question to be decided is based upon the need for maintenance, and it must be shown that where the person seeking maintenance is a child, then that sum must be 'required' for his or her maintenance. A further important point raised by this case is that 'beyond the mere fact of blood relationship there must be something as being a moral claim to be maintained or something of that kind for a claim to be made against the deceased's estate' (p 547 B).

In this case, the plaintiff was 47 years old at the time of his father's death in 1990. His parents had separated in 1945 when he was aged two. The deceased had never maintained his son, nor had there been any contact between them throughout the whole of this period. The plaintiff was a company director who lived in a property valued at some £350,000 and enjoyed a 'comfortable' standard of living. The trial judge concluded that there had been no good reason for the father's failure to maintain his son, thus failing to honour the 'moral and financial obligations' towards the applicant during his minority, and he awarded the plaintiff £40,000. The charities who were to benefit from the deceased's estate appealed. In allowing the appeal, it was held that the purpose of the 1975 Act was not to 'punish or redress past bad or unfeeling parental behaviour where that behaviour does not still impinge on the applicant's present financial situation'. The plaintiff had relied upon s 3(1)(d), which invites the court to have regard to:

> 'any obligations and responsibilities which the deceased had towards any applicant for an order ...'

It was clear that, in this case, the father's failure to maintain had no lasting impact on his son. As Sir John May said:

> '[The Act] ... was not passed ... to enable a court, perhaps many years after the event, to make retrospective reparation to a person in respect of whom a deceased had failed, years earlier, to comply with a legal or familial or moral obligation where any effect of that failure had not continued up to the deceased's death' (p 550 B).

By s 25(1) of the 1975 Act, 'child' includes an illegitimate child and a child *en ventre sa mere* at the death of the deceased. However, the phrases 'child of the family' and 'treated by the deceased as a child of the family ...' (s 1(1)(d)) are not defined in the Act. In *Re Leach (Deceased)* (1985), Slade LJ thought that the words 'treated by the deceased as a child of the family ...' referred to the behaviour of the deceased towards the potential applicant. So long as there had been the requisite behaviour during the relevant period it did not matter that the 'treatment' had ceased prior to the demise of the parent. The Act does not refer to the 'subsistence of the marriage' but 'in relation to the marriage', and this was deemed wide enough to encompass the behaviour of the stepmother towards her stepdaughter after the death of her husband, the applicant's father. It was proposed that the court should not be persuaded to adopt a '... too rigid and technical construction ...' in respect of these words. Therefore treatment after the marriage had ended could be relevant behaviour upon which to make an application under the Act.

The case law on this subject is not large, but it would be wise to consider the following decisions in addition to the case mentioned above: *Re Debenham (Deceased)* (1986), *Re Coventry (Deceased)* (1979), and *Re Callaghan (Deceased)* (1985).

6.5 Financial provision under the Children Act 1989

The relevant provisions are to be found at s 15 and Schedule 1 of the 1989 Act, and an application for financial provision is included within the definition of family proceedings under s 8(4) of the Act. This means that s 8 orders may, if appropriate, be made. Paragraph 1(1) of Schedule 1 states that the following may apply for an order:

- a parent. This includes, in addition to the child's natural parents, any party to a marriage in relation to whom the child is a child of the family;
- a guardian;
- any person in whose favour a residence order is in force.

A 'child' for the purposes of the legislation may include someone over the age of 18 years. (See para 2(1)(a) and (b) of Schedule 1.)

In deciding whether or not to make an order, the court must have regard to the following factors:

(a) the income, earning capacity, property and other financial resources which each person mentioned in sub-paragraph (3) has or is likely to have in the foreseeable future;

(b) the financial needs, obligations and responsibilities which each person mentioned in sub-paragraph (3) has or is likely to have in the foreseeable future;

(c) the financial needs of the child;

(d) the income, earning capacity, if any, property and other financial resources of the child;

(e) any physical or mental disability of the child;

(f) the manner in which the child was being, or was expected to be, educated or trained.

The court must also have regard to whether that person has assumed responsibility for the maintenance of the child, knowing that the child was not his and whether or not any other person is liable to maintain the child.

The factors to which the court is to have regard are unexceptional, the majority appearing as factors for consideration in applications under the Matrimonial Causes Act 1973 and the Domestic Proceedings Magistrates' Courts Act 1978.

In *Pearson v Franklin* (1994), the Court of Appeal considered whether the father should transfer to the mother his interest in the joint tenancy of the home for the benefit of the children. The parties, who were not married, had twins aged two. They were joint tenants of a property rented from a housing association. The mother left the home taking the children with her, while the father continued to live in the property. The relationship had broken down and there was little prospect of their ever resuming cohabitation. The mother, who was living in 'wholly unsatisfactory accommodation', applied to the county court for a specific issue order that she be allowed to reside in the property, with the children but in the absence of the father. The judge refused her application and the Court of Appeal dismissed her appeal. The court was of the view that the most appropriate remedy would be for her to make an application under s 15 and Schedule 1 of the Children Act. A transfer of the father's interest in the joint tenancy to the mother would give her an exclusive right to occupy the home. The court was of the opinion that '... the availability of a remedy under s 15 is confirmation of the unavailability of a remedy under s 8'. In other words, s 8 orders were not to be seen as ouster orders under another name. Reliance was placed upon the Court of Appeal decision in *K v K (Minors: Property Transfer)* (1992). In that case it was held that the words 'the benefit of the child' in the relevant section of the

Guardianship of Minors Act 1971 (now incorporated into the Children Act) were not confined to financial benefit nor giving the child a beneficial interest in the property. The court did have jurisdiction to order a parent to transfer to the other parent his or her interest in the joint tenancy of the family home. The effect of such an order is to exclude one parent from the home, and this should not be done without careful consideration of all the circumstances and the effect that such an order would have on the party excluded from the property. Thorpe J in the former case considered that:

> 'The right to apply for the transfer or settlement of the property, including tenancies, is the effective remedy for a parent who has not married and who needs the only available home to enable him or her to care for the child or children after the final separation of the couple' (p 143 H).

Sir Stephen Brown P held in *K v H (Child Maintenance)* (1993) that s 1 of the Children Act did not apply to applications for financial provision. Section 1 is principally directed at orders relating to the upbringing of the child, the administration of his property, or the application of income arising from it. Thus a 'straightforward' application for financial provision was not governed by the provisions in s 1, and the child's welfare is not considered to be of paramount importance. This is further confirmed by reference to s 105 of the Act, which defines 'upbringing' in relation to any child to include care of the child but not his maintenance (s 105 (1)).

It should be emphasised that these provisions are designed to provide financial and other support during the child's dependency relationship with the parent, with the limited exceptions outlined above based upon special need or where the 'child' is in full-time education or receiving vocational training (see *T v S* (1994)). The point was further emphasised by Ward J in *A v A (A Minor: Financial Provision)* (1994), where he stated that 'property adjustment orders should not ordinarily be made to provide benefits for the child after he has attained his independence' (p 661 G).

Children of unmarried parents also have access to the powers for capital provision contained in Schedule 15. Rachel Wingert (in *Capital Provision for Children of Unmarried Parents* (1994) Fam Law 194) expressed the belief that practitioners are increasingly seeking the transfer of property for the benefit of children. She points out that, to date, there has been little judicial guidance on the application of these provisions. It was pointed out by the Law Commission in its 1982 Report on Illegitimacy (No 118) that '... courts lean against making substantial capital orders in favour of the children of a marriage ... but [these additional powers] could be useful in some circumstances'. In the absence of specific judicial guidance, it is suggested that one looks at the divorce case law, and in particular at *Lilford (Lord) v Glynn* (1979). In *Kiely v Kiely* (above), Booth J was of the opinion that 'Lump sum orders in favour of children, and in particular children whose parents are of limited means, are rare ...'. The impact of the continuing financial obligations imposed by the Child Support Act will mean that the caring parent is less likely to be able to negotiate a property transfer in return for reduced maintenance payments. There would, of course, be no discernible benefit to the child, as either a property transfer or a Mesher Order will secure the property for the day-to-day needs of the child. To order an outright transfer might benefit the child once he has attained his majority, but that is plainly outside the scope of the Children Act provisions.

6.6 The Child Support Act 1991

The government White Paper, *Children Come First* (1990) (Cmnd 1263), gave an indication of why there was a need for a thorough overhaul of the approach to maintenance collection and enforcement. It stated that the system of maintenance was 'unnecessarily fragmented, uncertain in its results, slow and ineffective'. It was a system largely based upon judicial discretion, so that individuals with broadly similar financial needs could find themselves treated differently depending on the court and, sometimes, its location. Different courts were involved in decision-making, and the enforcement of maintenance orders and financial provision could, as has been seen, be applied for under a variety of statutes, each having a different purpose and philosophy. The government was also concerned about the growing number of single parent families who were increasingly reliant upon state benefits. Figures produced at the time the Act reached the statute book in 1991 highlighted an increase of over 20% in those claiming Income Support in a three year period from 1988, up from 727,000 to 895,000. At the same time, the numbers of single parent families receiving financial support from the absent parent had fallen to only 23% in 1991, from a figure of 50% a decade earlier. It was claimed that the amounts awarded were often too low and that the levels of maintenance arrears were too high. The conclusion was:

> '... the cumulative effect is uncertainty and inconsistent decisions about how much maintenance should be paid. In a great many instances, the maintenance award is not paid or the payments fall into arrears and then take weeks to re-establish. Only 30% of lone mothers and 3% of lone fathers receive regular maintenance for their children.

More than 750,000 lone parents depend on Income Support. Many lone mothers want to go to work but do not feel able to do so.'

The Child Support Act was therefore an attempt to bring a degree of rationality and consistency into an area of law that seemingly pleased very few. The idea was that the assessment, collection and enforcement of child maintenance would be administered through a new organisation called the Child Support Agency. Calculations would be based upon an agreed formula in an endeavour to achieve a consistent approach to all applicants, thus removing one of the main criticisms levelled against the operation of the old system through the courts.

The principle underpinning the legislation is relatively uncontentious, that absent parents should continue to make significant contributions to the financial support of their children. This reflects the philosophy of the Children Act in that parental responsibility survives the breakdown of the parents' marriage or relationship, and that rights, duties and responsibilities continue to flow from the ongoing legal relationship between parent and child. Section 1(1) of the Child Support Act states quite clearly that, for the purposes of the Act, 'each parent of a qualifying child is responsible for maintaining him'. By s 3(2), The absent parent is defined as follows:

'The parent of any child is an 'absent parent' in relation to him, if:

(a) that parent is not living in the same household with the child; and

(b) the child has his home with a person who is, in relation to him, a person with care.'

By s 3(3), the 'person with care' is defined in the following terms:

'... a person

(a) with whom the child has his home;

(b) who usually provides day-to-day care for the child (whether exclusively or in conjunction with any other person); and

(c) who does not fall within a prescribed category of person.'

For the sake of completeness, the other key definition is of a 'qualifying child'. This is defined in s 3(1) which provides that a child is a 'qualifying child' if:

'(a) one of his parents is, in relation to him, an absent parent; or

(b) both of his parents are, in relation to him, absent parents.'

A child is someone under the age of 16, or someone under the age of 19 who is receiving full-time education at school, but this definition does not embrace someone who is receiving advanced education. A 'qualifying child' includes both an adopted child and a child born to a couple by artificial insemination by donor, unless it is proved that the husband did not consent. This latter issue is likely to be the subject to judicial scrutiny in the near future. *The Times* (1995) 3 October reports that the husband of a woman who conceived by artificial insemination by donor is claiming that, for the purposes of the Child Support Act 1991, the child is not legally his. The child, a girl, was born in July 1985 after the couple had visited a clinic for artificial insemination using anonymous donor sperm. The husband registered the birth giving his name as that of the father. The Human Fertilisation and Embryology Act 1990 makes it clear that a man who signs a fertility clinic consent form is legally the father of the child. These rules did not apply in 1985 at the time of the child's birth. As a result, it is likely that the Child Support Agency will have to take the father to court in order to obtain a ruling on the matter. After the couple separated in 1993, the father paid maintenance amounting to £120 per week, later reducing the voluntary payment to £80 and finally terminating the payments altogether. The argument would appear to be that the present law does not apply to him as he is not the biological father of the child. However, the better view would appear to be that the father's actions are consistent with him accepting responsibility for the child. He named himself as the father at the time of the registration of the child's birth; he maintained the child whilst he and his wife were cohabiting; and he voluntarily assumed financial responsibility for the child once they had separated. Baroness Warnock, who chaired the inquiry into human fertilisation and embryology which reported in 1984, is quoted as saying that she was convinced that the husband would have to pay for the child's upkeep, considering it morally unjustifiable that his 'biological distance from the child' should result in a court coming to the conclusion that he was not responsible for the maintenance of the child. Thus when the parents are living apart, the 'absent parent' – the one who is not caring on a day-to-day basis for the child – will be required to pay child support through the Agency, which is part of the Department of Social Security.

One of the initial concerns about the Act was that it appeared to be 'benefit driven,' in that if the Agency were successful in increasing the amount that absent parents paid to caring parents, then the amount of state benefit paid out would, in consequence, be reduced. In the first report of the House of Commons Social Security Committee – The Operation of the Child Support Act, Session 1993–4, HC 69 (1993) – the objective of ensuring that there are 'substantial savings in the social security budget' is given prominence. 'The committee believes that taxpayers have for too long been asked, in effect, to pick up maintenance bills that should have been met by absent parents' (para 18). The Agency was expected to save taxpayers £530 million in the first year. For an assessment of the Report, see John Eekelaar, *Third Thoughts on Child Support* (1994) Fam Law 99. This must, though, be set against the cost of running the Agency, which was initially estimated to be about £400 million.

6.6.1 The role of the courts

The court's role as a result of the Child Support Act coming into force was outlined by David Burrows in his article entitled *Child Support Act 1991: The Court's Role, Amendments and Other Issues* (1993) Fam Law 301. The initial consequence was that a court in every financial relief case involving a family with qualifying children had to be made aware of the likely outcome of an assessment under the Act. The reason for this is that a court must consider the factors in s 25(2) of the Matrimonial Causes Act 1973, including the financial obligations and responsibilities each party has, or is likely to have, in the foreseeable future. There is also the statutory requirement that the court should consider the contributions each party is likely to make to the welfare of the family. Reference should also be made to the article at (1994) Fam Law 96 by Helen Meadows, which deals with child maintenance in light of the provisions of the 1991 Act and considers the 'residual functions of the court'. It points out that, while the purpose of the Child Support Act is to deprive the courts of the opportunity to assess child maintenance, there are still likely to be occasions when the court will retain the ability to '... exercise their old powers, at least on a transitional basis, and some cases in which the courts retain exclusive jurisdiction'. These situations are considered later in this chapter.

There is a phased implementation procedure, by which the Act should be fully operational by April 1997. There are transitional arrangements to cover the period from April 1993 until April 1997. From April 1993, it was intended that all new cases, whether the caring parent was on benefit or not, would be taken by the Agency. Existing cases where the caring parent was on benefit would be subject to phased implementation over a three year period. These must be differentiated from caring parents who are not on benefit, whose cases will only be handled from April 1996, and then in four tranches depending on the person's surname. The courts will continue to have a limited role in the assessment of maintenance when the Act becomes fully operational (see above). The courts will continue to be involved in the redistribution of the matrimonial assets on divorce or nullity, and will make assessments as to the appropriate maintenance level for the parties as well as making capital provisions for both parents and children.

One of the early criticisms of the Act related to the apparent injustice suffered by those who had divorced before the Act came into force and whose divorces had proceeded on the basis of a 'clean break' between the parties. The problem was vividly highlighted in the case of *Crozier v Crozier* (1994). The marriage was dissolved in 1988 and there was one child of the marriage. In the ancillary proceedings, the parties agreed that the husband would transfer to his former wife his share of the matrimonial home. In return, she took over responsibility for the mortgage and would have full responsibility for maintaining the child. The consent order, which was made in 1989, was expressed to be 'intended to effect a full and final settlement of all financial and property claims arising between the parties from the breakdown of the marriage, whether present or future, save for child maintenance'. Subsequently, the husband was notified that his maintenance contribution had been assessed under the Child Support Act at £29 per week. He had been making a £4 per week contribution from the time his former wife had indicated in early 1993 that her earnings were insufficient to maintain herself and the child. The husband was living with another woman and her child, aged seven, and their child, aged two. The former wife was living with another man and they were set to marry in the near future. The former wife also had a child by the man she was to marry. The former matrimonial home had been sold and the proceeds of £20,000 were held on deposit. The husband claimed that the consent order had been undermined by the child maintenance assessment and it should be set aside to allow him to claim his share of the proceeds from the sale of the former matrimonial home. It was held by Booth J that a demand under the Child Support Act was not a reason for setting aside the consent order. She explained that, while a clean break could be achieved between the parties to a marriage, there could be no break from the obligation to maintain the child. The legal liability to maintain the child rested with both parents. The consent order, with its reference to ongoing maintenance, reflected the child's right to be maintained. The former wife was in receipt of state benefits and therefore the state was '... empowered to seek the recovery of its expenditure on benefit from a person who was liable for maintenance'.

As a result of this decision, it is unlikely that clean break settlements made prior to the Child Support Act coming into force will be reopened, simply because, in law, the obligation to maintain one's child stems from the common law and will not be affected by agreements made as part of a clean break divorce settlement between the parties. Whilst the legal reasoning may be correct, the complaint is essentially of a more practical nature. The settlement means that, from the outset, the parties are aware of their ongoing financial commitments and can plan accordingly. In the *Crozier* case, each party had a new relationship and there was a young child from each of the partnerships. Neither the husband nor wife was affluent, she being on Income Support and he, a self-employed joiner, earning £9,390 gross. The increased payment to the child of his first marriage would presumably put further financial pressure on the available income to support his second family. It is imaginable that, at the margins, the pressure could be so great on some new families that the result of the child maintenance assessment might be the demise of a second marriage, with all its attendant ramifications. Yet, in principle, absent parents should not be allowed to cast their responsibilities onto the taxpayer.

This case should be contrasted with the cases of *Smith v McInerney* (1994) and *Mawson v Mawson* (1994), both first instance decisions of Thorpe J. In the former case, the marriage had lasted 17 years and there were three children of the family. Under a separation agreement, the husband had transferred to his wife his half share of the matrimonial home and collateral endowment policies. In return, he was released from any future obligation in respect of mortgage payments and from any future obligation to maintain his wife and children. Despite this agreement, the husband did in fact pay his wife £200 per month for the benefit of the children until he was made redundant, when the payments ceased. Three years later, he applied for a property adjustment order and a lump sum order. It was held that as a matter of 'general policy' that what had been agreed between the parties in the past should be upheld unless there were overwhelming reasons why the agreement should be varied. However, the judge found that as the wife had asserted her rights under the agreement, the husband also should have the benefit of the contract. He was therefore held to be entitled to the return of monies which he had voluntarily paid prior to his redundancy. The important point, though, was the conclusion reached that, as he was likely to be assessed by the Child Support Agency, and having transferred his interest in the matrimonial home to his wife, '... in reality the husband would be paying twice to discharge the same obligation'. The husband was therefore entitled to an indemnity from the wife in respect of any substantial periodical payments extracted from him by the Agency. This case can be reconciled with *Crozier* in that both judges acknowledged that the obligation under the Child Support Act is not affected by the existence of an agreed divorce settlement. However, they can be distinguished on the basis that, in the latter case, consideration was given to the likely impact of a child support assessment on an existing order.

In the *Mawson* case, the proceedings for financial relief by the wife were withdrawn pending an assessment by the Child Support Agency. The husband was assessed to pay £596 per month. The judge took this into account, ordered the transfer to her of the husband's share of the matrimonial home and a lump sum payment of £2,000. Maintenance to the wife was assessed at £150 per month, which should terminate after three months. The court held that a balance had to be struck between the desirability of securing the child's financial future and the need to 'uphold the message from the amendments to the 1973 Act that the wife's financial dependence upon her former husband should be brought to an end as soon as possible'. In the event, the judge extended the maintenance period to 12 months. The amount of maintenance assessed under the Act was clearly far in excess of what a court would have been likely to order, and it is interesting to speculate on how much this influenced the judge in reaching his decision as to the amount of maintenance to be paid to the wife and the duration of that support.

For an assessment of the *Crozier* decision, see Abbott, D, *Child Support and the Clean Break: Once a Parent* ... New Law Journal (1994) Vol 144 p 244, and Helen Meadows, *Child Support Act 1991: Setting Aside Clean Beak Consent Orders* (1993) Fam Law 635.

From April 1995 it has been possible for the Agency to depart from the formula assessment in the light of clean break settlements made before 5 April 1993, providing that a departure from the formula would be fair to both parents *and* the taxpayer.

6.6.2 The assessment

The calculation of the final maintenance assessment is a complex affair, and undergraduates are unlikely to be invited come to grips with the finer points of forms CSC1 and CSC2. CSC1 relates to the 'standard case' of one absent parent, whereas CSC2 deals with 'multiple absent parents'. The parents will be required to provide detailed financial information.

Stage One deals with the maintenance requirement, which provides scale allowances for each child. For example, a qualifying child under 11 will receive an allowance of £15.95. Children between 11 and 15 receive £23.40, and at 16-plus, the figure is currently £28.00. To these figures are added allowances for the parent as carer. For one or more children under 11, the allowance is £46.50. If there are no children under 11 but one or more between 11 and 13, the allowance is £34.88, and finally, if there is one or more children between 14 and 16, then the figure is £23.25. A Family Premium figure of £10.25 is added, and if the person with care does not have a partner, then another £5.20 is added. From the total is deducted Child Benefit at the prevailing rates, £10.40 for the first child and £8.45 for each subsequent child.

Stage Two identifies the mother's assessable income, including whether or not she is in receipt of Income Support. Earnings are shown gross, with deductions made for income tax, national insurance and pension contributions. If there is any further income, that must be added. If the child has any income, that also must be declared. The mother's exempt income is then calculated, and that accords with the 'parent as carer' allowance in Stage One. Any housing or travel costs are then added to the exempt income, as is any property transfer allowance.

The father's assessable income is then determined upon the same basis, although, in practice, this is likely to be substantially higher than the mother's by dint of the fact that he will not receive any allowances for the children, as they are likely not to be living with him. He will have an adult single allowance of £46.50.

Stage Three is the assessment, based upon a formula which is too detailed to account for in this summary, but applying the figures from Stages One and Two, a maintenance assessment figure is calculated.

Stage Four identifies and determines the father's 'protected income'. To his £46.50 allowance is added a further £26.50 if he has a partner, his housing costs, council tax and what is referred to as the 'prescribed amount'. The protected income figure is an assessment of what the father requires in order not to fall below subsistence level. The maintenance assessment from Stage Three is then deducted from the total disposable income of the father. If the figure for disposable income is higher than the protected income figure, then the final maintenance assessment figure will accord with the maintenance assessment from Stage Three.

Stage Five is the 'Final Calculation', where 30% of the net income of the father is calculated. If the result is greater than the provisional final maintenance assessment, then the assessment remains unchanged. If it is not, then the final assessment will be based upon 30% of the father's net income.

The CSC2 calculations are based upon similar principles but are more complex, because there is more than one absent parent to take into account, for example where the mother has had children by different men.

Please note that all figures shown above are correct at the time of writing and relate to the assessment year 1995-96.

6.6.3 Criticism of the Child Support Act

As Maggie Rae put it when reviewing the Child Support Agency's First Annual Report in the *New Law Journal* (1994) Vol 144, p 970:

> 'Supporters of the Child Support Agency are few and far between these days and we tend to keep ourselves carefully hidden from view. Unhappily, the First Annual Report of the operations of the Agency gives more ammunition to those who call for repeal than those of us who still want reform.'

In broad terms, the criticisms have centred upon the unfairness and rigidity inherent in adopting a formula approach to child maintenance. Comparisons were made with other jurisdictions which have similar schemes, particularly the United States and Australia, where it was suggested there is far more flexibility in approach. Public condemnation of the work of the Child Support Agency has been intense, although one must have some sympathy as it was not the Agency which created the legislation. The Agency was not assisted in reaching its targets by changes to the formula which were introduced in February 1994 following a report from the House of Commons Social Security Select Committee. Other criticisms have been levelled at the lack of a suitable appeal system, the unfairness in largely ignoring the additional expenditure connected with a second family, and the failure to take into account legitimate expenses such as travelling and the high cost of maintaining contact with the child.

The Secretary of State for Social Security introduced a White Paper in January 1995 entitled *Improving Child Support*, which attempted to deal with the three major criticisms of the Act:

- that the formula was intrinsically unfair;
- that the system was inflexible;
- that the Child Support Agency was unable to process cases efficiently.

Changes to the formula were introduced in April 1995. The major improvements are that no more than 30% of an absent parent's net income will be payable as child support. This is, in effect, a reduction of over 20%. Allowances are to be given for travel to work, and there will be an allowance to take account of pre-1993 property transfers. There may also be a reduction in the amount of maintenance paid to a former spouse.

A departure from the formula will be allowed where additional expenditure has been incurred which has not been taken into account by the formula and hardship will be the result if an adjustment is not made. The clean break settlements before 1993 can also be taken into account as a reason for departing from the formula.

The system for departures from the normal maintenance assessment are contained in Child Support Act 1995 which reached the statute book in July of that year. The Act will have a phased implementation, and the key provisions will come into effect in the 1996-97 financial year. The first provisions were brought into effect on 5 September and 1 October 1995, but the major provisions will not become law until sometime in 1996-97. The application of the 1991 Act has now been deferred in respect of situations where written maintenance agreements were made before the 5 April 1995 or where there is a child maintenance order in force. In effect, the court will continue to have jurisdiction in such cases. However, this deferment does not apply to cases where the carer is in receipt of Income Support, Family Credit or Disability Working Allowance. Additionally, if the man assessed is denying parentage, the Child Support Agency may now apply for a declaration of parentage not only at the outset of any application, but also throughout the period that an assessment is in force. Provision is also made for the payment of compensation to carers who are in receipt of Family Credit or Disability Maintenance Allowance in circumstances where maintenance is reduced as a result to changes in the child support legislation.

The new system of 'departure orders' will hopefully mitigate some of the difficulties which have ensued from the strict adherence to the formula. A number of grounds for departure are specified in the Act, eg extra costs arising from long-term illness or disability of the applicant or a dependant. The Act is designed to help improve the operation of the system and includes the provision for payment in prescribed circumstances of a 'child maintenance bonus' (see s 10).

In order to create sufficient time for the Child Support Agency to improve its performance, the government announced in December 1994 that there was to be an indefinite deferment in respect of taking on new cases where the person with care had been receiving benefit prior to April 1993. Non-benefit cases were to have been taken on in 1996, but it would appear that the likelihood of this date being met is slim. The courts will thus continue to have a role in assessing maintenance.

As Maggie Rae commented:

> 'These and other changes will, it is hoped, enable the CSA to offer a better service. This is vital if the system is to command respect. At the end of the day it will not matter that the formula has been improved and the departure system introduced, if the Agency cannot deliver.'

The maintenance assessment will be reviewed annually, and this may well be instigated by the absent parent if his or her circumstances have dramatically changed in that period. If there is a belief that the assessment has been calculated incorrectly, then a review can be requested, and that should be undertaken within 28 days of making the request. There is the right of appeal to the Child Support Appeal Tribunal, but significantly, legal aid will not be available for the tribunal hearing.

6.6.4 The Child Support Act – conclusion

The major question is whether the damage limitation exercise carried out by the government will succeed in redeeming the legislation and the Agency in the eyes of the public. The changes which were announced in 1995 seem to have helped to reduce the flow of critical comment and public condemnation of the Act and the Agency. What is certain is that the next two to three years will be critical as far as this piece of legislation is concerned.

Summary of Chapter 6

Financial Provision for Children

Financial provision for children can be made available in a variety of ways, depending on the type of proceedings and the statute under which an application is made. Provision can go to the child or, more usually, to the custodial parent, to be used for the benefit of the child.

The concept of 'child of the family' becomes important in this respect where financial provision is being sought from a person who is not the mother or father of the child. This is particularly important in respect of financial provision under the Matrimonial Causes Act 1973. The test, as was observed in an earlier chapter, is based upon whether or not the child has been treated as a child of the family. Crucial to this analysis is the existence of a family within which the child has been treated as a child of the family (see *M v M* (1981)).

The key sections of the Matrimonial Causes Act are ss 23, 24 and 25.

Provision can be made for a 'child' over 18 providing, he or she is receiving instruction at an educational establishment.

The Child Support Act 1991 has limited the ability of matrimonial courts to award financial provision. The intention is that all maintenance assessments will be determined by reference to a formula, and the court will only have a discretion in respect lump sum awards, property adjustment orders and in respect of maintenance certain situations listed at s 8 of the Child Support Act, eg if the child suffers from a disability and in consequence requires additional payments.

Financial provision is also available under the Domestic Proceedings and Magistrates' Courts Act 1978, but the jurisdiction has been severely curtailed in respect of secured and unsecured periodical payments as a result of the Child Support Act 1991.

Financial provision made be ordered in family proceedings, in which case the provisions of s 15 and Schedule 1 of the Children Act 1989 apply. In deciding whether or not to make provision, the court is bound to have regard to the factors listed at Schedule 1 para 4(1). Section 1 of the Children Act does not apply to applications for financial provision (see *K v H (Child Maintenance)* (1993)).

The major piece of legislation relating to the assessment of maintenance for a child is the Child Support Act 1991, which came into force in April 1993. The legislation was framed after the publication of the White Paper entitled *Children Come First* (1990) (Cmnd 1263) which highlighted the deficiencies of the existing system, being 'unnecessarily fragmented, uncertain in its results, slow and ineffective'. The Act therefore was seen as an attempt to bring a degree of rationality and consistency into the law. The principle underpinning the legislation is that absent parents should continue to make a significant contributions towards the financial support of their children. See s 3(2) for the definition of absent parent.

The assessment and collection of maintenance from the absent parent is undertaken by the Child Support Agency, which is part of the Department of Social Security.

There have been numerous criticisms of the Act and its effect one of the first being that no account had been taken when making an assessment of the fact that a divorce had been agreed on the basis of a 'clean break'. Absent parents who had adhered to the agreed financial arrangements at the time of the divorce were suddenly faced with a massive hike in maintenance payments for their children, and in consequence felt very aggrieved that no allowance had been made for the terms of the divorce settlement (see, for example, *Crozier v Crozier* (1994)).

However, do contrast the outcome of *Crozier* with the decisions, both at first instance, in *Smith v McInerney* (1994) and *Mawson v Mawson* (1994).

The major criticisms of the Act are:

- as a result of adopting a 'formula' approach to maintenance assessment, there was insufficient flexibility to deal with individual difficulties;
- the formula itself was intrinsically unfair;
- the Agency was unable to process cases in an efficient manner.

As a result of intense media pressure, the impact of the legislation was reviewed by the House of Commons Social Security Select Committee. Its findings, published in early 1995, have resulted in changes, including the power for the Agency to take into account 'clean break' settlements prior to 1993. The future is still not certain, but the changes introduced in 1995 should help those affected by the legislation to believe that when the Act was introduced in 1993.

Chapter 7

Adoption

7.1 Introduction

The courts were first empowered to make adoption orders in 1926 as a result of the Adoption of Children Act of that year, which in turn was based upon the recommendations of the Tomlin Committee (*Report of the Child Adoption Committee* (1925) (Cmnd 2401)). Prior to 1926 there had been a completely unregulated market in young children, with commission being earned by professional agents for facilitating informal adoption arrangements between natural parents and potential 'adopters'. By 1921, public disquiet had been such that the government set up the Hopkinson Committee on Adoption. The result was the *Report of the Committee on Child Adoption*, which clearly favoured legislation to create the necessary framework for adoption to be legalised. The Committee defined adoption as:

> '... a legal method of creating between a child and one who is not a natural parent of the child an artificial family relationship analogous to that of parent and child.'

As Jolly and Sandland point out in *Political Correctness and the Adoption White Paper* (1994) Fam Law 30:

> 'From the passage of the first Adoption Act in 1926 the law has premised on the "closed" model of adoption. This holds that the function of adoption is the discrete reallocation of the unwanted babies of single women to "respectable" homes ... However, over the last 25 years the demography of adoption has changed radically ...'

The Compact Oxford English Dictionary defines adoption in this way:

> 'to take voluntarily into any relationship which he did not previously occupy ... to take as one's own child conferring all the rights and privileges of childship, or such of them as the law permits to be thus conferred.'

The consultation document *Review of Adoption Law: Report to Ministers of an Interdepartmental Working Group* (1992) defined the fundamental purpose of adoption as:

> '... securing a permanent home for a child by transferring the child, for virtually all purposes, from the birth family to a new adoptive family and severing the links with the first.'

It was proposed that adoption should continue to have this effect. One of the main advantages of adoption is the permanent status it confers upon the relationship between the child and the adoptive parents in the expectation of bringing with it security and stability to all parties. This in turn requires a commitment to be given by the prospective adopters. In addition to the benefits which accrue to the new legal parents, adoption creates legal relationships between the child and members of the adoptive parents' families.

There has been further legislation since 1926, culminating in the current statutory provision, the Adoption Act 1976. The Children Act 1989 makes only small changes to the 1976 Act. Section 12 of the 1976 Act, as amended, states that an Adoption Order:

> '... is an order giving parental responsibility for a child to the adopters, made on their application by an authorised court.'

Section 39(2) provides:

> 'An adopted child shall, subject to subsection (3) be treated in law as if he were not the child of any person other than the adopters or adopter.'

Subsection 39(3) refers to adoption of a child by one of its natural parents as sole adoptive parent, in which circumstances subsection 39(2) has no effect in respect of entitlement to property.

The transfer of parental responsibility can only occur as a result of a court order, and any 'informal' care arrangements made between parents and others will not accomplish the legal transfer of parental responsibility.

The number of adoption orders made continues to decline although there appears to be a strong demand from would-be adoptive parents. This is attributed to the decline in the numbers of babies and children available as a result of better use of contraception, abortion, and society being more prepared to tolerate single motherhood and cohabitation. Currently between 6,000 and 7,000 children are adopted each year, a figure nearly 50% lower than 15 years ago. The judicial statistics for 1994 show that adoption orders fell by 6% to 6,326. It should also be borne in mind that between 40 and 50% of all adoptions are made to step-parents, giving a truer picture of the extent of adoption by 'strangers' to the birth parent.

The main adoption agencies for England and Wales are the local authorities, and s 1 of the 1976 Act established a duty whereby every local authority was to

> 'establish and maintain within their area a service designed to meet the needs, in relation to adoption of

(a) children who have been or may be adopted;

(b) parents and guardians of such children; and

(c) persons who have adopted or may adopt a child

and for that purpose to provide the requisite facilities, or secure that they are provided by approved adoption societies.'

7.2 Welfare of children

The Adoption Act 1976 does not make the welfare of the child the paramount consideration. This is because there are other, perhaps equally important, considerations, for example the interests of the natural parent and the prospective adopters. Section 6 states:

> 'In reaching any decision relating to the adoption of a child a court or adoption agency shall have regard to all the circumstances, first consideration being given to the need to safeguard and promote the welfare of the child throughout his childhood; and shall so far as is practicable ascertain the wishes and feeling of the child regarding the decision and give due consideration to them having regard to his age and understanding.'

Lord Simon in *Re D (An Infant) (Parent's consent)* (1977) at pp 160-161, commenting on s 6, stated:

> 'In adoption proceedings the welfare of the child is not the paramount consideration (ie outweighing all others) as with custody or guardianship; but it is the first consideration (ie outweighing any other) which may well have been no more than elucidatory and confirmatory of the pre-existing law, though the new statutory provisions are explicit that in adoption proceedings it is the welfare of the child throughout childhood which must be considered, and not merely short-term prospects.'

In *Re W* (1984), Cumming-Bruce LJ, reflecting on the distinction between 'paramount' and 'first consideration', said:

> 'What precisely the distinction is I find it unnecessary, fortunately, to define. It is manifestly an extremely fine distinction. But the difference in language does have this effect, that in custody ... welfare becomes paramount in the weighing exercise over all other considerations, including the interests of all grown-ups. Parliament evidently decided ... that though the welfare of the child should be the first consideration, it is the first among a number of considerations which will themselves depend upon the particular circumstances of the individual case, both as to the number of those considerations and, of course, their weight.'

In practice, it means that only if the court considers that adoption, or freeing for adoption, will promote the child's welfare does it go on to the second stage and consider the issue of parental consent (see Balcombe LJ in *Re E (A Minor) (Adoption)* (1989)). This view was also accepted and applied by Butler-Sloss LJ in *Re D (A Minor) (Adoption: Freeing Order)* (1991), when the court held that the welfare test under s 6 had to be considered 'first and separately from the test under s 16(2)(a) of the 1976 Act of whether the parent was unreasonably withholding consent' *Re U (Application to free for adoption)* (1993) confirms that this is indeed the correct legal approach to the issue.

However, the *Adoption Law Review* recommended that the welfare principle in adoption law should be brought into line with that in the Children Act, but only in circumstances where parental consent had been obtained to such a course of action. It is also useful to reflect on whether the paramountcy principle should be relevant only during the child's minority. The *Adoption Law Review* recognised that there are adopted children who have a particularly positive experience during their minority but 'subsequently experience difficulties in the area of personal identity'. Undoubtedly there are many complex decisions which need to be taken before an adoption order is granted, and in the interests of consistency it is suggested that the factors listed in the Children Act at s 1(3) should be equally applicable to adoption. The Review goes on to propose that there should be two additional considerations, *viz*:

- the likely effect on the child's adult life of any change in legal status;
- the relationships which the child has with his parents, his siblings, other relatives and any other relevant persons, the value to the child of them continuing, and the likelihood of them continuing if the order is or is not made.

The adoption court should also, it is proposed, be under an obligation to consider whether the making of the order would be better than making no order at all. It will be recalled that this is consistent with the principle in s 1(5) of the Children Act 1989.

7.3 Freeing for adoption

The freeing procedure, which has been criticised in the *Adoption Law Review*, is designed to declare the child is free to be adopted. This is done under s 18 of the Adoption Act 1976 which states:

> 'Where on an application by an adoption agency, an authorised court is satisfied in the case of each parent or guardian of the child that

(a) he freely, and with full understanding of what is involved, agrees generally and unconditionally to the making of an adoption order; or

(b) his agreement to the making of an adoption order should be dispensed with on a ground specified in section 16(2);

the court shall make an order declaring the child free for adoption.'

The 'freeing' procedure owes its genesis to the Houghton Committee Report of 1972 – *Report of the Departmental Committee on the Adoption of Children* (Cmd 5107) (HMSO, London). The presumed benefits were:

- that the mother could agree in principle to have her child adopted prior to approaches being made to prospective adopters; and
- that if the child was already in the care of the local authority, then action could be taken, again at a preliminary stage, in order to dispense with parental consent before moving forward to identify prospective adopters.

Under s 18(5), on the making of a freeing order, parental responsibility for the child is given to the adoption agency. This means that the local authority had complete control over the child and the right to place him where the authority believes to be best. Once the adoption application is made, then there ought to be no opposition from the natural parents as their agreement would have been secured or dispensed with as part of the 'freeing' process. Butler-Sloss LJ, in *Re H (A minor) (Freeing Order)* (1993), considered the application to free for adoption to be a 'valuable procedure and, in circumstances such as where the child is not yet placed or may have only recently been placed, it may be of particular value'. She went on to say that the procedure can also prove to be of value to foster parents wishing to adopt because it protects them from the trauma of contested proceedings, and generally avoids parents and potential adopters having to be kept apart to protect the identity of the potential adopters. The freeing order is deemed to be the equivalent of an adoption in depriving natural parents of 'their very parenthood'. This view is reinforced by reference to the Law Commission's Report No 172, para 2.11, which states:

'But the parents should not be deprived of their very parenthood unless and until the child is adopted or freed for adoption.'

The Court of Appeal held in *M v C and Calderdale Metropolitan Borough Council* (1993) that once a freeing order was made a parent became a 'former parent' by virtue of ss 18(5) and 19 of the 1976 Act, with no rights other than to be informed whether an adoption order had been made and very limited rights under s 20 to apply to revoke the freeing order. Therefore, in the context of the Children Act 1989, a 'former parent' could not apply for a s 8 order. An unmarried father who had not applied for parental responsibility for the child under the Children Act 1989 is not considered to be a 'parent' for the purposes of the Adoption Act 1976.

In principle, once the freeing order is made, there is no reason why contact between the natural parents and the child should not continue, but in practice this may act against the long-term interests of the child. If, for example, the judge concludes that existing contact with the natural parents has not resulted in any positive benefits to the child, then it could well be decided that parental contact should be discontinued.

The *Adoption Law Review* (1992) expressed concern that insufficient weight appeared to be given to parental lack of agreement at the 'freeing' stage. It has been stated by the Court of Appeal (see *Re C (A Minor) (Adoption: Parental Agreement: Contact)* (1993)) that in considering whether a child should be freed for adoption, a two-stage sequential approach should be followed. The first related to the need to promote the child's welfare, and the second to decide if any parent was unreasonably withholding agreement. If the court decided that adoption is in the child's interests, then it is difficult to comprehend how any weight can be given to the views of the parents. The consequence of making the freeing order is that the parents lose all their legal rights and responsibilities in respect of their child and, in effect, paramountcy is being accorded to the welfare of the child when the legal requirement is simply to regard it as the first consideration. The Review proposes a new test, that of:

> '... the court being satisfied that the advantages to a child of becoming part of a new family and having a new legal status are so significantly greater than the advantages to the child of any alternative option as to justify overriding the wishes of a parent or guardian.'

Balcombe LJ in *Re C* (1993) (above) has referred to this balancing exercise between the welfare of the child and the rights of the parents in the context of adoption as 'a difficult legal, moral and social problem ...' (p 270 G).

An example of where the court took account of the mother's views and desire to maintain contact is *Re P*

(Adoption: Freeing Order) (1994). In this case the local authority applied to free the children for adoption. The judge formed the view that contact between the mother and children should continue, as he was impressed with the relationship between them. He ordered that contact should continue as a precondition to adoption. He dispensed with the mother's agreement but ordered that there should be contact by the mother to the children four times a year. The mother appealed on the basis that the judge should not have dispensed with her agreement. The Court of Appeal allowed the appeal in part. The court ruled that the judge could not make an order which had the effect of binding the prospective adopters at the moment of adoption or thereafter. It was acknowledged that the judge had tried to protect the mother's position regarding contact, but it was decided that it would be preferable to take account of her views regarding contact, in the adoption proceedings. The freeing order was set aside on the basis that, given the judge's views on the desirability of contact, it created more difficulties for the local authority in the search for a family. Butler-Sloss LJ was of the opinion that 'whether or not there should be continuing contact, is ... a matter that should be dealt with on the adoption application' (p 1005 A).

7.4 Parental agreement

It will be apparent, simply from reading the foregoing discussion on freeing orders, that it is desirable that all parties are in agreement that an adoption should take place. However, in reality, and quite understandably from a parental perspective, that agreement may not always be forthcoming. A parent is defined for the purposes of the adoption legislation as any parent who has parental responsibility for the child under the Children Act 1989. The agreement of the unmarried father is not required unless he has acquired parental responsibility under s 4 of the Children Act 1989. It should, though, be noted that an unmarried father who has a contact order but not parental responsibility is not required to give his consent to the adoption. The more emotive issue is whether an unmarried father who does not possess any order in respect of his child, but who has, over the years, built up a strong relationship with his child, should have to give his consent to the proposed adoption. The *Adoption Law Review* suggested that, where there was a genuine relationship with the child, the father should be given the opportunity to discuss the adoption plan and 'any alternatives to it'. A guardian for these purposes is defined as anyone appointed in accordance with the provisions of s 5 of the Children Act 1989. This could be someone appointed by a parent to act on his or her behalf in the event of that parent's death, or by a court, to have parental responsibility for the child. Section 18(1) provides the agreement of each parent or guardian may be dispensed with if any one of the grounds listed at s 16(2) of the 1976 Act is satisfied. Section 16(2) lists the grounds as follows:

'That the parent or guardian

(a) cannot be found or is incapable of giving agreement;

(b) is withholding his agreement unreasonably;

(c) has persistently failed without reasonable cause to discharge his parental responsibility for the child;

(d) has abandoned or neglected the child;

(e) has persistently ill-treated the child;

(f) has seriously ill-treated the child.

It is proposed to consider each ground in turn but without a doubt it is s 16(2)(b) which has proved to be the most controversial and at the same time problematic.

7.4.1 Adoption Act 1976 s 16(2)(a)

In *Re F* (1970), it was held that if, after taking all reasonable steps, the parents could not be found or were incapable of giving agreement – for example, because of political considerations there were no practical means of communicating with the parent – then consent could be dispensed with. Similarly, in *Re R* (1966), the child was a refugee from a totalitarian state, and any attempt to contact the parents, who were still in that country, would put their lives at risk. It was held that the adoption process could continue without parental agreement. Note that, in this case, the adoption went ahead even though the parents had no idea of what was being proposed.

In the former case, the infant had lived with the adoptive parents for some four years. The mother had not visited the child for over three years and efforts to find her had been unsuccessful. Five months after the order dispensing with consent was made, the mother reappeared, claiming that she had only just heard of the order. The court allowed her appeal on the basis that all reasonable steps had not been taken to find her, despite communicating to the mother's last known address and advertising in the press.

7.4.2 Adoption Act 1976 s 16(2)(b)

Much of the guidance on the correct interpretation to be given to this subsection dates from decisions of the House of Lords in the 1970s. Many would take the view that it is reasonable for any parent to withhold consent to his or her child's adoption given the irrevocable nature of the exercise. Consider, for instance, the case of a surrogate mother who, having handed over the baby to the 'parents', decides that she wishes to keep her child and refuses to consent to the adoption of the baby. The baby, in such circumstances, might be made a ward of court, whereupon the court would have to decide if the proposed arrangements were in the best interests of the child. However, if the matter is taken purely in the context of adoption, and the mother consistently refuses to sign adoption papers, then the court would be forced to consider whether or not the mother is unreasonably refusing to give consent. In one recent case, reported in *The Times* (1995) 3 October, a surrogate mother who had accepted £8,000 in exchange for her baby was reported to have started court action in order to have the baby returned to her. The baby was six months old. Earlier in the year, a Scottish court had awarded interim custody of the child to the couple. The mother had been artificially inseminated with the husband's sperm, and he was therefore the natural father of the child. In circumstances that are unusual, it is perhaps difficult to determine what is reasonable and what is not. However, the welfare of the child will probably dictate that he is adopted by the couple, assuming that the bonding process has progressed normally and that there is no reason why the couple should not adopt the child. However, it is always likely to be a question of fact on a case-by-case basis whether or not to withhold consent is unreasonable.

Three cases deserve attention in the first instance. *Re W* (1971) is to be considered the leading authority. The baby was born to an unmarried mother who already had two illegitimate children. She placed W for adoption within a few days of his birth and did not see the child again before the adoption proceedings. Having initially signified her consent to the adoption, she then changed her mind. The county court judge considered she was unreasonably withholding the consent. The mother appealed. The Court of Appeal, in allowing her appeal, emphasised that a high degree of culpability on the part of the mother towards the child must be shown in order for her to be deprived of her right to it. The prospective adopters appealed. The House of Lords allowed the appeal and sought to lay down guidelines to be adopted by judges when considering such applications. Indeed Balcombe LJ in *Re C (A Minor) (Adoption: Parental Agreement: Contact)* (1993) spoke of the principles of law applicable to this question being well established, and went on to cite the key parts of Lord Hailsham's speech in *Re W*. Lord Hailsham said:

> '... the test is reasonableness and nothing else. It is not culpability. It is not indifference. It is not failure to discharge parental duties. It is reasonableness, and reasonableness in the context of the totality of the

> circumstances. But, although welfare *per se* is not the test, the fact that a reasonable parent does pay regard to the welfare of the child must enter into the question of reasonableness as a relevant factor. It is relevant in all cases if, and to the extent that, a reasonable parent would take it into account. It is decisive in those cases where a reasonable parent must so regard it ... in an adoption case, a county court judge applying the test of reasonableness must be entitled to come to his own conclusions, on the totality of the facts, and a revising court should only dispute his decision where it feels confident that he has erred in law or acted without adequate evidence or where it feels that his judgment of the witnesses and their demeanour has played so little part in his reasoning that the revising court is in a position as good as that of the trial judge to form an opinion.'

The conclusion was that reasonableness was to be assessed on the basis of whether a reasonable parent in the same circumstances would give consent, rather than assessing whether the particular parent had reasonably withheld consent. If the particular parent had made a decision to withhold consent which, in all the circumstances, the reasonable parent could and may have made, the court should not dispense with consent.

In the recent case of *Re O (Transracial Adoption: Contact)* (1995), the judge was faced with opposition from the mother, who was Nigerian, to the adoption of her daughter in this country. He referred to the view that:

> '[the] reasonable Nigerian mother, looking at all the relevant criteria with objectivity, would see that R's need for security in the Ws' family throughout the second half of her minority is a decisive consideration which cannot be met by anything other than or anything less than acceptance of the adoption order.'

Significantly, the judge was also of the opinion that, in circumstances where the wishes and feelings of the child were in conflict with those of the guardian, it may be necessary to take the child's wishes into account.

The second case to consider is *O'Connor v A and B* (1971), where Lord Reid considered that, whilst the child's interests came first, 'considerable weight' should be given in 'proper cases' to the claims of natural parents and the adopting family. Lord Guest thought 'strong reasons' must be shown for dispensing with consent, particularly where the parents are married and have accommodation and wish to have the child.

Their Lordships thought that of particular importance was any evidence of instability on the part of the parents and the disruptive effect of moving the child from the home of the proposed adopters, assuming that he had been there for some time, as with a child in a long-term fostering arrangement.

The third case is *Re D (An infant) (Parent's consent)* (1977). This was a case where there appeared to be fundamental differences of opinion between judges in the Court of Appeal and the House of Lords. The House restored the order made by the county court judge in allowing the mother's and stepfather's appeal against the Court of Appeal decision. A homosexual father had refused to consent to the adoption of his son by the child's mother (the man's former wife) and her new husband (ie the stepfather). The father acknowledged that he was a practising homosexual who had, for a number of years, engaged in 'intimate associations with a number of men' and that at present he was living with a youth of 19. He claimed a genuine affection for his son and guaranteed that if contact were to continue, his son would not be exposed to his father's lifestyle or influenced by his friends. He was prepared to have access under supervision. The mother and stepfather wished for the boy to be fully integrated into their new family unit, and indeed the stepfather had assumed full financial responsibility for the maintenance of the boy. The local authority was in favour of the adoption taking place. The county court judge found the father to be withholding consent unreasonably to his child's adoption, since the reasonable father would wish to protect his child 'even if it meant parting from his son forever so that he could be free from this danger' (of homosexuality). He also thought that the father had 'nothing to offer the child at any time in the future'. The Court of Appeal concluded there was no immediate danger of the child being subjected to homosexual influences and allowed the appeal. It was not contended that the judge had erred in law, only that he had reached the wrong conclusion on the basis of the evidence. It was held by the House that an objective standard had to be applied in seeking to determine whether or not the decision made by the father in his individual circumstances was reasonable. Relying upon the decision in *Re W* (1971), it was stated by Lord Wilberforce that a direction to dispense with consent should be given sparingly and only in rare and exceptional cases.

In *Re F* (1982), the child had been separated from his mother for some three years after being seriously assaulted by the mother and her partner, as a consequence of which the local authority eventually obtained a care order. The court dispensed with the mother's agreement on the basis that adoption 'would be the most appropriate course which gave [the child] a settled and secure home'. No reasonable parent would have concluded that the child would benefit from contact with his mother throughout his childhood.

In a more recently reported case, *Re E (Adoption: Freeing order)* (1995), Bracewell J stated that the current legal framework is that set out by Butler-Sloss LJ in *Re D* (1991) at p 52 E. After citing the celebrated passage from Lord Hailsham's speech in *Re W* (1971), she refers to Lord Reid's question in *O'Connor v A & B* (1971), *viz*, 'Would a reasonable parent have refused consent?' She goes on:

> '... this involves consideration of how a parent in the actual circumstances of the mother, but (hypothetically) endowed with a mind and temperament capable of making reasonable decisions, would approach a complex question involving a judgment as to the present and the future and the probable impact upon the child, *per* Lord Reid in *Re D* (1977).'

She goes on to refer to the greater emphasis given to the welfare of the child as one of the factors. However, the 'critical factor' is deemed to be the chance of a successful reintroduction to, or contact with, the natural parent in assessing the reaction of the hypothetical reasonable parent. The test is to be applied at the time of the hearing. In the context of the *Re E* case, the judge concluded that any order for contact would be 'disastrous', and that on all the evidence and, despite the mother's legitimate sense of grievance against the local authority for failing to maintain contact with her, there were overwhelming advantages for the child in adoption.

7.4.3 Adoption Act 1976 s 16(2)(c)

It was stated in *Re P* (1962) that the obligations of a parent must include:

- the natural and moral duty of a parent to show affection and care towards the child; and
- the duty to maintain the child both financially and economically.

A rather strict approach to this subsection was taken by Baker J in *Re D (Minors) (Adoption by parents)* (1973), when he stated that the failure envisaged by s 16(2)(c) must be of:

> 'such gravity, so complete, so convincingly proved that there can be no advantage to the child in keeping continuous contact with the natural parent who has so abrogated his duties that he for his part should be deprived of his own child against his wishes.'

7.4.4 Adoption Act 1976 s 16(2)(d)

This and the final two grounds are rarely used. 'Abandoned or neglected' implies culpability, and it has been suggested that the conduct ought to be such as to warrant prosecution under s 1 of the Children and Young Persons Act 1933. This deals with cruelty to persons under the age of 16 caused by wilful assault, ill treatment, neglect, abandonment ...

7.4.5 Adoption Act 1976 s 16(2)(e)

The key word here is 'persistent', which implies a course of conduct over a period of time. In *Re A (A minor) (Adoption: Dispensing with Agreement)* (1979), serious assaults over a 21-day period were regarded as sufficient to establish persistent ill treatment.

7.4.6 Adoption Act 1976 s 16(2)(f)

This subsection does not apply unless (because of the ill treatment or for other reasons) the rehabilitation of the child within the household of the parent or guardian is unlikely (s 16(5)). The decision on rehabilitation need not be referable to the ill treatment and, in consequence, it is suggested that this should be determined by reference to s 6, placing the child's long-term welfare as the first consideration.

7.5 Contact

Adoption has, over the last 20 years, become much more of an open, less secretive procedure. Section 51 of the Adoption Act 1976, as amended by the Children Act 1989, permits the disclosure of the birth records of adopted children, providing that the adopted person has attained the age of 18. There has been an increasing tendency in recent years to acknowledge that the maintenance of contact between an adopted child and his or her birth family may be beneficial. One example would be the situation where a teenager is adopted and contact with parents and siblings may well be in the child's long-term interests, building upon existing relationships. There is an increasing responsibility being assumed by adoption agencies in keeping links alive by acting as intermediaries between the various groups.

The White Paper, *Adoption: The Future* (1993) (Cmd 2288) stressed that it may be sensible and humane to encourage an open adoption approach, provided that the prospects for a secure and successful adoption are not jeopardised. It is proposed that adoption agencies will have three main functions concerning contact:

- to endeavour to keep open the possibility of voluntary contact between adopted children and their birth family;
- if there is to be no contact, to counsel birth parents as to the desirability of being kept informed about the child's progress;

- to work closely with adoptive parents and consider with them the advisability or otherwise of contact continuing between the child and the birth parents. Wherever possible the wishes of the child should be taken into account.

Regard should be had to the judgment of Simon Brown LJ in *Re E (A Minor) (Care Order: Contact)* (1994) at pp 154-155. In support of the views expressed in the White Paper, he said:

> '... although the value of contact may be limited by the parents' inadequacy, it may still be of fundamental importance to the long-term welfare of the child, unless, of course, it can be seen that in a given case it will inevitably disturb the child's care ... contact may well be of singular importance to the long-term welfare of the child: first, in giving the child the security of knowing that his parents love him and are interested in his welfare; secondly, by avoiding any damaging sense of loss to the child in seeing himself abandoned by his parents; thirdly, by enabling the child to commit himself to the substitute family with the seal of approval of the natural parents; and, fourthly, by giving the child the necessary sense of family and personal identity. Contact, if maintained, is capable of reinforcing and increasing the chances of success of a permanent placement, whether on a long-term fostering basis or by adoption.'

The judge recognised that there was an ongoing debate about the merits of open as opposed to closed adoption but acknowledged that 'there will undoubtedly be cases ... in which some face to face contact is clearly desirable ...'.

The *Adoption Law Review* had considered the question of openness in the adoption process in some detail (see para 4 at p 9). Adoption, it was stated, had 'traditionally been a somewhat closed and secretive process in which many children have been shielded from knowledge about, and contact with, their birth families'. Openness can, of course, take many different manifestations, and the extent to which more openness can be brought into the process should be determined by reference to all the circumstances on a case-by-case basis. The *Review* was concerned to alter perceptions about adoption and to urge all those involved in the process to recognise that more openness could in some cases have very positive benefits. There has, in practice, been an increasing recognition that a child's knowledge about his or her antecedents could be instrumental in helping to create a positive self-identity for the child. Openness can occur at the pre-adoption stage, for example by arranging for the birth parents to meet the prospective adopters, or by encouraging the birth parents to share information about their family with the prospective adopters. If this could be achieved, then it is likely to lead to a feeling of security, in that the child would be less likely to believe that he or she had been rejected by the birth parents. It could also lead to an arrangement whereby information was passed at regular intervals from the birth family to the adopters for onward transmission to the child. The *Review* also called for more openness in the court process. For example, there could be more disclosure of information held on court records, subject only to there being compelling reasons why information should not be disclosed. Adoptive parents are counselled at an early stage in the adoption process to prepare them for the ordeal of telling the child that he or she is adopted. This is regarded as essential. As the *Review* commented: '... It is hoped that it would now be extremely rare for an adopted child to grow up without knowing of his or her adoptive status.'

The Court of Appeal has recently given guidance on the appropriate procedures involved in applications for leave to apply for direct or indirect contact after adoption. In *Re T (Minors) (Adopted Children: Contact)* 1995, the court believed that guidance was necessary because differing views had been expressed in *Re C (A Minor) (Adopted Child: Contact)* (1993) and *Re T (A Minor) (Contact after Adoption)* (1995). The correct procedure, so as not unnecessarily to disturb the adoptive parents, was for the application for leave to remain in the county court unless there were compelling reasons to transfer it to the High Court. The Official Solicitor should only rarely be brought in as a respondent. The procedure is designed to act as a filter to save persons who had the care of children from being vexed by applications which lacked merit.

The House of Lords had ruled in *Re C (A Minor) (Adoption: Conditions)* (1988) that the court had the power to impose any terms or conditions it thought fit when making an adoption order, and this included the ability to make provision for access to a member of the child's natural family where it was clearly in the child's best interests. It was further decided that compliance with such an order would be enforceable by committal proceedings. The House was of the opinion that, in normal circumstances, it was desirable that there should be a complete break on adoption. Nor would a court be inclined to impose terms or conditions regarding access to members of the child's family if the adopting parents disagreed with those terms or conditions. The previous authorities, *Re B (MF) (An Infant)*, *Re D (An Infant)* (1972) and *Re G (DM) (An Infant)* (1962) had established that the 'ordinary rule' cutting off contact could be disregarded in the exceptional case, where a court is satisfied that the best interests of the child warrant continued contact with the birth parents (see Rees J in *Re J (A Minor) (Adoption order: Conditions)* (1973)). Oliver LJ put it this way in *Re V (A Minor) (Adoption: Dispensing with agreement)* (1987):

> 'To put it another way, any such condition, if it is not to be repugnant to the notion of adoption, must recognise that, in the ultimate analysis, the question of access or no access is for the adopters to decide in the exercise of their parental rights.'

This was vividly illustrated by the recent case of *Re T (Adoption: Contact)* (1995). The child was the subject of a care order and was placed with prospective adopters. The mother had agreed to the child's adoption but had requested that she be allowed to resume contact with her child on two or three occasions each year. For their part, the prospective adopters were prepared to allow contact once each year. The mother was supported by the local authority and the guardian *ad litem*, but there was opposition to the arrangements for contact being included in the adoption order. The judge ordered that there should be contact '... not less than once a year' and included an order to that effect. The adopters appealed against the need for an order. In allowing the appeal, the Court of Appeal indicated that, in deciding such a question, the welfare of the child was the primary consideration. It was felt that the mother ought to place her trust in the adopters and that for their part, the finality of an adoption order should not be threatened. They would, for example, have to return to court if they wished contact to be discontinued if the requirement for contact had been included in the adoption order. To make no order would give the adopters the flexibility they needed to establish the new family unit. The right course of action in these circumstances was to include in the adoption order a recital of the intention of the adopters of allow contact between the child and the natural parent, and make it clear that the court believed that an order to that effect was unnecessary.

Of great importance will be the agreement of the adopters to such a course of action. The Court of Appeal was of the view that there was no reported case which indicated that such an order had been imposed upon prospective adopters. This was made very clear by Lord Ackner in *Re C (A Minor) (Adoption: Conditions)* (1988), when he said that a court would only impose terms and conditions as to access to the child's natural family '... in the most exceptional case'. To do so, he suggested, would be to create a potentially frictional situation '... which would be hardly likely to safeguard or promote the welfare of the child'.

The adoption of children who are subject to care orders has occasionally brought local authorities into conflict with the courts. At the hearing of the care proceedings it is likely that the court will wish to be appraised of the plans formulated by the local authority for the future welfare of the child. Volume 3 of the Department of Health's *Children Act 1989 Guidance and Regulations: Family Placements* requires a local authority to put forward a 'care plan', and in *Manchester City Council v F* (1993), Eastham J thought that a care plan 'so far as is reasonably possible' should accord with the *Children Act Guidance and Regulations*, particularly if it was the ultimate intention of the local authority to place the child for adoption.

There is nothing particularly contentious about this course of action, except in the case itself the contents of the care plan were challenged by the guardian *ad litem*, in that there was insufficient information to permit him to make an unqualified recommendation. The local authority and the guardian then cooperated, with the result that a consensus was reached. However, and this is the significant point, the court would not endorse an attempt by the guardian to enquire into the feasibility of the local authority's long term proposals. The difficulty is that once adoption has been considered to be the most appropriate course of action, confidentiality arises under the adoption regulations, and any further action by the social services department might jeopardise or possibly usurp the functions of the fostering and adoption panel. It does mean, however, that there is real potential for the local authority to amend the plan at some future stage and act in a way which does not accord with the plan 'endorsed' by the court.

One way out of this dilemma is for the court to make a ruling on contact under s 34 of the Children Act 1989. As was forcefully pointed out in *Re B (Minors) (Care: Local Authority's Plans)* (1993), parliament had given the court, not the local authority, the duty to decide on contact between the child and those concerned with a s 34(1) application. The court can, as a result, require the local authority to justify its long-term plans, but only to the extent that it is intended to exclude contact between the parent and the child. Therefore, in exceptional circumstances, a court could intervene. Otherwise, as Butler-Sloss LJ said, it would make a mockery of the paramountcy principle of the welfare of the child, '... subordinating it to the administrative decision of the local authority in a situation where the court was seized of the contact issue'.

There may be circumstances where contact between the birth family and the adoptive family is entirely inappropriate, for example if the birth family is harassing the adoptive family.

The *Adoption Law Review* proposes responding to this type of problem by allowing a court to attach a non-molestation order to the adoption order. The non-molestation order could be granted either to the child or to the adoptive parents depending on whether it was the child or adoptive parents who were being harassed or molested.

7.6 Inter-country adoptions

The number of adoptions involving children from overseas has traditionally been very low, averaging under 100 each year until 1990. In that year, political, social and economic problems experienced in Eastern Europe led to a significant number of children being brought to the United Kingdom for the purpose of adoption. The majority of these children came from Romania. This whole process is fraught with difficulty, not least in ensuring, as far as possible, that the natural parents are aware of what is going to take place. Many children will, sadly, be orphans, but this fact will need to be verified if possible. With the numbers of 'domestic' babies available for adoption at an all time low, to adopt a child from overseas presents desperate potential adopters with an opportunity they might not otherwise have to acquire a child of their own. Yet no one would wish to see an illicit international trade in young children being encouraged, nor is it desirable to offer material or financial inducements to poor parents in order to secure their agreement to the adoption of their child. The White Paper stresses that the wishes of prospective adopters in this country should be respected and, in all suitable cases, supported and facilitated.

The United Kingdom is a signatory to the Hague Convention on the Adoption of Children (1965) and reference should be made to s 17 of the Adoption Act 1976 which embodies the terms of the Convention into English law. Sadly, only three countries ratified the Convention. Further discussions took place at the Hague in 1992 and led to the Hague Convention on Inter-country Adoption 1993. Currently over 60 countries have signed the 1993 Convention. The recent critical review of adoption law and practice should, in the not-too-distant future, lead to the passing of a new Adoption Act, and the 1993 Convention should be incorporated into English law. The Convention recognises that an inter-country adoption may offer the possibility of a permanent home to a child for whom such a luxury is unavailable in his or her own country. A stated objective of the Convention is to prevent the '... abduction, the sale of, or traffic in, children'.

7.6.1 The Hague Convention 1993

The objects of the Convention are stated to be:

> '(a) to establish safeguards to ensure that inter-country adoptions take place in the best interests of the child and with respect for his or her fundamental rights as recognised in international law;
>
> (b) to establish a system of cooperation amongst Contracting States to ensure that those safeguards are respected and thereby prevent abduction, the sale of, or traffic in children;
>
> (c) to secure the recognition in Contracting States of adoptions made in accordance with the Convention.'

It should be noted that the Convention covers only adoptions which create a permanent parent-child relationship. The commitment of so many countries to the task of ensuring that inter-country adoptions are successfully processed is in stark contrast to the 1965 Convention. Only three countries ratified that Convention: the United Kingdom, Austria and Switzerland. Convention orders made in one country are enforceable in the other two, but it will be immediately apparent that, given the small numbers of signatories, the impact of the Convention upon English law is minimal, although it is incorporated into the law by the Adoption Act 1976.

The current position is that a foreign adoption order is recognised in this jurisdiction if it is a Convention order made under the Adoption Act 1976 or falls within the ambit of the Adoption (Designation of Overseas Adoptions) Order 1973. Twenty four foreign and 40 Commonwealth countries are specified under the order and are referred to as 'designated countries'. The *Adoption Law Review* makes the point that, '[i]n practice, the list of designated countries has had little relevance to inter-country adoption'. This is because, in many of those countries, inter-country adoption is not possible because the law of the country '... does not offer the opportunity of a foreshortened legal process which inter-country adopters generally see; a period of residence is usually necessary for investigation and supervision of the placement'. When the list was drawn up in 1973, the adoption procedures in those countries broadly accorded with the practice in the United Kingdom. Twenty years on, this is not always the case.

Adoption orders from non-designated countries are not recognised in the United Kingdom, with the result being that children adopted in one of these countries will have to be adopted again once they are resident in the United Kingdom.

In practice, then, prospective adopters in the United Kingdom may apply to adopt a child from either a designated or non-designated country, providing that country accepts inter-country adoption applications. Different procedures will apply depending on the decision taken by the prospective adopters, and it should be pointed out that there are likely to be variations in the adoption procedures and requirements as between different designated countries. For example, in some countries an adoption order will not be made final until a probationary period has been completed. In other countries a child is permitted to leave without an adoption order having been made, with the result that the prospective adopters will have to make an application to the United Kingdom court to adopt the child once they have returned. The Adoption Act 1976 bestows the status of protected child upon the child, who will, in effect, be viewed as a private foster child.

7.7 Transracial adoption

Bromley and Lowe comment that '... it is a hotly disputed issue as to whether it is desirable to have transracial adoptions at all' (pp 414-5, 8th edn).

The White Paper concludes that there is no current evidence to show that, as a result of transracial adoption, children will suffer identity problems or prejudice. The government is not proposing to introduce legislation to ensure that those professionals involved in such adoptions 'take approaches which are based on common sense ... and not ... on ideology'. Jolly and Sandland (above) comment that 'ideology', or value judgments, will always be part of adoption law. The White Paper on adoption does not signal the end of ideology. The issue was sympathetically addressed by Sir Stephen Brown P in *Re JK (Adoption: Transracial Placement)* (1991). The child, who was aged three, had been born to a Sikh mother who was seeking a divorce from her husband. The child was illegitimate and the mother freely placed her for adoption at birth. She was placed with foster parents, to whom she became very attached, and at the time of the hearing was described as a 'normal, happy, little girl who had settled firmly into that family and was regarded as a fully integrated member'. The local authority wished to place her for adoption with a Sikh family, but it had proved impossible, as a stigma attached to illegitimate children in that community. The local authority was not supportive of the foster parents when they expressed their desire to adopt the child, claiming it was contrary to its policy guidelines. The issue for the court was whether the child should be removed, because of her racial and cultural background, from the only home and 'parents' that she had known, for placement with an unidentified family. The child was made a ward of court. It was held that the child was happy and well looked after. She had a secure home and went to the same school as her adoptive brother and sister. There were children of mixed race at the school. The court was reassured that the prospective adopters would assist the child to follow her own Sikh traditions and culture and seek assistance if necessary. A psychiatrist was of the opinion that the child would suffer psychological harm if she were to be removed. It was decided that the wardship should continue, the child remaining with the foster parents, and they were given leave to commence the adoption process with the help of an independent agency.

7.8 Step-parent adoption

Step-parent adoptions account for approximately half of all the adoption orders made in the jurisdiction. The role of the adoption agency in such cases is to supervise the child pending the adoption hearing and to submit a report to the court. The White Paper has suggested radical changes to this practice and proposes a new Parental Responsibility Agreement to which the non-custodial parent will signify acceptance. The Agreement would then be registered with the court. One benefit to flow from this proposal, if accepted, is that the natural parent will not be forced formally to have to adopt his or her child. The *Adoption Law Review* considered it '... anomalous that the parent who is caring for the child should also become an adoptive parent. It can be disturbing for a birth parent and child to have the birth certificate replaced by an adoption certificate on which the birth parent is shown as an adoptive parent' (para 19.3). A further advantage is that the child's links with the other natural parent will not need to be severed, eg after the divorce of the parents. The response in the White Paper was predictable given that both the Houghton Committee on the Adoption of Children in 1972 and the *Adoption Law Review* in 1992 were less than enthusiastic about the presumed benefits of step-parent adoptions. Where a natural parent is dead, there can be fewer objections if the survivor remarries and together they wish to secure total legal rights over the child. Even so, there may be ongoing benefits to the child through maintaining a legal link with grandparents or other relatives. However, looked at from the child's point of view there would appear to be few, if any, positive benefits to accrue from the 'finality' of adoption, especially if the child is at an age where he or she has built up meaningful relationships with the extended family of his natural parents. The Parental Responsibility Agreement would, it appears, act in a similar way to a parental responsibility order under s 4 of the Children Act 1989, which may be obtained as a result of an agreement reached with the mother. The government is therefore intent upon providing alternatives in an attempt to discourage step-parent adoptions rather than prohibit them by law, on the basis that, in some circumstances, they might be justified – for example, where the other parent has never acted in a parental capacity and contact with members of that side of the birth family has been minimal or non-existent. Of course, many children who figure in step-parent adoptions have no father figure other than the step-parent, and many are illegitimate. It is suggested that for those who fall into this category the new proposals will be of little benefit.

The *Adoption Law Review* also expressed concern at the 'relative incidence of breakdown of second and subsequent marriages'. If there is a divorce between the parent and step-parent, it is a distinct possibility that the natural parent and child may wish to revert to the legal position prior to the adoption and re-institute the relationship with the child's birth family. The *Review* therefore recommended that a step-parent adoption order should be capable of being 'undone' where the marriage has ended as a result of divorce or death. In the former case, the divorced step-parent would have to give his consent, and so too the child if aged over 12.

7.9 *Inter vivos* guardianship orders

The White Paper also considered the needs of relatives and foster parents, and proposes an alternative to adoption for those in these categories. The *inter vivos* guardianship order would be available to supplement the residence orders that courts may already make in such cases. Foster parents would acquire a 'foster-plus' status, strengthening their position but without prejudicing the child's ongoing links with his or her birth parents. Orders would extend up to the age of 18 and would enable the guardian to appoint another in the event of his own death before the child reaches the age of 18. The *inter vivos* order would emphasise the permanence of the relationship, and no application could be made to dissolve it without the leave of the court. Parental responsibility would be shared with the birth parents.

7.10 Who may adopt?

The current legal position is that if two people wish to adopt, they must be married to each other. This may seem unfair to those in a long-term relationship who are denied the opportunity to have equal joint rights in respect of the child. This issue was faced by Cazalet J in *Re AB (A Minor) (Adoption: Unmarried Couple)* 1995. The couple had lived together in a stable relationship for over 20 years. The child was born in May 1990 and had made his home with the applicants on a fostering basis since 1992. The court was satisfied that the child's long-term future lay with the applicants, but being unable to make a joint adoption order, the judge made one in favour of the foster father. He then went on to consider an application by the couple for a joint residence order. The court accepted that it had powers under s 11(4) of the Children Act to make such an order. If a residence order were to be made in favour of the female partner, this could give the impression that the child was to be expected to live only with her, and that was not the reality of the situation. A joint residence order would therefore reflect the circumstances of the case. The judge also made it clear that he was not seeking to circumvent the provisions of s 14 of the Adoption Act 1976, which provides that no more than one person could apply for an adoption order apart from a married couple. The effect of this decision is that the female partner, while gaining parental responsibility for the child, does not acquire the full rights that she would have attained if she had been granted an adoption order.

If neither party is a natural parent of the child to be adopted, then each must be 21 or over. The Children Act has changed the position in respect of a natural parent. Providing that she or he is aged 18 and the spouse is 21 or over, then the adoption can proceed (Children Act 1989 Schedule 10 para 4). There is no upper age limit for adoption, although some adoption agencies discourage applications from people over 40 years of age.

The White Paper expressed concern that some agencies have been too restrictive when considering the ages of prospective adopters. It stresses that the approach ought to be that adopters have a reasonable expectation of retaining health and vigour to care for the child until he or she reaches majority. In short, the White Paper urges that a much less rigid approach be adopted towards the age of the applicants.

The matter was considered by the Queen's Bench Division in *R v Secretary of State for Health ex parte Luff* (1992). In this case, the couple were much taken by the plight of children living in orphanages in Romania. They were desirous of giving two of the children a fresh start in the West. The couple were aged 53 and 37 respectively. The male applicant, aged 53, was retired and had had a successful heart operation. Doctors had estimated his future life expectancy to be about 10 years. The Department of Health raised a query about his medical history and was informed by the consultant who had carried out the operation that, in his view, there were serious reservations about his suitability as a prospective adopter because of his short life expectancy. There was also a second opinion by a consultant cardiologist which was not adverse to the applicant. The outcome was that the Department of Health made an adverse recommendation to the Home Office and, in consequence, the Home Office rejected the application and refused permission for the children to immigrate to the United Kingdom. The telling factors were the children being put at the risk of an early bereavement, and that they could not look forward to a secure and settled life in the circumstances. The applicants sought an order of *certiorari* to quash the Department of Health's recommendation. The application was dismissed on the basis that what the children required more than anything was stability, and this could only be achieved by placing them for adoption with healthy people.

The White Paper also argues strongly for the retention of the presumption in favour of adoption by married couples. There are no proposals in the White Paper which would enable unmarried couples to apply jointly for adoption, although there is nothing to stop one person applying to adopt. Adoption by one person is provided for by s 15 of the Adoption Act 1976. The prevailing view appears to be that if a couple are not prepared to accept a formal commitment to each other, ie marriage, then why should adoption be different? (But see the views expressed in *Re AB* above.)

7.11 Conclusion

The whole of adoption law and procedure has been under review for the past four years. In addition to the *Adoption Review* in 1992 and the White Paper in 1993, the Department of Health, the Welsh Office and the Lord Chancellor's Department produced a consultation document in April 1994 entitled *Placement for Adoption*. The paper outlines proposals for the early consideration by a court of the adoption plan and, as far as possible, the elimination of unnecessary delay. The paper recommends that for uncontested adoptions the process should be 'simple and quick and consistent with a proper consideration of the child's needs'. It is proposed that an adoption order may be granted in respect of a child aged 12 or more only with the agreement of the child. The only grounds on which a court may consider dispensing with consent would be if the child were incapable of giving or withhold agreement. In contested adoptions, the paper recognises that the court's role is crucial where there is a conflict between the agency's plans and the wishes of the child's family. In such circumstances, it would appear crucial to allow the court to consider the issue before the child is placed with the prospective adopters. Views were sought on whether there should be orders endorsing a general adoption plan in addition to 'specific placement orders'. This latter order would grant parental responsibility to the prospective adopters. The order would lapse after 12 months.

Primary legislation is, at the time of writing, still awaited, and one must view with concern, if not suspicion, the comment in the White Paper that the government intends that the proposals should be implemented in ways that ensure no extra costs. This view is reiterated in the 1994 document on placement for adoption.

Adoptions are now fewer and more likely to involve older children, and therefore the proposal that children over 12 should consent to their adoption is to be welcomed. Of course, many of these children will have developed links with their birth parents and extended family, and therefore the commitment to more open and flexible adoption procedures is to be applauded.

Inter-country adoption procedures need to be streamlined, and changes are long overdue in respect of step-parent adoptions and giving greater security to long-term foster parents. The White Paper envisages that, in domestic adoptions, the balance between the rights and interests of the child, adoptive parents and birth parents will be defined afresh. If there is to be permanent severance between birth parent and child, then there must be shown to be clear advantages over less permanent options such as s 8 orders.

The finality of adoption orders was recently put to the test in *Re B (Adoption order: Jurisdiction to set aside)* (1995). In this case, the applicant was born to an English mother and a Muslim Arab father in 1959. As a result of a genuine mistake, he was placed with a Jewish couple and subsequently adopted by them. A few years ago, he traced his natural mother and father and sought to have his adoption set aside on the basis that if the truth had been known at the time he would never have been placed with a Jewish couple. The Court of Appeal held that it had no inherent jurisdiction to set aside an adoption order which, on the face of it, had been granted after all the correct procedures had been complied with. Swinton Thomas LJ said:

> 'To allow considerations such as those put forward in this case to invalidate an otherwise properly made adoption order would, in my view, undermine the whole basis on which adoption orders are made, namely that they are final and for life as regards the adopters, the natural parents and the child.'

Adoption law, practice and procedure is under intense scrutiny, and draft legislation should be forthcoming in the not-too-distant future.

7.11.1 Adoption: the future

The government White Paper on Adoption was published in November 1993. The government considered the basic structure relating to adoption to be sound. However, it intends that there should be important changes in the law governing domestic and inter-country adoptions and in adoption procedures and practice. In respect of domestic adoptions, the following represents the extent of the changes to be introduced in the near future, designed to redefine the balance between the rights and interests of the child, the adoptive parents and the birth parents:

- recognition that the permanent legal severance of the relationship between the child and birth parents should be justified by clear and significant advantage to the child compared with less permanent options;
- recognition that the child's interests, wishes and feelings should be ascertained and given great weight and that he or she should have the right opportunity to influence decisions directly if of an age and understanding to do so;
- once an adoption is decided on, a careful judgment about contact between the child and his birth family, giving the views of the adoptive parents and the child the greater weight so that the prospects of a successful adoption are not undermined, and reasonable requirements for privacy respected;
- arrangements to encourage adoptive parents to inform adopted children of their status and backgrounds;
- new guidelines for all concerned with the adoption process emphasising the need both for skilled professional assessment and for common sense human judgments reflecting the value placed on traditional parenting and the need for stable and secure relationships between parents and between them and their children;
- common sense values in such matters as the age of adoptive parents and issues of race and culture in considering the best option for the child;
- a new structure for agencies' adoption panels to ensure that the full range of such judgments is brought to bear;
- new complaints and representation procedures for cases where people wishing to adopt feel that their application has not been fairly considered, or other complaints by any party to an adoption.

In addition there will be:

- separate procedures through which families already caring for children other than their own may adopt them, provided that all the usual adoption criteria are satisfied. This will, in suitable cases, give special recognition to the role of some foster parents and caring relatives and reduce the length and complexity of process for all concerned;
- simpler ways in which step-parents can share parental responsibility for a child of their spouse by a former marriage or relationship;
- ways other than adoption in which the relationship and the responsibilities of other carers and relatives can be recognised. These new alternatives to adoption would provide the opportunity for a child to enjoy a sense of permanence and stability greater than that provided by foster care arrangements.

In respect of adoption of overseas children by parents in this country, the government aims are:

- greater clarity and reliability of process, including a new duty on local authorities to help parents seeking an overseas adoption;
- greater involvement of voluntary adoption agencies as well as local authorities to handle overseas adoptions, as already occurs in domestic adoptions;
- a new and clearer relationship between legal processes here and in the child's country of origin;
- a more streamlined relationship between adoption and immigration processes;
- new protection against abuses such as neglect of the overseas birth parents' wishes or financial or other inducements to release for adoption.

The government will bring forward legislation to give effect to these objectives whenever the legislative timetable permits, but at the time of writing, a draft Bill has not materialised.

Summary of Chapter 7

Adoption

Adoption has been defined as 'a legal method of creating between a child and one who is not a natural parent of the child an artificial family relationship analogous to that of parent and child' (Tomlin Committee 1926).

The current law on adoption is contained in the Adoption Act 1976 which came into force in 1988. Section 39(2) of the Act states that 'an adopted child shall, subject to subsection (3) be treated in law as if he were not the child of any person other than the adopters or adopter'.

Parental responsibility will also be transferred upon the making of an adoption order. The Adoption Act 1976 does not make the welfare of the child as the paramount consideration. Section 6 requires the court or adoption agency to have regard to all the circumstances, 'first consideration being given to the need to safeguard and promote the welfare of the child throughout his childhood ...'.

Once a court considers that adoption will promote the child's welfare, then it goes onto the second stage of the process which is to consider the issue of parental consent.

A child has to be 'free' to be adopted, and s 18 provides that consent must be freely given by the parent(s) or that the court has dispensed with consent on the basis of the criteria in s 16(2) of the 1976 Act. In principle, once the child is freed for adoption, contact with the natural parents should cease, but in practice this does not always occur as it may act against the long-term interests of the child.

Section 16(2) lists the reasons which allow the court to dispense with parental agreement to adoption. The most controversial is s 16(2)(b) that the parent or guardian is withholding consent unreasonably. The leading cases are:

Re W (1971)
O'Connor v A and B (1971)
Re D (An Infant) (Parent's consent) (1977)

Statements from these cases have recently been applied in *Re D* (1991) and *Re E (Adoption: Freeing Order)* (1995).

Over the last 20 years, adoption has become a much more open process, and in some cases, perhaps involving older children, contact is maintained with the birth parents. The recent White Paper: Adoption: The Future (1993) (Cm 2288) argued that it may be 'sensible and humane' to encourage open adoption provided the prospects for a secure and successful adoption are not jeopardised. Judicial support for this may be found in the judgment of Simon Brown LJ in *Re E (A Minor) (Care Order: Contact)* (1994).

There has also been a significant increase in the number of people seeking to adopt foreign children, particularly from war torn areas of Eastern Europe and the slums of large South American cities. Inter-country adoptions are governed by the Hague Convention (1993), based upon the mutual recognition of each country's adoption orders. The success of this Convention will depend upon the number of countries deciding to become signatories, which in turn depends upon the existence of well developed adoption procedures in the countries in question.

Step-parent adoptions account for approximately half of all the orders made in this country. The recent *Adoption Law Review* (1992) and the White Paper saw few benefits from the present system, and it is proposed that a Parental Responsibility Agreement should be available as an alternative to an adoption order. The White Paper also proposes that there should be alternatives to adoption for relatives and foster parents and recommends the creation of *inter vivos* guardianship orders which would supplement residence orders. These orders would emphasise the permanence of the relationship and no application could be made to dissolve the order without the leave of the court.

There are a limited number of people who are allowed to adopt, the major category being married couples. Adoption by a single person is also allowed, but there is, as yet, no provision for unmarried couples to apply jointly for an adoption order. Adoption law has been under review for the last three years, and draft legislation should be forthcoming in the near future.

Chapter 8

Wardship

8.1 Introduction

> 'While there has been a significant decline in wardship, it is still in active use, particularly where there are highly contentious issues over residence, allegations of abuse in respect of which the relevant local authority has decided not to take care proceedings, and in cases with an international aspect ... as well as cases where the issue is publication of material concerning a child ... In such cases the matter should be transferred to the High Court and the Official Solicitor should be invited to represent the child.'

The above quotation is taken from the Children Act Advisory Committee Report for 1993/94 and neatly summarises the present role of the wardship jurisdiction, a jurisdiction which, since the Middle Ages, has offered, in one form or another, the opportunity to resolve problems connected with the property and the well-being of children.

The Law Commission Working Paper No 101 entitled *Family Law: Review of Child Law: Wards of Court* (1987) defined a ward of court as 'a child whose guardian is the High Court'. The result of a child being made a ward of court was stated by the Commission to be twofold: that no important step in the child's life could be taken without the leave of the court and secondly that any court order or direction must be consistent with the principle that the welfare of the child is the first and paramount consideration.

The history of wardship is neatly summarised by Heilbron J in *Re D (A Minor)* (1976). She refers to wardship as being 'a very special and ancient jurisdiction' which had its origins in the 'sovereign's feudal obligation as *parens patriae* to protect the person and property of his subjects'. The obligation was first cast upon the Chancellor, passed to the Chancery Court, and in 1970 came to rest in the Family Division of the High Court. Justification for the unique role played by the jurisdiction was given by Lord Eldon LC in *Wellesley v Duke of Beaufort* (1827), where he stated:

> 'This jurisdiction is founded on the obvious necessity that the law should place somewhere the care of individuals who cannot take care of themselves, particularly in cases where it is clear that some care should be thrown around them.'

He also opined that it had always been the principle of the court not to risk incurring damage to children 'but rather to prevent the damage being done'.

In the Middle Ages, and particularly when the Court of Wards was operating between 1540 and 1660, the focus was not so much on the welfare of wards but upon their property. The decline of property-related matters and the rise of welfare-related issues commenced in the 18th century, and by 1893 Lord Justice Kay was able to state in *R v Gyngall* (1893) that wardship:

> '... is essentially a parental jurisdiction and that description of it involves that the main consideration to be acted upon in its exercise is the benefit or welfare of the child ... the Court must do what under the circumstances a wise parent acting for the true interests of the child would or ought to do.'

A major point worth emphasising at an early stage is that the jurisdiction is not one created by statute. It may loosely be described as an 'inherent jurisdiction' emanating from the Crown and being developed under the aegis of the common law. That is not to say that the jurisdiction has not been affected by parliamentary intervention. For example, in 1949 the Law Reform (Miscellaneous Provisions) Act simplified procedural requirements and opened up the jurisdiction to a wider, less affluent audience. Just as the 1949 Act paved the way for expansion of the jurisdiction, the Children Act 1989 has resulted in the role of wardship being substantially reduced in favour of new remedies provided under s 8 of the Act.

At the heart of the matter is whether or not children will benefit from having the status of ward bestowed upon them. Family proceedings include proceedings under the jurisdiction of the High Court in relation to children and wardship, and therefore, if the particular question can be effectively resolved under the Children Act, then the wardship jurisdiction ought not to be invoked. This is not to deny that the court has a discretion to allow wardship proceedings, but a blind eye cannot be turned to the intention of the Children Act 1989 to reduce the need to resort to the jurisdiction. It is instructive to consider the statement of Waite LJ in *Re CT (A Minor) (Wardship: Representation)* (1993), where he considers the status of wardship in light of the Children Act 1989:

> 'The scheme of the Children Act 1989 is to establish a statutory code for both the private and public law field. It implements proposals in the Law Commission's Final Report, Family Law: Review of Child Law: Guardianship and Custody (1988) ... of which a major objective was stated to be the reduction of the need to resort to the wardship jurisdiction of the High Court ... The jurisdiction is not only circumscribed procedurally. The

> courts' undoubted discretion to allow wardship proceedings to go forward in a suitable case is subject to their clear duty, in loyalty to the scheme and the purpose of the Children Act legislation, to permit recourse to wardship only when it becomes apparent to the judge ... that the question which the court is determining in regard to the minor's upbringing or property cannot be resolved under the statutory procedures in Part II of the Act in a way which secures the best interests of the child; or where the minor's person is in a state of jeopardy from which he can only be protected by giving him the status of ward of court; or where the court's functions need to be secured from the effects, potentially injurious to the child, of external influences (intrusive publicity for example) and it is decided that conferring on the child the status of ward will prove a more effective deterrent than the ordinary sanctions of contempt of court which already protect family proceedings.'

The statement from the Children Act Advisory Committee Report, with which this chapter begins, bears testimony to the fact that the jurisdiction is still to be taken seriously. At its zenith in 1991, originating summonses numbered just under 5,000. Currently, numbers are unlikely to reach 10% of that figure.

Examples of the considerations relevant in deciding whether or not to invoke the jurisdiction are to be found in *Re T (A Minor) (Wardship: Representation)* (1993). A girl aged 13 wished to leave the adoptive couple who were her lawful parents and go to live with her natural family. She had obtained leave to make an application for a residence order in favour of her aunt, with whom she initially wished to live. She sought the advice of a solicitor who was satisfied that she had sufficient maturity and understanding of the issues to enable him to accept her instructions. Her adoptive parents strongly opposed the application and they proceeded to institute wardship proceedings, thus ensuring that the court would have to determine, as a preliminary issue, which was to be the appropriate forum. T argued that it was inappropriate that she should be made a defendant in the wardship proceedings and thus, possibly, have her views put by a guardian *ad litem*. It was further maintained that exactly the same issues arose in the wardship proceedings as those under the s 8 application, where she would be capable of giving her own instructions.

In the Court of Appeal, Waite LJ was minded to permit recourse to wardship only where it was apparent that any matter relating to the upbringing or property of the child could not be resolved under the statutory procedures, while at the same time securing the best interests of the child. He referred to the greater impact of wardship orders to provide an effective deterrent, where one is needed, as opposed to the 'ordinary sanctions of contempt of court which already protected all family proceedings'. Of particular concern was control of the media with respect to 'intrusive publicity' or 'where the minor's person was in a state of jeopardy from which he could only be protected by giving him the status of ward'. (Reference should be made to rule 9.2A of the Family Proceedings Rules 1991 as amended by the Family Proceedings (Amendment) Rules 1992 SI No 456 on when and in what circumstances a child need not be represented by a next friend or guardian *ad litem*.)

In the event, the Court of Appeal decided to allow the child's appeal and discharge the wardship order.

The purpose of this chapter is to outline the development of the wardship jurisdiction since 1949, paying attention to its use by local authorities in the period 1970-1991 thereby providing reasons why restrictions were imposed upon the use of the jurisdiction by local authorities. Section 100(3) states:

> 'No application for any exercise of the court's inherent jurisdiction with respect to children may be made by a local authority unless the authority have obtained the leave of the court.'

The chapter will also consider the current role of wardship and highlight aspects of the jurisdiction which make it a particularly beneficial one when dealing with those unique, one-off type of cases which occasionally do surface and for which there is no obvious forum for adjudication.

The search would be long and arduous if one were seeking a body of reported case law between 1950 and 1970. It simply does not exist. This is not to deny that the wardship jurisdiction was used, and occasionally abused, during this period, for example, to quote Latey J in *Re X (A Minor) (Wardship: Restriction on publication)* (1975):

> '... I ... think it unlikely that the court would make a wardship order when a child was brought in as a vehicle to achieve some ulterior objective – a commercial one, for example.'

Applications in the early 1950s were under 100, and a decade later were still relatively low at around 250. Wardship was occasionally used by parents in a last ditch attempt to control their recalcitrant children, although it is probably accurate to suggest that wardship, to be effective in such circumstances, needed the cooperation of the ward, usually to ensure that an undesirable relationship should be brought to an end.

In *Re B (JA)* (1965), a 42 year old married man was restrained from communicating with a teenage girl, but for every successful case it is possible to highlight one which achieved little or no success at all. *Re F* (1977) bears ample testimony to the fact that resort to the jurisdiction can have the opposite effect to that required by the parents. In that case, a 15 year old girl had formed an association with a man, aged 28, who, in the words of Lord Denning MR, was 'a very bad character. He has a long criminal record with 18 convictions. He took drugs and wore long hair. He was one of a hippy gang who did no work but squatted in empty premises. He gave this young girl drugs. He had sexual intercourse with her, knowing that she was only 15. She thought that she was in love with him'. Despite the granting of the wardship order in favour of the parents, she would not return home and eventually went to live in a local authority hostel.

Wardship also had a role to play in endeavouring to assist a parent in combating the evils of kidnapping of the child by the other parent. That the role has been dramatically curtailed is a result of the introduction of the Child Abduction and Custody Act 1985, which gives effect to the Hague and European Conventions (see Chapter 9). Wardship, however, may still be useful if a child is brought within the jurisdiction from a non-convention country or abducted to such a country.

The Law Commission has described the wardship jurisdiction as (para 3.53 Law Commission Working Paper 101 1987):

- an alternative jurisdiction;
- an independent jurisdiction;
- a supportive jurisdiction;
- a review or appellate jurisdiction.

Local authority interest in the jurisdiction increased throughout the period 1970-1991. Indeed, despite the extensive statutory provisions available to local authorities when discharging child care duties, the High Court was, in 1974, prepared to endorse recourse to the wardship jurisdiction. In *Re B (A Minor) (Wardship: Child in Care)* (1974), Lane J was of the opinion that there were cases where the existence of a wardship order would be of value both to the child and to the local authority. The authorities, she said, confirmed:

> '... that the court has power to make a wardship order notwithstanding the existence of a care order in favour of a local authority.'

Dunn J was even more emphatic in his commitment to wardship, even though a juvenile court had discharged a care order. The local authority remained unconvinced that the action was in the child's best interests and promptly sought a wardship order. In his judgment in *Re D (A Minor) (Justices' decision: Review)* (1977), he made the following statement:

> 'Far from local authorities being discouraged from applying to the court in wardship ... they should be encouraged to do so, because in very many of these cases it is the only way in which orders can be made in the interests of the child, untrammelled by the statutory provisions of the Children and Young Persons Act 1969.'

The major reasons why wardship proved popular to both local authorities and parents in the context of child care legislation are not difficult to ascertain. In particular the Children and Young Persons Act 1969 did not include a 'probability' provision, ie for a child to be taken into care it had to be established that 'his proper development is being avoidably prevented or neglected or he is being ill-treated'. No account could be taken of the risk of future harm, ie it was more probable than not that he would suffer at some time in the future. Wardship was therefore seen as a way to 'fill the gap' in the statutory code. However, see the ingenious interpretation offered by the House of Lords in *D v Berkshire County Council and Others* (1987).

Parents also had a limited role in proceedings and often sought recourse to the jurisdiction in an attempt to gain via the prerogative jurisdiction what was denied to them through the statutory scheme. Parental ability to seek review of the exercise of local authority discretionary powers by invoking the wardship jurisdiction was limited by the decision of the House of Lords in the case of *A v Liverpool City Council* (1981). The House was firmly of the opinion that the exercise of the jurisdiction should be 'closely circumscribed' (Lord Roskill) although confirming that wardship is 'never extinguished merely because the child is in the care of the local authority'. The appropriate mechanism to challenge the exercise of discretionary powers was deemed to be judicial review.

8.2 The current position

What, then, are the essential features of the wardship jurisdiction since the Children Act 1989 limited local authority access to the jurisdiction? Section 8(3)(a) of the 1989 Act confirms that wardship proceedings are to be treated as family proceedings, which means that any s 8 order is available to the court if it should wish to exercise this option in the best interests of the child.

The Supreme Court Act 1981 (s 41) states that wardship proceedings must be commenced by originating summons, but the crucial decision for any legal advisor must be to decide whether an invocation of the jurisdiction is preferable to an application under the Children Act 1989 for a specific issue or prohibited steps order. If there is a dispute between parents over the upbringing of their child, then s 8 would seem to provide sufficient power to the court to resolve the matter by way of a specific issue order, albeit leave might have to be obtained by those who are not parents and do not have a residence order in their favour (see s 10(1)(a)(ii)). It has yet to be decided whether recourse to wardship would be appropriate if leave to apply for a s 8 order were to be refused. Hale J alluded to the point in *C v Salford City Council* (1994), and was of the opinion that:

> '... it would have been a bold decision, to say the least, to say that although I was against them on the leave criteria I should nevertheless permit them to proceed in wardship proceedings.'

In the case itself, the court granted leave to foster parents to apply for a residence order in respect of their foster child who suffered from Down's Syndrome. The child had been made a ward of court four days before the application for leave was lodged and the judge was quite clear that no material advantage would accrue to the child by maintaining the wardship order. Two reasons were advanced as to why the continuation of the wardship order might have been apposite. First, that the Official Solicitor could continue to be involved, and secondly that as it was an exceptional and difficult case. These arguments did not carry the day. The Official Solicitor had made it clear that he would wish to be involved were the wardship order to be discharged. The comment by the judge regarding the second issue is perhaps more significant. She stated:

> 'It is an exceptional and extremely difficult case, but again it can be decided in exactly the same way in the Children Act jurisdiction as it can be decided in the wardship jurisdiction.'

Ultimately, the courts will have to determine the extent of the interrelationship, if any, between the statutory code and the wardship jurisdiction. However, it is scarcely credible that the court would permit access to the wardship jurisdiction in circumstances where the applicant has chosen not to apply for leave under s 10 of the Children Act unless there is an overriding reason why the best interests of the child are better served by recourse to wardship.

The High Court may decline jurisdiction in wardship for other reasons, as both common law and statute have imposed some restrictions on its use. In *Re F (In utero)* (1988), the Court of Appeal determined that a court has no jurisdiction to make an unborn child a ward of court. This is unsurprising given the decision by Sir George Baker P in *Paton v Trustees of British Pregnancy Advisory Services and another* (1978) to the effect that a foetus cannot, in English law, have any right of its own until it is established that it has an existence independent from that of the mother. The difficulty which would arise if a foetus were to be given similar rights to a child centres on the welfare principle. To place the interests of the foetus above all other interests, including those of the mother, is a recipe for conflict which the Court of Appeal in *Re F* was unprepared to sanction. May LJ spoke of 'insuperable difficulties' in seeking to enforce an order against the mother, particularly if the mother failed to comply with the order. Should a mother be forced by the High Court to give up smoking or drinking alcohol during her pregnancy, given that there could be harmful side effects on the foetus? Or suppose the mother is a drug addict as in *D v Berkshire County Council* (1988): how could the interests of the foetus be protected in such circumstances? Ironically, May LJ did comment that the facts of the case would have prompted to exercise the jurisdiction if it existed!

Section 100(2)(a) of the Children Act 1989 denies a wardship court the jurisdiction to 'require a child to be placed in the care, or put under the supervision, of a local authority'. The court formerly possessed the power so to do under s 7(2) of the Family Law Reform Act 1969, but, as s 100(i) of the 1989 Act states, rather tersely, 's 7 ... shall cease to have effect'. However, once jurisdiction has been established, the courts have been slow to acknowledge that limits should be imposed in respect of the extent of the jurisdiction. In *Re X (A Minor)* (1975), Roskill LJ considered that 'no limits to [the] jurisdiction have yet been drawn and it is not necessary to consider ... what (if any) limits there are to that jurisdiction'. Sir John Pennycuick, however, while agreeing in theory that wardship was an 'unrestricted jurisdiction to do whatever is considered necessary for the welfare of the ward', thought it was 'quite impossible' in practice to protect a ward against everything which might result in harm. The jurisdiction, he said, must be exercised with due regard for the rights of outside parties, there must be a 'proper balance' between the rights of the ward and those outside parties. In *Re X* (1975), the balancing exercise centred around interfering with the right of free publication in order to save a 14 year old girl from the trauma of reading passages in a book due for publication which portrayed her father as utterly depraved, indulging in sordid and degrading conduct, and as one who was 'obscene and drank to excess'. The court acknowledged that the right of free speech and free publication were at least as important as the rights of individuals and refused to order that the offending passages should be deleted from the book. It is worth noting that the welfare of the child was not considered to be the first and paramount consideration, as neither the custody nor the upbringing of the child were in question.

Wardship has become an increasingly important jurisdiction in helping to determine the ambit of press reporting of issues concerning children. In *Re M and another (Minors) (Wardship: Freedom of publication)* (1990), the issue facing the court was whether information regarding the removal of two wards from the care of foster parents should be publicised. The *dicta* of Sir John Pennycuick in *Re X* (1975), together with that of Booth J in *Re L (A Minor) (Wardship: Freedom of publication)* (1988), was applied. The Court of Appeal confirmed that the welfare of the children was not paramount and, as such, an injunction preventing publication should not automatically be granted. If, indeed, it was thought necessary to grant an injunction, it should 'be no wider than necessary to protect the welfare of the children'. Uninhibited press publicity would, in the majority of cases, be detrimental to the interests of any children, but an injunction which concealed the identity of the children while allowing the article to discuss local authority decision-making was deemed acceptable.

Booth J in *Re L* (1988) had emphasised that the mere fact that a child was a ward of court did not impose an absolute prohibition on the publication of any information leading to the identification of the ward. It is incumbent upon the judiciary to be clear and precise when framing the terms of any injunction in order to ensure that there was no undue or unnecessary restriction imposed upon the press. How should the court carry out this balancing exercise? Neill LJ considered the question in *Re W (A Minor) (Wardship: Freedom of publication)* (1992). The following are the guidelines suggested by the judge:

- The court will attach great importance to safeguarding the freedom of the press.
- Account must be taken of Article 10 of the Convention for the Protection of Human Rights and Fundamental Freedoms, designed to safeguard the 'freedom to hold opinions and to receive and impart information and ideas without interference by public authority'.

- There must be exceptions to the Convention of which the protection of children must be of significance.

- The welfare of the child is not the paramount consideration when carrying out the balancing exercise.

- The 'nature and extent' of the public interest in the matter will be an important factor. A distinction ought to be drawn between cases of mere curiosity and where the press is commenting upon a subject of genuine public interest.

- Invariably a story can be told without the need to identify the ward, although it was acknowledged that some wider identification may occur in the process of disseminating the facts.

- The imposition of any restraint should be to prevent any risk of harassment to the ward or those closely associated with him or her.

- Any restraint must be unambiguously expressed, and it should be noted that a court cannot protect a ward against distress occasioned by reading the publication in question.

The case in question concerned the placing by a local authority of an adolescent boy with foster parents, two men who had had a stable homosexual relationship over a considerable period of time. The boy had a disturbed background which had included involvement in homosexual activities with men much older than himself. *Mirror Group Newspapers* wished to publish an article about the matter. The local authority sought and obtained an *ex parte* injunction to restrain publication, which was confirmed at a later hearing. The newspaper's appeal was allowed to the extent that publication could take place providing no attempt was made to identify the boy but allowing the local authority to be identified. The court recognised and accepted that there was a risk that the ward could be identified but presumably expected the newspaper to do everything possible to minimise the risk of that occurrence.

Control of the media in the context of criminal proceedings was examined in *Re R (A Minor) (Wardship: Restrictions on publication)* (1994). In criminal proceedings, the trial judge has powers under s 39(1) of the Children and Young Persons Act 1933. This section gives a discretion to the court to direct that a newspaper report should not reveal the name, address, or school of the child, nor 'include any particulars calculated to lead to the identification' of any child or young person connected with the proceedings. Nor should any photograph be published which would result in identification. Note that s 49 of the Act seeks to achieve a similar result in respect of proceedings in a youth court, except that the restrictions are mandatory. However, s 49 of the Criminal Justice and Public Order Act 1994 makes minor changes to the restrictions in the context of youth courts. Juveniles who are 'unlawfully at large' may now be named and their photographs published. This, however, is not automatic, and the court must be satisfied that the juvenile has been charged with or convicted of:

- a violent offence;
- a sexual offence; or
- an offence punishable in the case of an adult with imprisonment for 14 years or more.

In *Re R* (1994), the father of a young girl was facing trial on a charge of kidnapping her, and the events surrounding his arrest had attracted considerable media attention. Pictures of the child, her parents and their names has been disclosed. The child had become a ward of court soon after the parents had separated in 1988. Some six months after the father's arrest in June 1993, *The Independent* newspaper published the father's account of the circumstances surrounding his abduction of his daughter. The child's guardian *ad litem* sought an injunction restraining publication of any material relating to the ward or likely to lead to her identification. The father opposed the injunction on the basis that it would inhibit the media from reporting his trial, which was imminent. An order under s 39 of the Children and Young Persons Act 1933 is only effective from the commencement of the trial, and the judge felt that the ward would gain greater protection if the injunction were continued, thus, in effect, preventing any reporting of the trial. The father's appeal was allowed. The court confirmed that where a ward was the victim of an alleged criminal act it was up to the trial judge to impose restrictions under s 39. The significant point from the case is the view of two judges who doubted whether a wardship judge had the power to make an order restraining publication of the reporting of criminal proceedings. Wards could not be protected from adverse publicity unless the 'effective working of the court's jurisdiction' is threatened, which in this situation was not the case, given that there had been enormous publicity at the time of the father's arrest. There is a clear statement of principle in the judgment of Millett LJ that parliament had entrusted trial judges, not wardship judges, with the responsibility to determine whether fair and accurate reporting of criminal proceedings should be restricted. See the Contempt of Court Act 1981 s 4 and also the case of *Re H-S* (1994) and the statement of principle that where an injunction is sought which will impose a restraint upon the freedom of the press in order to protect the identity of a child, then the matter should be transferred to the High Court. In this case the county court had jurisdiction by virtue of the fact that the parents of the children had been divorced in 1984.

The Children Act Advisory Committee Report for 1993-94 refers to 'special category cases' where the inherent jurisdiction of the High Court may be invoked rather than having recourse to a s 8 specific issue order. There is some potential for confusion in the terminology, for while wardship is undoubtedly an exercise by the court of its inherent jurisdiction, the Children Act appears to recognise an inherent jurisdiction separate and independent from wardship. It would appear that the inherent jurisdiction, as distinct from wardship, does not offer all-embracing protection of the latter jurisdiction. The Children Act Advisory Committee Report refers to it in this way:

> '... unlike the Children Act, it enables the court to take a continuing supervisory role in the upbringing of the child, since each important step in the life of a ward requires the approval of the court.'

A recent example of where the Court of Appeal had to consider the interrelationship between the wardship jurisdiction and the statutory code is *Re W (Wardship: Discharge: Publicity)* (1995). The father had issued wardship proceedings and the mother had obtained interim care and control of the four children of the marriage. Later, the mother agreed to the children living with their father. Sadly, from the mother's point of view, the children indicated that they did not wish to continue to see their mother. There continued to be conflict between the various members of the family, culminating in access between the mother and her children ceasing in 1993. The father sought to end the wardship but his application was refused. An order was also made preventing both the father and the children from giving information to the media. The father appealed against both orders. The Court of Appeal continued the wardship stating that no comparable protection could be achieved under the Children Act. A prohibited steps order was deemed inappropriate because it could not anticipate how the father might act in the future. Nor was such an order likely to be effective in preventing the publication of information about the children. As a result of the wardship order being maintained, the Official Solicitor continued to be involved and 'could act as a buffer between the parents'. The father had acted in the past in a less than objective way. seeking publicity which was detrimental to the well-being of the children. 'Thus wardship can afford the boys some degree of protection from the father's actions'. Balcombe LJ thought it arguable that a prohibited steps order '... may not be used to prevent some non-parental activity such as publishing information about the child, because this is not a step in meeting parental responsibility ...'. However, one is left in no doubt that wardship would not have been continued '... unless it offered advantages to the boys which could not be secured by use of the orders available under the Children Act 1989'.

Wardship and the inherent jurisdiction have proved valuable jurisdictions when dealing with medico-legal cases, often requiring life or death decisions to be taken. Whether the inherent jurisdiction is the appropriate legal framework within which to proceed was considered in *Re O (A Minor) (Medical Treatment)* (1993). The issue was whether or not a child born prematurely to Jehovah's Witness parents should be allowed blood transfusions in the event of an emergency arising which threatened the chances of her survival. The child was subject to an Emergency Protection Order and the local authority was in the process of seeking a care order in order to acquire the necessary parental responsibility from which they could authorise appropriate medical treatment. Given the gravity of the situation, Johnson J had little doubt that any application under the Children Act should be transferred to the Family Division as quickly as possible. Any *ex parte* application for authority to use blood or blood products could be dealt with by a judge of the Family Division. Applications should 'ordinarily be made under the inherent jurisdiction of the court', as wardship is specifically prohibited under the provisions of s 100(2)(c) if the child is already the subject of a care order.

The judge also refers to the flexibility of the system which provides for at least one judge of the Family Division being available night or day to deal with emergency applications.

Reference should also be made to the decision of Thorpe J in *Re S (A Minor) (Medical Treatment)* (1993). In this case, again revolving around the desirability of giving blood transfusions to the child of Jehovah's Witness parents, the local authority sought leave under s 100 to invoke the inherent jurisdiction and the parents sought a prohibited steps order under the Children Act s 8. The local authority application succeeded.

At the time of writing, the latest reported case which highlights the value of the court's inherent jurisdiction is *Devon County Council v S* (1995), in which Thorpe J refused to accept that s 100 of the Children Act should be construed in a restrictive way. The local authority, he said, was not seeking to have 'protective powers' conferred upon it but was inviting the court to exercise those powers under its inherent jurisdiction, without which significant harm might befall the children. Section 100(2), it will be recalled, states:

> 'No court shall exercise the High Court's inherent jurisdiction with respect to children ...
>
> (d) for the purpose of conferring on any local authority power to determine a question which has arisen, or which may arise, in connection with any aspect of parental responsibility for a child ...'

There are, however, numerous cases of great significance, where the wardship jurisdiction has been invoked in order to resolve medico-legal problems, albeit these cases were decided before the Children Act 1989 came into force in October 1991. *Re R (A Minor) (Wardship: Medical treatment)* (1991) is a case in point, decided, as it was, in July 1991. The court held that when exercising its wardship jurisdiction, the High Court had the power to consent to medical treatment even though the ward was competent to consent. It was also stated that the wardship court had an 'overriding power' not possessed by natural parents to refuse consent or forbid, if ward consented, if the court thought that in giving consent the ward would be acting against his or her own best interests. The decision of Lord Donaldson MR has not passed without comment, but it does appear to have been accepted as a correct statement of law in *Re W (A Minor) (Medical treatment)* (1992) *per* Balcombe LJ. It is perhaps worthwhile spending some time in analysing the judgments delivered by the Court of Appeal, as various statements of principle are established. In particular, all three judges allude to the fact that the High Court's inherent jurisdiction in relation to children is equally exercisable whether or not the child is a ward of court. Lord Donaldson MR states:

> 'Indeed the only additional effect of a child being a ward of court stems from its status as such and not from the inherent jurisdiction, eg a ward of court cannot marry or leave the jurisdiction without the consent of the court and no important or major step in a ward's life can be taken without that consent.'

Balcombe LJ acknowledges that before the Children Act came into force the inherent jurisdiction in respect of children was invariably exercised through the wardship jurisdiction. The 1989 Act makes the distinction 'clear for all to see' and he was of the opinion that wardship was only 'machinery' and that the court's inherent jurisdiction could be exercised irrespective of whether the child was a ward of court. There is further proof, if proof indeed were needed, that there are limitations on the exercise of the jurisdiction, albeit the 'theoretical position' is that the jurisdiction is limitless.

Re D (1976), perhaps more than any other wardship case, illustrated the great strength of the jurisdiction in being able to respond quickly to what the judge referred to as a 'novel situation'. The mother of an 11 year old girl suffering from Sotos Syndrome feared that she might be seduced at a young age and possibly give birth to an abnormal child. She therefore determined that the correct course of action was to seek to have the girl sterilised. Wardship proceedings were initiated by the educational psychologist treating the girl in order to prevent the operation from taking place. This again illustrates another strength of the jurisdiction, that anyone who claims to have the best interests of the child at heart can institute proceedings. The High Court agreed that the operation should not take place, particularly as it involved the 'deprivation of a basic human right, ie the right of a woman to produce'. Therefore if such an operation were to be performed for non-therapeutic reasons and without her consent (she was deemed incapable of giving consent), then it amounted to a violation of that right.

It is suggested that sterilisation, and perhaps abortion cases, may now fall into that special category where the appropriate course of action is to invoke the inherent jurisdiction of the High Court and not necessarily the wardship jurisdiction. That there is still some doubt about the veracity of this statement is confirmed in a case reported as a news item in *The Times* (1995) 5 October. The issue to be decided was whether a mentally handicapped girl aged 17 should have an abortion. Pringle J, sitting in the High Court in Belfast, accepted that the girl would be unable to cope with pregnancy, motherhood or having the child adopted. The Western Health Board brought the case, having previously made the child a ward of court. A consultant gynaecologist had given evidence to the effect that the girl did not know that she was pregnant, and further evidence was submitted by a psychiatrist who suggested that if the pregnancy continued a mental breakdown was a strong possibility. The judge emphasised that in his opinion the abortion was '... clearly in the girl's best interests'. The girl was 12 weeks pregnant when the judge gave his approval for the abortion to be performed. So what is there left for the wardship court? One clearly defined area would be in support of the legislation which seeks to prevent child abduction and kidnapping. For example, in *Re M (A Minor) (Abduction)* (1994), the Court of Appeal decided, given the very unhappy circumstances, that a 13 year old boy should be made a ward of court rather than return to his home jurisdiction of Ireland, from which he had run away, willingly aided by his father who lived in England. It was for the wardship court then to consider how the long-term interests of the boy would best be served.

The Children Act Advisory Committee Report (1993/4) refers to 'highly contentious issues over residence' and 'allegations of abuse in respect of which the relevant local authority has decided not to take proceedings', but the better view appears to be that wardship is very much becoming a residual jurisdiction and that the majority of cases formerly dealt with by recourse to wardship will fall to be decided under the provisions of the Children Act or the inherent jurisdiction. Its future, then, is very much in the hands of lawyers and the courts. Will lawyers continue to consider the jurisdiction as having an advantage over the statutory provisions and the inherent jurisdiction? Does the public interest demand that such an ancient jurisdiction should not disappear in its entirety, given that single issue cases of great public interest are bound to arise from time to time? The truly unique features of the wardship jurisdiction, so eloquently attested to by Lord Scarman in *Re E (SA) (A Minor) (Wardship)* (1984), should not be forgotten:

> 'But a court exercising jurisdiction over its ward must never lose sight of a fundamental feature of the jurisdiction that it is exercising, namely that it is exercising a wardship, not an adversarial jurisdiction. Its duty is not limited to the dispute between the parties: on the contrary, its duty is to act in the way best suited in its judgment to serve the true interests and welfare of the ward. In exercising wardship jurisdiction, the court is a true family court. Its paramount concern is the welfare of its ward. It will, therefore, sometimes be the duty of the court to look beyond the submissions of the parties in its endeavour to do what it judges necessary. When a ... parent persuades the court that it should make a child its ward, the court takes over the ultimate responsibility for the child.'

Any child within the jurisdiction can be made a ward of court. British subjects owe allegiance to the Crown, and as the inherent jurisdiction is based upon the concept of parens patriae, the necessary link is established. Those children who do not owe allegiance to the Crown will, however, not be at a disadvantage provided they are within the jurisdiction. In practice, the basis of the jurisdiction for non-British subjects is whether or not there is an immediate need for the child to receive the assistance of the court. In *Re B-M (Wardship: Jurisdiction)* (1993), it was stated that the English wardship court had jurisdiction irrespective of the child's nationality, if either:

- the child was physically present in England and Wales; or
- England and Wales was the habitual residence of the child.

As the mother and father were both habitually resident in England and Wales at the date of the wardship order, then so was their child – and the court had the power to make her a ward of court.

Wardship proceedings are commenced by issuing an originating summons under s 41 of the Supreme Court Act 1981. The effect of this is that the child immediately becomes a ward, but there is a 21-day period in which a date should be agreed for a hearing before a district judge. Failure to comply with this procedure will result in the wardship lapsing.

It is suggested that in the context of a university LLB course, the major focus for study will be the interrelationship between the inherent jurisdiction, Children Act 1989 and the wardship jurisdiction.

Summary of Chapter 8

Wardship

Wardship is in decline, but not a terminal decline. The Children Act Advisory Committee Report 1993/4 confirms that the jurisdiction is still active 'where there are highly contentious issues over residence, allegations of abuse in respect of which the ... local authority has decided not to take care proceedings, and in cases with an international aspect ...'.

A ward of court is a child whose guardian is the High Court. This means that no important step in a child's life may be taken without the leave of the court. Additionally, any decision taken must be consistent with the principles that the welfare of the child is the first and paramount consideration.

Wardship is an ancient jurisdiction dating back to the Middle Ages and had its origin in the sovereign's feudal obligation as *parens patriae* to protect the person and property of his subjects.

Wardship is not a statutory jurisdiction although the Children Act has, through the specific issue order, removed much of the wardship jurisdiction. Rather, it may be described as an 'inherent jurisdiction' which has been developed under the aegis of the common law. In *Re T (A Minor) (Wardship: Representation)* (1993), the Court of Appeal stated that wardship should only be used if matters relating to the upbringing and property of the child could not be resolved under the statutory procedures, while at the same time securing the best interests of the child. The Law Commission described the wardship jurisdiction as:

- an alternative jurisdiction;
- an independent jurisdiction;
- a supportive jurisdiction;
- a review or appellate jurisdiction.

Much use was made of the jurisdiction by local authorities in the period 1970 to 1991, but now, leave must be obtained before a local authority can commence wardship proceedings. (Children Act s 100(3)).

The current position is that wardship proceedings are designated as family proceedings under the Children Act, which means that any s 8 order may be made providing it is justified by reference to the best interests of the child. However, the Children Act prevents a wardship court from placing a child in the care of a local authority.

Wardship has become an important jurisdiction when deciding the ambit of press reporting of issues concerning children.

See *Re M and another (Minors) (Wardship: Freedom of publication)* (1990) and *Re W (A Minor) (Wardship: Freedom of Publication)* (1992).

Some confusion may have been introduced as a result of the Children Act referring to the 'inherent jurisdiction' which appears to be separate and independent from the wardship jurisdiction. The distinction, it is suggested, is to be found in the fact that wardship results in the court taking a continuing supervisory role for the child, since each important step in the life of the ward requires the approval of the court.

Wardship has proved particularly valuable in the context of medical cases. See *Re D* (1976) as a striking example of the effectiveness of the wardship jurisdiction.

Any child within the jurisdiction can be made a ward of court, and proceedings are commenced by way of originating summons, the effect of which is that the child becomes a ward of court immediately.

Addendum

The value of the wardship jurisdiction has once again been demonstrated in the case of a 13 year old English girl, Sarah Cook, who, with her parents blessing 'married' an 18 year old Turkish waiter whom she had met on holiday. The girl has now been made a ward of court and the President of the Family Division has ruled that she should be brought back from South-East Turkey 'forthwith'. He also ruled that should she return she would not again be allowed to leave the jurisdiction without the court's permission (*The Times*, 25 January 1996).

Chapter 9

Child Abduction

9.1 Introduction

The removal of children by their parents, or by one parent, from one jurisdiction to another is of increasing concern. A coherent response to the difficulties caused by abduction was worked out in the 1980s, and England and Wales now has legislation, criminal and civil, which, taken together, forms a comprehensive code aimed at combating the problem.

Abduction from the jurisdiction may result in the child being taken to Scotland or Northern Ireland or to any other jurisdiction in the world. The Family Law Act 1986 addresses the problem of 'local' abduction. This legislation was necessary because, prior to the Act coming into force, a custody order issued by a court in England and Wales could not be enforced, nor indeed would it have been recognised, in another part of the United Kingdom. A broad range of orders relating to children are now recognised and enforceable throughout the kingdom, eg s 8 Children Act 1989, a wardship order, or an order granted under an exercise of the inherent jurisdiction, providing it gives care of a child to any person or provides for contact with or the education of a child (see s 1(1)(d) of the Family Law Act 1986). In order to be effective, the order must be registered in the 'receiving' jurisdiction. This means that a court in that jurisdiction may treat the order as if it had originally been made by that court.

These orders are referred to as Part I orders (see s 1 of the 1986 Act). The court does not have to give automatic effect to such orders. Section 30 permits orders to be 'stayed' and s 31 gives a court the power to dismiss enforcement proceedings. Sections 33 to 37 give the court wide powers in relation to ordering the disclosure of a child's whereabouts, recovery of the child, and even surrendering of a person's passport.

9.2 Criminal law

Child abduction was made a criminal offence as a result of the Child Abduction Act 1984, and this becomes complementary to the common law offence of kidnapping. However, there is authority to support the proposition that the statutory code should be invoked in preference to the common law offence. In *R v C* (1991), Watkins LJ stated, at p 260 D:

> 'It is our firm opinion that prosecutors should, in future, avoid altogether charging anyone with child kidnapping at common law.'

Despite this seemingly clear statement of principle, there is the suggestion in the judgment of Watkins LJ that if there are exceptional circumstances, then such a course of action may be merited.

Lord Brandon in *R v D* (1984) alluded to four factors which 'amply justified the decision to prosecute the father for kidnapping ...' albeit it must be remembered that the Child Abduction Act 1984 was not in force at the time. The question was whether the matter should be treated as a contempt of court or prosecuted as the offence of kidnapping. Bearing in mind that parents will invariably act in ways which are perceived to be in the child's best interests, then a charge of common law kidnapping may appear inappropriate. Lord Brandon thought, as a matter of policy, that parents who snatch their children who are wards of court should be dealt with as a contempt of court rather than make them subject to a criminal prosecution. A charge of common law kidnapping should only be brought if ordinary, right-thinking people would immediately and without hesitation regard the act as criminal in nature. However, the offence exists, and even though it is unlikely to be called upon, the four factors referred to by Lord Brandon may be taken into account. They are:

- '[t]he appalling nature of the father's conduct' (he terrified the mother by having 'two thugs' with him when he snatched the child);
- the repetition of his conduct, albeit without the two thugs;
- the fact that the child was a ward of court, and on each occasion was removed from the jurisdiction;
- that the father had committed a series of other offences.

The common law offence would be applicable where the child is over 16, as the 1984 applies only to those under 16. The Director of Public Prosecutions (DPP) must give consent to bring a prosecution.

The statutory offence is stated thus:

> '... a person connected with a child under the age of 16 commits an offence if he takes or sends the child out of the United Kingdom without the appropriate consent' (s 1 Child Abduction Act 1984).

Section 1(2) states that a person is connected with a child for the purposes of the section if:

'(a) he is a parent of the child;

(b) in the case of a child whose parents were not married

to each other at the time of his birth, a person who there are reasonable grounds for believing to be the father of the child;

(c) a guardian of the child;

(d) a person in whose favour a residence order is in force with respect to the child;

(e) a person who has custody of the child.'

The offence is not committed if:

- the appropriate consent is given; or
- he is a person in whose favour there is a residence order, because such a person has, by virtue of the residence order, the ability to remove the child from the jurisdiction for up to one month (see s 13(2) of the Children Act 1989).

Section 1(5) also provides a defence based upon belief that the other person has consented or would consent if he was aware of all the relevant circumstances. Presumably the requirement here is for an honest belief consistent with the criminal law principles regarding mistake. Nor would it appear necessary for the belief to be based upon reasonable grounds, although, in practice, the less reasonable the grounds the less likely a jury is to conclude that the belief was honestly held (see *R v Gladstone Williams* (1987)).

The subsection also provides a defence if it can be shown by the accused that he had taken all reasonable steps to communicate with the other person but had been unable to do so, or that the other person has unreasonably refused his consent. This latter defence will not apply if the other person is someone in whose favour a residence order is in force or who has custody of the child.

Section 1(3) relates to those who can give the appropriate consent. They are:

- the child's mother;
- the child's father, if he has parental responsibility;
- any guardian of the child;
- any person in whose favour there is a residence order in force with respect to the child;
- any person who has custody of the child;

or

- the leave of the court granted 'under or by virtue of the Part II of the Children Act 1989'

or

- if a person has custody, the leave of the court which granted that custody.

In practice, this means that one parent cannot lawfully take the child out of the jurisdiction without the consent of the other, assuming the normal situation where both have parental responsibility. The Matrimonial Causes Act 1973 s 1(2)(d), requires a positive consent before a decree nisi will be granted on the basis of two years' separation. However, there is nothing in the Child Abduction Act 1984 which suggests that one parent needs to take steps to give consent. The suggestion, therefore, is that, providing there is knowledge of the circumstances, then acquiescence is all that will be necessary to ensure that the consent requirement is fulfilled.

If the parents are unmarried and the father does not possess parental responsibility, then the mother can act unilaterally. If the father had doubts as to whether or not the mother would return with the child, then an application for a prohibited steps order could be made or the child made a ward of court.

Section 2 of the 1984 Act creates the offence of child abduction by other persons and the key words here are 'take and detain'. These actions relate to children under 16 years of age and it must be shown that they have been taken or detained without lawful authority or reasonable excuse. The section recognises the right of parents and those entitled to lawful control not to have a child removed or kept out of their lawful control. Case law on all aspects of the Child Abduction Act 1984 is hardly plentiful, but s 2 was considered by the Court of Appeal in *R v Leather* (1993). The court concluded, perhaps unsurprisingly, that all that was required to commit the *actus reus* of the offence was the removal of the child from lawful control. It certainly did not require, nor did the section even contemplate, the geographical removal of the child. In this case, the accused had urged children aged between 10 and 14 to accompany him, purportedly to search for a lost bicycle. They went with the appellant and removed themselves from his presence when they chose so to do. The accused did not at any time attempt to touch or molest them, and they visited places they were familiar with and to which their parents had, in the past, allowed them to go. The court was adamant that if the parents had known the circumstances they would not have consented to the children going away with the accused, albeit for only a short distance. A child is taken for the purposes of the offence if the defendant 'causes or induces the child to accompany him or any other person ...' (s 3(a)).

The existence of the Child Abduction Act 1984 may be reassuring to many parents. However, parents need to be aware of the practical steps which may be taken in an attempt to defeat a potential abductor. The help of the police should be sought if there is a real likelihood of removal, in order that attempts can be made to prevent a criminal offence taking place. The police can, of course, arrest, providing there is reasonable cause to suspect someone of attempting to remove a child from lawful custody of his or her parents or of taking or sending the child outside the United Kingdom without appropriate consent.

If the intervention of the police is too late then the port alert system can be mobilised. *Practice Direction* (1986) dictates that the police need to be satisfied that the threat of removal is 'real and imminent'. 'Imminent' means that action is not being sought simply as a means of 'insurance'. The request for assistance should be accompanied by as much detail as possible regarding the child and the alleged abductor, eg descriptions, passport numbers, and nationality. Any travel details should also be notified, for example that he or she is expected to attempt to leave the jurisdiction by sea rather than by air. The child's name will remain on the list for four weeks and is then automatically removed.

9.3 International abduction

The chances of a speedy recovery of children abducted from the United Kingdom will be enhanced if they are taken to a country which is a signatory to one of the two Conventions created to help combat the problem. The two Conventions are:

- The Hague Convention on the Civil Aspects of International Child Abduction.
- The European Convention on Recognition and Enforcement of Decisions Concerning Custody of Children and Restoration of Custody of Children.

Although established in 1980, they were not given effect in the United Kingdom until 1986 when the Child Abduction and Custody Act 1985 came into force. These Conventions, which are based upon differing premises, apply to children removed from the United Kingdom and to those brought to England and Wales from Convention countries. Sadly, not all countries are signatories, and therefore the impact of the legislation is nullified when children are taken to 'non-convention' countries.

The objective of the two Conventions remains the same, the major difference being that a court order determining custody rights is required before the European Convention can be invoked. 'Custody' is taken to include a decision relating to 'access' to a child. It will probably be sensible to deal with each one in turn.

9.3.1 The Hague Convention

The Hague Convention has no geographical limits imposed upon which countries may be signatories. In *Re F (Child Abduction)* (1995), Millett LJ stated that the Convention was:

> '... an international convention and it is to be hoped that its terms will receive a similar interpretation in all the contracting states. It is to be construed broadly and in accordance with its purpose without attributing to any of its terms a specialist meaning which it may have acquired under domestic law.'

And in the same case, Butler-Sloss LJ considered that it was the duty of the court to 'construe the Convention in a purposive way and the make the Convention work'. She stated it to be against the philosophy of the Convention for one parent 'unilaterally, secretly and with full knowledge that it is against the wishes of the other parent ... to remove the child from the jurisdiction of the child's habitual residence'.

The Child Abduction and Custody Act 1985 creates a procedure whereby a central authority in one country will communicate with the central authority of the receiving country in order to expedite the return of the child(ren). Although an applicant can approach the overseas central authority, it is preferable if an approach is made to the central authority for England and Wales, which is the Lord Chancellor's Department. In Scotland, the functions are discharged by the Secretary of State.

An interesting account of the French approach to the Hague Convention is to be found at (1993) Fam Law 148 in an article entitled *The Hague Convention on Abduction and Beyond ... Conflicting aims, different solutions – The French Practice* by Alain Cornec. The author recognises that the same questions have been asked of both the English and French courts, yet '... the innovative solutions reached have been very different'. He maintains that the French decisions prevent the Convention from being used as an instrument of blackmail in parallel divorce proceedings, while the English decisions emphasise the importance of taking account of the child's interests between the order for return and the eventual decision of the court in the country of habitual residence. As to the former point, examine the decision of the French *Cour de Cassation* (outlined at p 150, Horlander 1992). This case decides that any acceptance by the aggrieved parent of the removal of the child must be unambiguous and that the possibility of an action against the abductor under the Hague Convention cannot be traded for the renunciation by the mother of her right to financial relief in any divorce proceedings. The article asserts that in a review of eight French cases, the abductor on seven occasions was the mother.

Schedule 1 of the 1985 Act deals with the scope of the Hague Convention. Article 3 establishes that the Convention is designed to inhibit the wrongful removal or retention of a child. A removal or retention is considered wrongful if it is in breach of rights of custody attributed to a person, an institution or any other body, either jointly or alone ... under the law of the state where the child 'was habitually resident immediately before the removal or retention'.

It is a prerequisite to the invocation of the Act that these rights were actually being exercised or would have been exercised but for the removal or retention. It is immediately apparent that consideration will need to be given to the following terms:

- Wrongful removal
- Wrongful retention
- Habitual residence

It must also be remembered that a court order is not required. The Hague Convention seeks to restore to individuals the ability to exercise rights over a child which have been, or will be, denied because of the wrongful removal or retention. Professor Nigel Lowe and Michael Nicholls of the Central Authority for England and Wales, in an article entitled *Child Abduction: The Wardship Jurisdiction and the Hague Convention* (1994) Fam Law 191, concluded that the warding of a child as a result of issuing an originating summons gives the High Court immediate control over the child, thus bestowing upon the court rights of custody for the purposes of Article 3 of the Hague Convention. However, they point out that, in all probability, this does not prevent those with parental responsibility and those looking after a child having rights of custody as well as the court. It is also suggested by the authors that to make a child a ward of court prior to a Convention application may prevent a subsequent change in the child's habitual residence, and this may determine the outcome of the case. The final caveat is that, under English law, a Convention application takes precedence over wardship proceedings, and therefore a defendant who makes a child a ward of court will not be able to prevent a foreign applicant from seeking a remedy under the terms of the Convention.

Lord Brandon in *Re H; Re S* (1991) regarded removal and retention as mutually exclusive concepts, and defined them in the following way:

> 'For the purposes of the Convention, removal occurs when a child, which has previously been in the State of its habitual residence, is taken away across the frontier of that state; whereas retention occurs where a child, which has previously been for a limited period of time outside the State of its habitual residence, is not returned to that State on the expiry of such limited period. That being so ... removal and retention are basically different concepts so that it is impossible either for them to overlap ... or for either to follow upon the other.'

This principle has been consistently adopted and applied in subsequent cases. In *Re S (Minors) (Child Abduction)* (1994), it was stated that 'wrongful retention under the Convention is not a continuing state of affairs'. The requirement is for one parent to be able to demonstrate there has been a 'specific event at a specific point in time' in order to constitute the act of wrongful retention. It follows from this that whether or not there has been a wrongful removal or retention will, in every case, be an issue of fact. See also *Re B (A Minor) (Abduction)* (1994), confirming that all that is required is a single occasion when wrongful retention occurred.

The removal or retention of the child must breach the rights of custody attributed to a person before it can be considered wrongful. This raises the question of how narrowly should the term 'rights of custody' be construed. It will be obvious that an unmarried father who has not acquired parental responsibility under the Children Act 1989 (s 4) could be said not to possess any 'rights of custody'. In *Re B (A Minor) (Abduction)* (1994), the Court of Appeal had to decide whether the father of a child aged 6 who, under the relevant laws of Western Australia did not possess any legal rights over the child because he was not married to the mother, could invoke the Hague Convention when the child was not returned to Australia by her mother who was residing in Wales. It held that the Convention had to be construed 'broadly' and that courts should be slow to attribute any specialist meaning to the term 'rights of custody'. This allowed the court to confirm the decision of the judge at first instance who ordered the child's immediate return to Australia. The judge had concluded that the father had acquired rights under the Convention, first through his active role in the care of the child, secondly the status which the mother had bestowed upon him by indicating that his consent was necessary before the child left the jurisdiction, and finally the expressed desire by the mother that the father should have 'joint guardianship' with the father having 'sole custody'. This latter commitment had not been sanctioned by the maternal grandmother. The court also held that as the mother and grandmother had been untruthful with the father in order to obtain his consent to the removal, the consent given was obtained by the deceit and was not a 'true consent'.

Waite LJ had 'no difficulty' in bestowing a broad connotation to the word custody given the purposes of the Hague Convention. These were, he said, '... in part at least, humanitarian'. The objective is to spare children from further disruption to their lives contingent upon their parents relationship breakdown. The arbitrary removal of children from a settled environment can only be resisted if courts make it absolutely clear that 'rights of custody' will be given the widest possible meaning, thus discouraging the potential abductor from imagining a more sympathetic hearing will be attainable in the 'receiving' jurisdiction. The judge went on to state that the expression 'rights of custody' when used in the Convention therefore needs to be construed in the sense that will best accord with that objective. 'In most cases that will involve giving the term the widest sense possible.'

Consideration should be given to the House of Lords decision in *C v S (A Minor: Abduction: Illegitimate child)* (1990) which appears at first sight to be at odds with the decision in *Re B*. The facts were very similar in that the mother removed the child from Western Australia to Britain. The parents were not married and the father had not acquired any legal rights over the child. The House held the removal to be lawful as it was not a breach of any of the rights of custody possessed by the father at the time of the removal. Waite LJ in *Re B* was satisfied that *C v S* could be distinguished primarily because, in the former case, the mother had been absent from the child for over one year and that the father had day-to-day care of the child prior to his removal, and the mother's recognition that the father had to consent before his child could be taken from the jurisdiction.

Closely related to the issue of 'rights of custody' is the requirement that the child is habitually resident in the State which bestows those custody rights 'immediately before the removal'. In *Re K (Abduction: Consent: Forum Conveniens)* (1995), Waite LJ refers to habitual residence as '... an ephemeral concept', and in *C v S*, Lord Brandon warned that the expression 'habitually resident' should not be seen as a term of art. Having said that, the Convention does not give any guidance as to its meaning. Reference is made by Lord Brandon to the 'ordinary and natural meaning' of the words. He goes on to point out that a decision should ultimately be reached after considering the following:

- that it is a question of fact to be decided by reference to all the circumstances of the case;
- a person may cease to be habitually resident in a country in a single day; and
- if a young child is in the sole lawful custody of the mother, the child's habitual residence will be the same as hers.

In *C v S*, the mother had left Western Australia with the child with the settled intention that neither she nor the child should continue to be habitually resident there. Therefore the removal of the child was not wrongful because it did not breach the father's custody rights, nor was the retention unlawful because the child was not habitually resident in Australia when the mother made the decision not to return the child. (In order to avoid confusion, note that the case of *C v S* is also referred to in some reports as *Re J*.) As to how the law is applied, see the decision in *Re B (Child Abduction: Habitual Residence)* (1994). Here, the unmarried parents separated and the mother, with the agreement of the father, brought the child to England with the intention of settling here. However, within a few weeks she had returned to Canada with the child in order to attempt a reconciliation with the father. Three months later she decided the reconciliation had failed and, without consulting the father, brought the child back to England. The father issued an originating summons under the Hague Convention seeking the child's return. It was decided that the child ceased to be habitually resident at the time the mother left Canada for the first time, and the attempted reconciliation was for an insufficiently long period for a settled intention to be formed to regard Canada as her habitual residence. In practice, the issue of whether the child was habitually resident in a particular jurisdiction is likely to be a matter of fact determined by reference to all the evidence. So, for example, in *Re F (A Minor) (Child Abduction)* (1992), the judge had concluded that the family had indeed left England with the settled intention of taking up permanent residence in Australia and rejected the father's contention that they had merely been on an extended holiday. Crucial to this finding was the fact that the family had sent by sea 19 packing cases, although the father sought to explain this by saying 'we did not take any major household items such as a sofa or television set with us – only such items as would make our extended stay enjoyable'. Another significant factor was the father's acquisition, soon after arrival, of forms intended to permit him to apply for residential status in Australia.

9.3.2 Returning the child

It is quite clear under Article 12 that where a child has been wrongfully removed or retained, the courts in the Contracting State should not be concerned with the merits of the case but work on the presumption that the child should be returned. If the period to have elapsed since the removal or retention is less than 12 months, the court should order the return of the child 'forthwith'. Even if the period is over 12 months, the presumption is in favour of an immediate return 'unless it is demonstrated that the child is now settled in its new environment'.

Article 12 must be considered together with Article 13, which grants a discretion to the court to refuse to order the child's return for one or more of the following reasons:

- That the person ... having the care of the child was not exercising the custody rights at the time of the removal or retention.
- That the person had consented to or subsequently acquiesced in the removal or retention.
- That there is a grave risk that the return would expose the child to 'physical or psychological harm or would otherwise place the child in an intolerable situation'.

A child may also object to his return being ordered providing he has 'attained an age and degree of maturity at which it is appropriate to take account of its views'.

Let us therefore examine the issues raised by Article 13. The cases referred to will deal only with children removed from another Contracting State, but it is probably fair to assume that in the overwhelming majority of cases courts in all Contracting States will act in accordance with Article 12 and return the child. Article 13 should not be seen as diminishing the commitment to ensure the immediate return of the child.

The following points can be extracted from the judgment of Stuart-Smith LJ in *Re A* (1992):

- Acquiescence cannot occur unless there is an awareness, in general terms, of rights possessed by one parent against the other.

- This seems to require a knowledge of one's legal rights under the Hague Convention and that the other parent's act in removing or retaining the child is unlawful.

- It is preferable if the acceptance of the situation is communicated in 'clear unequivocal words or conduct and the other party must believe that there has been an acceptance'.

- It should be recognised that the party purporting to acquiesce may be in some emotional turmoil because of the circumstances and that courts should question whether or not there is 'real acquiescence'.

The later decision of *Re AZ (A Minor) (Abduction: Acquiescence)* (1993) confirms that the terms of the Convention require courts to be slow to infer acquiescence, particularly if the perception is held that one parent has, because of the circumstances, no real choice in the matter. In such circumstances, there may well be an agreement that the child should remain with the abductor for a temporary period in order to see how things develop or work out. The Vice-Chancellor, Sir Donald Nicholls, thought that at a later stage a court should:

> '... look at all the circumstances and consider whether the parent has conducted himself in a way that would be inconsistent with him later seeking a summary order for the child's return. That is the concept underlying consent and acquiescence in Article 13. That is the touchstone to be applied.'

Waite LJ in *Re S (Minors) (Abduction: Acquiescence)* (1994) refers to the 'common thread' running through the case law. He believes that acquiescence is primarily established by inferences drawn from an objective survey of 'the acts and omissions of the aggrieved parent'. Yet that does not exclude taking into account subjective factors, although care needs to be taken not to give undue weight to such elements. The central question, echoing the words Sir Donald Nicholls in *Re AZ*, was stated to be:

> '... has the aggrieved parent conducted himself in a way that is inconsistent with his later seeking a summary return?'

In *Re R (Child Abduction: Acquiescence)* (1995), the Court of Appeal urged that correspondence and conversations between parents should be taken as a whole. So, to extract a single sentence from a four-page letter, speculate as to its meaning and then treat it as evidence of acquiescence was to be deprecated. The court reiterated the demand for clear and unambiguous evidence of acceptance of the situation.

What weight should be placed on the views of the children? The Children Act 1989 places the wishes of the children as one of a series of factors to be taken into account in deciding what is in their best interests. There is no such statutory endorsement that the children's wishes will be particularly influential in the decision-making process. The underlying purpose of the Convention must never be forgotten, ie the speedy return of the child so that outstanding matters of concern can be dealt with by the court where the child has his or her habitual residence. English courts have retained the flexibility to treat each case on its merits by refusing to lay down a minimum age below which a child's wishes will not be taken into account. In *B v K* (1993), children aged nine and seven expressed an opinion against returning to their former habitual residence, which was relied upon by the court as a ground for refusing to adhere to the underlying presumption of the Convention. This view was reiterated in *S v S (Child Abduction)* (1992), with the court stressing that it is only in exceptional circumstances that the immediate return of the child should be refused. However, the court did accept the objections to return put forward by a nine year old girl who wished to remain with her mother in England. The judge at first instance had taken into account the girl's views, as put to a court welfare officer, to the effect that she had a 'strong dread of going back to France and feels more comfortable in England'.

The Court of Appeal will be slow to overturn the decision of the first instance judge unless the conclusion reached is plainly wrong. This could include taking into account the wrong principles or failing to take account of some relevant factor. However, as *G v G* (1985) points out, the Court of Appeal will not rehear the case nor substitute its own judgment for that of the judge at first instance unless the decision was plainly wrong. The case thus establishes that the principles applicable when the Court of Appeal is exercising its general appellate jurisdiction will be equally applicable when it is reviewing cases involving the welfare of children. The court has no general power to substitute its own preferred solution to that of the judge at first instance who will usually have had, and taken, the opportunity to speak with the parents and child. Only where the judge at first instance has exceeded the generous ambit within which judicial disagreement was reasonably possible, and was plainly wrong, should the Court of Appeal impose its own solution.

There is dicta to support the proposition that what is required is specific inquiry into the child's ability to understand the implications of not returning to his or her home country. In *Re R* (1995), the objections of brothers aged seven and six to the return to their father in the United States proved to be decisive. In the Court of Appeal, Balcombe LJ stated:

> 'Were it not for the boys' objections, this would be the clearest possible case for the application of the Convention.'

However, that view was not shared by Millett LJ in the same case:

> 'The children were ordinary little boys ... of average maturity ... their views were firmly held and based on reasonable grounds. But I cannot accept that, given their age and maturity, it was appropriate to take their views into account ... It follows that ... the court was bound to order the boys to be returned to Illinois'.

A court needs always to be conscious of the fact that a child's views can be influenced by the opinions of the carer parent. Given the purpose of the Convention, a court should be seeking to ascertain whether or not the child has objections to returning, not whether he prefers the mother to the father or vice versa. In practice, however, it may prove virtually impossible to dissociate the two, and as Butler-Sloss LJ said in *Re M (A Minor) (Child Abduction)* (1994), it would be 'artificial' if a court were to seek so to do.

Further consideration was given to this issue in the recently reported case of *Re K (Abduction: Child's Objections)* (1995). In this case, the parents lived in the USA until the mother visited England and informed the father that she was not returning to the USA. The mother accepted that the children were being wrongfully retained in England. The mother claimed the father had acquiesced in the unlawful retention and additionally that one of the children was terrified of returning to the USA. She argued that the child was old enough to have her wishes taken into account. The court accepted that the child's 'age and degree of maturity were consistent with her chronological age and that she objected to being returned to the USA'. The court was of the view that this fact alone did not resolve the dilemma of whether she was mature enough for her views to be taken into account. For example, the court was unclear as to precisely the nature of her objection to returning to the USA. The court concluded that the child did not have the requisite degree of maturity for her views to determine the outcome of the proceedings. The court ordered the return of the children in accordance with the terms of the Hague Convention. The crucial question to be decided appears to be whether the child 'understands the distinction between an order for her immediate return to the USA for her future to be decided and an objection to her return in any circumstances' (*per* Wall J). The judge also drew attention to the fact that the policy of the Convention can be 'easily circumvented by unscrupulous parents imposing on their suggestible children fears and anxieties which if uncritically accepted could persuade the court into orders which would frustrate the purpose of the Convention'.

In conclusion, it is suggested that the child's views, together with an assessment of the likely consequences of the child's return, should be the major factors when deciding whether the exceptional circumstances exist thereby justifying a failure to adhere to the aims of the Convention.

9.3.3 Grave risk of physical or psychological harm

Article 13(b) permits a court to refuse to return a child if there is a grave risk that the child will be physically or psychologically harmed. Intriguingly, the Article also identifies the possibility of the child being placed in an intolerable situation as an alternative ground upon which to base a refusal to return. In *Re G* (1995), the court held that the children, all aged under three, were emotionally dependent upon the mother. If they were to be returned to the father in Texas, the mother inevitably would return with them. She was suffering from a severe agitated depressive state and was in considerable danger of becoming psychotic. The court took the view that the mother was likely to suffer a severe mental breakdown were she to return to the USA with the children, and that that would place the children at grave risk of psychological harm or place them in an intolerable situation.

Judges are bound to find themselves with difficult balancing tasks to be carried out. The Article appears to require a focus on the likely effect of the return of the child to its habitual residence but surely this must be set against an assessment of the likely psychological consequences of refusing to return the child. Of course, the welfare of the child is not the paramount consideration in such cases, arguably the paramount concern is to return the child as soon as possible: the 'primary purpose', as Thorpe J put it in *N v N (Abduction: Article 13 Defence)* (1995). Thus where the issues are finely balanced, the presumption should be in favour of returning the child.

A court should also be wary of one parent manipulating the situation so as to put great psychological pressure upon the child, which it would then be argued would be exacerbated by any impending return. An obvious example would be a mother's refusal to accompany the child back to their former home. In *Re C (A Minor) (Abduction)* (1989), Butler-Sloss LJ was not prepared to permit such conduct by a mother to defeat the purpose of the Convention. 'Nor should the mother, by her own actions, succeed in preventing the return of the child who should be living in his own country and deny him contact with his other parent'.

The recently reported case of *Re F (Child Abduction: Risk if Returned)* (1995) is a vivid illustration of how Article 13(b) can be used in order to prevent the child from being returned to his place of habitual residence. The court accepted that the mother had wrongfully removed her child from the father in breach of his custody rights in the state of Colorado. In removing the child, the mother had rendered nugatory the father's ability to exercise his custody rights, and this amounted to a clear breach of the Hague Convention. When it came to considering the position under Article 13(b), it was accepted by the court that '... a very high standard is required to demonstrate grave risk and an intolerable situation'. The mother and grandmother had made very serious allegations against the father, in particular of his violence towards the child and the extremely deleterious effect it had on him. Butler-Sloss LJ pointed out that there were serious difficulties inherent in proving grave risk of physical or psychological harm or in demonstrating that the child would be placed in an intolerable situation if returned. She was of the opinion that, of the cases under Article 13(b) which had reached the appellate court, in none had the required standard been reached. As such, this is a significant case, being the first to attain that standard, although the judge expressed 'considerable hesitation' in coming to the conclusion that the child should not be returned to the USA. The fact that the child was the recipient of much of the father's violence was obviously a significant factor in persuading the judge to reach the conclusion that she did. The child had also witnessed acts of violence and uncontrollable temper directed at his mother. On one occasion, that father had expelled the mother and child from the matrimonial home, and in consequence the police were called. This led to the father threatening to kill both the mother and child. The court saw the child as a victim of the matrimonial discord between the parents and not a 'bystander'. The child also suffered from asthma, and the effect upon him of this behaviour was extremely serious. The physical manifestation of all this behaviour was that he started to wet his bed regularly and to have nightmares where he screamed out in his sleep. He was settled at the maternal grandmother's home in Wales, and the bedwetting and nightmares gradually ceased and his overall behaviour and demeanour changed for the better. However, when informed that he might have to return to his father if the mother's appeal was lost, his unsettling behaviour returned and he became aggressive towards other children in his class at school. The court thus came to the conclusion that there was significant risks to the child's security and stability if he were to be returned to the USA. Perhaps the approach to Article 13(b) is best summed up by Sir Christopher Slade at p 43(F):

> '... I understand that the courts of this country are only in rare cases willing to hold that the conditions of fact, which give rise to the courts' discretion ... They are in my very quite right to be cautious and to apply a stringent test. The invocation of Article 13(b), with scant justification, is all too likely to be the last resort for parents who have wrongfully removed their child to another jurisdiction.'

Under Article 12 of the Convention, the abductor is offered the opportunity to demonstrate that 'the children are now settled in their new environment' providing that more than one year has elapsed since the abduction. This gives rise to a discretion under Article 18 as to whether or not to return the children. The key question here is the meaning of the word 'now' in Article 12. In *Re N (Minors) (Abduction)* (1991), Bracewell J concluded that the word should refer to the commencement of the proceedings, and not in the sense of the day of the hearing, as any delay may prejudice the outcome. She was of the opinion that the degree of settlement which needed to be demonstrated was more than 'mere adjustment to the surroundings'. 'Settled' in this context has two constituents. In the first place, it involved a physical element of being established in a community or environment. Secondly, it had an 'emotional' constituent denoting security, stability and permanence. The emphasis, therefore, is placed upon the connection between the child and his or her environment, and not on the relationship with the parent. The focus of attention will be the school, home, friends, activities and opportunities. If the application is brought within a year, then Article 12 will normally be invoked without delay and the child returned.

9.3.4 Discretion

The case of *Re K* (1995) (above) raises the interesting point of whether or not the court will have a discretion to order the return of a child even though the terms of the Hague Convention are not fulfilled. In this case, the parents were American citizens who had one son and had divorced in 1991. The father lived in Houston, Texas, and by order of the Texan divorce court had staying contact with his son. The mother, the principal carer of the child, moved to England and remarried. The father reluctantly agreed that the child should accompany her on the basis that he had no choice given the circumstances. The child and the father maintained contact, and on occasions the child returned to Texas to stay with his father. Although the parents had agreed that the child should accompany the mother to England, there was a breach of the divorce court order that the child should not be removed from Texas without the court's permission. The mother eventually commenced family proceedings in England in which an interim residence order was made in her favour. However, the father had also returned to the Texas court seeking a modification of the original order, thus giving him interim sole care. The father ultimately resorted to the Hague Convention, seeking the return of his son to Texas in order to allow the Texan court to determine the issue. The judge at first instance and the Court of Appeal concluded that the child was not habitually resident in Texas at the time the breach of the court order occurred, and therefore there had been not been a wrongful retention as required under the terms of the convention before a child can be returned. The father therefore could not establish a right to the mandatory return of the child. Counsel for the father then argued that, given the fact the court accepted that it appeared to be in the child's best interests for the Texan court to resolve the matter, international comity between jurisdictions demanded that the child should be returned. The Court of Appeal was impressed by this argument. It was pointed out that the two jurisdictions were very similar in terms of the approach to the resolution of such disputes. Each accepted that it was obliged to act in the best interests of the child, '... both systems adopt the same child-centred and pragmatic approach to cases involving children. Both operate under the same sense of urgency and in the same spirit of comity with each other. Each has available to it a court welfare service equipped to make enquiries not only within its own territory but also through their colleagues working in the other jurisdiction'. The conclusion, as Waite LJ stated, was:

> 'The two systems of law are so similar in approach and in execution that the order which eventually emerges (whether from London or Houston) will lay down a regime for future residence, contact and maintenance that will be expressed (differences of legal terminology apart) and enforced identically in either jurisdiction.'

The English proceedings were therefore stayed in order to allow preparations to be made for an early return to the USA. There had been a disproportionate emphasis placed upon the concept of habitual residence, with the court at first instance seemingly concluding that the child should remain in England simply because this was his place of habitual residence. The Court of Appeal, for the reasons stated above, thought otherwise. The decision was undoubtedly made easier as a result of the similarities between the two jurisdictions, both procedurally and in respect of the principles to be applied. Whether or not the court would have ordered the child's return to a less compatible jurisdiction is more debatable.

For an analysis of the main case law up to the end of 1993, see the two articles by Christina Sachs at (1993) Fam Law pp 530 and 585 *et seq* entitled *Child Abduction – The Hague Convention and Recent Case Law*. The author concludes that the case law demonstrates that the courts '... have consistently shown a broad and purposive approach to its [ie The Hague Convention] interpretation ... [thus] ... ensuring the prompt return of abducted children to the jurisdiction of their habitual residence, while giving due weight to the exceptional circumstances which may prevent this'.

9.4 The European Convention

As the title of the Convention suggests, its terms are limited to European signatories, and only if the applicant has been granted a 'custody' order. This includes a decision relating to access to the child. The purpose of the Convention mirrors that of the Hague Convention in creating a network of states committed to the speedy return of abducted children to their place of habitual residence. Reference should be made to Schedule 2 of the Child Abduction and Custody Act 1985 to ascertain the scope of the Convention.

The European Convention may be invoked where there has been an 'improper removal' of a child 'across an international frontier in breach of a decision relating to his custody which has been given in a Contracting State and which is enforceable in such a State'. Improper removal also includes the failure to return a child where one parent has had access to the child or there has been a 'temporary stay in a territory, other than that where the custody is exercised'. Although the legislation and Convention refer to 'custody' and 'access', concepts which have been replaced by the terms 'residence' and 'contact' as a result of the Children Act 1989, the term 'decision relating to custody' is undoubtedly wide enough to embrace the new terminology. Article 1(c) defines the term this way:

> '... a decision of an authority in so far as it relates to the care of the person of the child, including the right to decide on the place of his residence, or to the right of access to him.'

Article 4 outlines the basic procedure to be adopted. The 'decision relating to custody' may be 'recognised or enforced' in a Contracting State through application to the central authority of that State. Once accepted under Article 4, then the central authority must act by taking appropriate steps without delay to discover the whereabouts of the child and, if necessary, institute court proceedings with a view to securing the enforcement of the 'custody decision'.

A perusal of a range of law reports will show that the European Convention is very much secondary to the Hague Convention, at least when it comes to usage. This is hardly surprising given the narrower scope of the European Convention, with its requirement for a court order to be in place. Case law relating to the Convention is less than plentiful. In *Re L (Child Abduction)* (1992), Booth J was asked to decide whether an Irish custody order vesting custody of the three children of the marriage in the father should be recognised, registered and enforced in England. The Irish order was granted on 8 October 1990, which was almost a year to the day prior to the ratification of the Convention by the British and Irish governments. The judge referred to the need for proceedings under the Convention to be taken expeditiously and without undue delay. She decided that the legislation should be construed so as to permit recognition and registration of orders made prior to the ratification of the Convention. This is one advantage that the European has over the Hague Convention, as *Re H* and *Re S* (1991) held that the convention only applied to wrongful removals or retentions occurring after the date on which the 1985 Act came into force (see s 2(2) of the Child Abduction and Custody Act 1985). It was accepted that under the Act there was a mandatory requirement that a subsisting decision relating to custody should be registered and that a court had only limited powers to exercise a discretion to refuse recognition. These powers are declared in Articles 9 and 10, the most potent likely to be the provision under Article 10, which allows the court to decide that the 'effects of the original decision are manifestly no longer in accordance with the welfare of the child'. This conclusion must be reached not as a result of the mere change of residence but by reason of a change in the circumstances 'including the passage of time'. Booth J expressed it this way in *Re L*:

> 'If I am to exercise my discretion under Article 10(1)(b), I have to be satisfied by reason of a change of circumstances, including the passage of time, that the effects of the original decision are manifestly no longer in accordance with the welfare of the child. It is a very high

burden of proof that rests upon the party who seeks to persuade the court to be so satisfied.'

Of course, most young children are likely to be adversely affected by the passage of time and the removal from one country to another, but it does not necessarily follow that the original decision is manifestly no longer in accordance with the welfare of the child.

The court was concerned, should it have been decided that the two children remain in England, that they would be separated from their brother on a permanent basis. The court decided that the order of the Irish court should be registered in this country and that the two children be returned to Ireland.

The date when the order, which is the subject of registration, is issued can be a crucial factor in a court's decision whether or not to recognise that order under the European Convention. In *Re M (Child Abduction)* (1994), the mother had brought the children from Ireland to England and refused to return with them to Ireland. She obtained, on an *ex parte* basis, interim residence orders in respect of the children some three weeks before the Dublin Family Circuit Court gave sole custody of the children to the father. He applied under the European Convention for the order to be registered in this jurisdiction. On refusing the father's application, Rattee J found that the Dublin court's order was plainly incompatible with the decision of the English court, albeit the English order had been obtained on an *ex parte* basis and was an interim order. Article 10(1)(d) allows a court to refuse recognition and enforcement if the decision is incompatible with 'a decision given in the State addressed'. The judge found that, as they had been in England for some 18 months, it was in accordance with the welfare of the children that they be allowed to remain. A decision on their long-term future would, therefore, be taken by the English and not the Irish court.

Recently, the Court of Appeal has confirmed that recognition of an order by an English court did not automatically mean that it would be enforced. The two words, 'recognition' and 'enforcement', as they appear in Article 10, were to be read disjunctively. One result of the decision in *Re H (A Minor) (Foreign custody order: Enforcement)* (1994), which is undoubtedly consistent with the wording of Article 10, may be to offer a glimmer of encouragement to those wishing to abduct their children to another jurisdiction if they believe courts are likely to be a little more sympathetic towards hearing arguments based upon the welfare principle. However, the court undoubtedly retains the maximum discretion to deal with each case on its merits, and this is, indeed, consistent with the welfare principle, if arguably not totally supportive of the underlying principle of the Convention.

It will be apparent that both the Hague and European Conventions will be applicable to many cases. The general principle is that the Hague Convention will take precedence over the European, given its greater flexibility in not being dependent upon the existence of a court order relating to the custody of the child.

The European Convention applies to any child under the age of 16 providing he or she has been improperly removed from their habitual residence.

9.5 Non-convention countries

There are a number of countries throughout the world which have not ratified the two conventions. If a child is abducted to one of these countries, very real difficulties are likely to ensue in trying to achieve the return of the child. The major difficulties confront parents of children abducted from this jurisdiction to a non-convention country. One option is to begin proceedings in that country, but this is likely to be time consuming, prohibitively expensive, and with no guarantee of success. The criminal law could perhaps be invoked if there is an extradition treaty between the two countries.

However, the position is much clearer if the child is brought from a non-convention country to England. The courts have been adamant that the principles underpinning the Hague Convention should apply. The principles were reiterated most recently in *Re M (Abduction: Non-convention country)* (1995) and stated thus:

> '(1) Normally, the best interests of children were best secured by having their future determined in the jurisdiction of their habitual residence.
>
> (2) The court, in determining a non-convention case, would take account of those matters which it would be relevant to consider under Article 13 of the Convention.
>
> (3) The essence of the jurisdiction to grant a peremptory return order was that the judge should act urgently.
>
> (4) In this area the principle of comity applies. It is assumed, particularly in the case of States which are fellow members of the European Union, that such facilities as rights of representation ... welfare reports, opportunities of giving evidence ... all of which are necessary to place the court in a position to determine the best interests of the child concerned, will be secured as well within one State's jurisdiction as within another.'

The two children at the centre of the dispute in this case were born in Italy in 1990 and 1992 respectively, of an English mother and an Italian father. In 1993 the parents' relationship broke down and the mother applied to an Italian court for a custody order in respect of each child. She was, however, advised that her chances of success were remote, and in consequence of this advice she brought the children to England and sought a residence order from the English courts. A month later, the father commenced custody proceedings in the Italian courts and obtained an order directing that the children were to live with him on an interim basis. He also filed an answer in the English proceedings. Wilson J granted an order for the children to return to Italy. The mother's appeal was dismissed. The Court of Appeal stated that the principles applicable to the Hague Convention were also '... *prima facie* those to be applied in all non-convention cases'. The father had given undertakings to the English court and the court had no reason to assume that the father would not fulfil his promises. It is assumed in these non-convention cases that the peremptory return of a child will accord with his or her best interests. As Waite LJ said '... in the absence of special circumstances, it will best serve the immediate welfare of the abducted child to have its long-term interests judged in the land from which it was abducted'. It should be noted that since this case was decided, Italy has become a signatory to the Hague and European Conventions. Nevertheless it does not inexorably follow that a child will be returned. In *D v D (Child Abduction: Non-convention country)* (1994), the Court of Appeal refused to order the children to be returned to Greece, as the mother had become pregnant by another man since bringing the children to this country and could not return to Greece. The court would not order the return of the children without their mother in whose care they had been for most of their lives. The Court of Appeal had no doubt that this was a case which should be heard by the court in the non-convention country and was critical of the mother:

> '... I am very aware of the injustice to the father since the mother has achieved a decision which her conduct does not merit. But this court is principally concerned with the welfare of the children.'

Do note that this case was one of consolidated wardship applications and would suggest that it may be more appropriate than an application for a s 8 order under the Children Act 1989. Cases such as this will invariably be complex, and wardship is a jurisdiction with a long pedigree in determining exactly which course of action will serve the best interests of a child.

The courts have to send out a clear signal to those in non-convention countries intent upon bringing their children within this jurisdiction. They must clearly understand that their children face the prospect of being returned to the country of their residence without delay. Occasionally it will be in the best interests of children not to be returned, but in the overwhelming majority of cases the welfare of the child will demand its return from whence it came. The courts were familiar with so called 'kidnapping' cases long before the 1985 Act became law. It is instructive to read the case of *Re L (Minors) (Wardship Jurisdiction)* (1974) described by Balcombe LJ in *Re S (Minors) (Abduction)* (1994) as 'the case from which all the relevant modern law derives ...' containing, as it does, the classic passage in the judgment of Buckley LJ, *viz*:

> 'To take a child from his native land, to remove him to another country where maybe his native tongue is not spoken, to divorce him from the social customs and contacts to which he has become accustomed, to interrupt his education in his native land and subject him to a foreign system of education, are all acts (offered here as examples and, of course, not as a complete catalogue of possible relevant factors) which are likely to be psychologically disturbing to the child, particularly at a time when his family life is also disrupted. If such a case is promptly brought to the attention of a court in this country, the judge may feel that it is in the best interests of the infant that these disturbing factors should be eliminated from his life as speedily as possible.'

9.6 The port alert system

The Child Abduction Act was brought into force in October 1984. As has been seen, it provides the framework for a workable and effective system which is aimed at discouraging parents and others from kidnapping or otherwise removing children from the jurisdiction. The aims of the legislation are also supported by the port alert system which became effective on 2 May 1986. If there is a real threat that a child is about to be removed unlawfully from the United Kingdom, application may be made by the applicant or his legal representative to any police station for assistance in helping to prevent the child's removal. In practice, this will be carried out at the applicant's local police station. The duty is placed upon the police and not the Home Office to alert immigration officers at ports in an attempt to prevent the child from leaving the jurisdiction. Prior to instituting the port alert system, the police will need to be satisfied that there is a real and imminent threat of removal. 'Imminent' means within 24 to 48 hours, and 'real' means that in seeking to invoke the procedure, '... the port alert is not being sought by or on behalf of the applicant by way of insurance' (*Practice Direction* (1986)).

It is not necessary to obtain a court order in respect of a child under 16 before police assistance can be sought, but if an order has been obtained, it should be produced. It follows that the system will be at its most effective if the applicant can provide as much detailed information as possible relating to the child and the person likely to be attempting to remove the child from the jurisdiction. In the case of a child who is a ward of court, evidence will need to be produced to verify the child's status, as no ward may be removed from the jurisdiction without the consent of the court. The applicant will also be asked to produce as much information as possible about the likely points of embarkation and times of travel. The child's name will remain on the stop list for four weeks and then be automatically removed unless a further application is made. Another measure which can be taken is to request that the passport office should not provide passport facilities to the minor, although there is every possibility that the child will be included on the parent's passport, thus rendering this procedure nugatory.

9.7 Conclusion

International child abduction is a growing phenomenon, and it is to be hoped that further ratifications of the Hague Convention will be made in the not-too-distant future. The English courts have consistently adopted the principle that the best interests of the child are coterminous with the return to the jurisdiction in which he or she had their home as Buckley LJ so graphically demonstrated in the passage cited above from *Re L*. Of one thing all judges are agreed: that the action decided upon must accord with the best interests of the child. It is clear that in enacting the 1985 Act, parliament was not departing from the fundamental principle that the child's welfare is paramount (see *G v G* (1991)). Having said that, the judiciary has to be convinced that the overseas jurisdiction will:

> '... apply principles which are acceptable to the English courts as being appropriate, subject always to any contra-indication such as those mentioned in Article 13 of the Hague Convention, or a risk of persecution or discrimination, but *prima facie* the court to decide is that of the State where the child was habitually resident immediately before its removal' (*Re F* (1991), *per* Lord Donaldson MR).

Summary of Chapter 9

Child Abduction

The problem of international child abduction continues to escalate, and England and Wales have legislation, both criminal and civil, with which to combat the problem. Abduction may occur within the United Kingdom or to any country in the world. The legal remedies available to meet the former difficulty are contained in the Family Law Act 1986, and those associated with overseas abduction are to be found in the Child Abduction Act 1984 and the Child Abduction and Custody Act 1985.

Criminal law

In respect of the criminal law, the common law offence of kidnapping is still recognised, but in practice, the statutory code under the 1984 Act will take precedence. The offence is committed if a person connected with a child under 16 takes or sends the child in question out of the United Kingdom without the appropriate consent. A person is connected with a child if, for example, he is a parent or guardian of the child or has custody or a residence order in respect of the child. Section 2 of the 1984 Act creates a second offence which may be committed by other persons who take or detain a child without lawful authority or reasonable excuse.

The Act has generated little case law, but for an example of how the Act may be used see *R v Leather* (1993).

International abduction

The Hague Convention and the European Convention attempt to provide a framework under which abducted children may be returned to the place of their habitual residence as quickly and speedily as possible. The objectives of the Conventions remains the same although the basis upon which the two Conventions may be invoked are different. In the latter case, a court order must exist which purports to determine custody rights. Custody in this context includes access. No such requirement exists in the case of the Hague Convention. Attention should be paid to Schedule 1 of the 1985 Act and in particular Articles 3, 12 and 13. In broad terms, the Hague Convention is designed to inhibit the wrongful removal or retention of a child. It is necessary to become familiar with the terms 'wrongful removal' 'wrongful retention' and 'habitual residence'.

There is a great deal of case law to assist in the above task. Concentrate on the following cases:

Re H; Re S (1991)

Re S (Minors) (Child Abduction) (1994)

Re B (A Minor) (Abduction) (1994)

C v S (Minor) (Abduction: Illegitimate child) (1990)

Re A (1992)

Re AZ (A Minor) (Abduction: Acquiescence) (1993)

Re R (Child Abduction: Acquiescence) (1995)

Reference should be made to Schedule 2 of the Child Abduction and Custody Act 1985 in order to ascertain the scope of the European Convention. The Convention may be invoked when there has been an improper removal of a child across an international frontier in breach of an enforceable decision relating to his or her custody. Refer to Articles 1(c), 4, 9 and 10 for the relevant detail. The following cases are important:

Re L (Child Abduction) (1992)

Re H and Re S (1991)

Re M (Child Abduction) (1994)

Re H (A Minor) (Foreign custody order: Enforcement) (1994)

Note that because of the wider ambit of the Hague Convention, it will usually take precedence over the European Convention.

Non-convention countries

This is perhaps the most unsatisfactory aspect of the law relating to child abduction. There are certain countries which are signatories to neither the Hague nor European Conventions. If a child is abducted to one of these countries, very real difficulties will ensue in trying to ensure the speedy return of the child. One option is to begin proceedings in that country, but this can be both costly and protracted with no guarantee of success. But the position is much clearer if the child is brought to this country from a non-convention country. The principles to be applied are to be found in the case of:

Re M (Abduction: Non-convention country) (1995)

See also the cases of:

D v D (Child Abduction: Non-convention country) (1994)

Re L (Minors) (Wardship: Jurisdiction) (1974)

Re S (Minors) (Abduction) (1994)

Index